# Christe Eleison!

## The Invocation of Christ in Eastern Monastic Psalmody c.350–450

JAMES F. WELLINGTON

PETER LANG
Oxford · Bern · Berlin · Bruxelles · Frankfurt am Main · New York · Wien

Bibliographic information published by Die Deutsche Nationalbibliothek.
Die Deutsche Nationalbibliothek lists this publication in the Deutsche Nationalbibliografie; detailed bibliographic data is available on the Internet at http://dnb.d-nb.de.

A catalogue record for this book is available from the British Library.

Library of Congress Control Number: 2014942487

ISSN 2235-1930
ISBN 978-3-0343-1789-4 (print)
ISBN 978-3-0353-0622-4 (eBook)


Hochfeldstrasse 32, CH-3012 Bern, Switzerland
info@peterlang.com, www.peterlang.com, www.peterlang.net



This publication has been peer reviewed.

Printed in Germany

# Contents

# Abbreviations

| | |
|---|---|
| AS | Analecta sacra spicilegio solesmensi parata |
| CSEL | Corpus scriptorum ecclesiasticorum latinorum |
| GCS | Die Griechischen christlichen Schriftsteller der ersten drei Jahrhunderte |
| *HTR* | *Harvard Theological Review* |
| OCA | Orientalia Christiana Analecta |
| OCP | Orientalia Christiana Periodica |
| PG | Patrologiae cursus completus. Series Graeca |
| PL | Patrologiae cursus completus. Series Latina |
| SC | Sources Chrétiennes |
| *SP* | *Studia Patristica* |

*To Hilary and Catherine*

# Introduction

For centuries the Jesus Prayer has been leading Orthodox Christians beyond the language of liturgy and the representations of iconography into the wordless, imageless stillness of the mystery of God. In more recent years it has been helping an increasing number of Western Christians to engage with God not only with the lips and the mind but also with the heart, and drawing them into a deeper contemplation through the continual rhythmic repetition of a short prayer which, by general agreement, first emerged from the desert spirituality of early monasticism.

It has been claimed that the earliest source to cite the standard formula of the Jesus Prayer, 'Lord Jesus Christ, Son of God, have mercy on me' (Κύριε Ἰησοῦ Χριστέ, υἱὲ τοῦ Θεοῦ, ἐλέησόν με), is the *Peri tou Abba Philēmon*,[1] a work dating from the sixth or early seventh century.[2]

This anonymous piece of writing relates to the teaching of an Egyptian hermit and to his rule of life in the later period of the Roman Empire in Egypt. In the *Peri tou Abba Philēmon* we encounter many of the words and concepts traditionally associated with the spiritual environment of the Desert Fathers. Throughout the narrative there is a pronounced emphasis on stillness (ἡσυχία), watchfulness (νῆψις), 'pray without ceasing' (ἀδιαλείπτως προσεύχεσθε), and secret or inward meditation (κρυπτὴ μελέτη), all of which are acknowledged to have played a part in the development of the Jesus Prayer.

1 *Philokalia tōn Ierōn Nēptikōn, Vol. II* (Athens: Astir Publishing Company, 1959), 241–52.

2 Irénée Hausherr, *Noms du Christ et voies d'oraison*, OCA 157 (Rome: Pontificium Institutum Orientalium Studiorum, 1960), 239–46; Gerald E. H. Palmer, Philip Sherrard and Kallistos Ware, ed. and trans., *The Philokalia. The Complete Text compiled by St Nikodimos of the Holy Mountain and St Makarios of Corinth, Vol. II* (London: Faber and Faber, 1981), 343–57; A Monk of the Eastern Church, *The Jesus Prayer* (Crestwood, New York: St Vladimir's Seminary Press, 1987), 37–8 note 5.

There is also, within this work, an important passage relating to another aspect of the ascetic discipline of this hermit:

> Once a certain brother who lived with him asked him: 'What is the mystery of contemplation?' Realizing that he was intent on learning, the Elder replied: 'I tell you, my son, that when one's intellect is completely pure, God reveals to him the visions that are granted to the ministering powers and angelic hosts'. The same brother also asked: 'Why, Father, do you find more joy in the psalms than in any other part of divine Scripture? And why, when quietly chanting them, do you say the words as though you were speaking with someone?' And Abba Philemon replied: 'My son, God has impressed the power of the psalms on my poor soul (οὕτω προετύπωσεν ὁ Θεὸς τὴν δύναμιν τῶν ψαλμῶν ἐν τῇ ταπεινῇ μου ψυχῇ) as he did on the soul of the prophet David. I cannot be separated from the sweetness of the visions about which they speak: they embrace all divine Scripture' (Πάσης γὰρ τῆς θείας Γραφῆς εἰσι περιεκτικοί).[3]

The purpose of this study is not to attempt to provide a comprehensive account of the steps leading up to the appearance of Κύριε Ἰησοῦ Χριστέ, υἱὲ τοῦ Θεοῦ, ἐλέησόν με in this sixth- or seventh-century narrative. Nor is its aim to prove any direct causal connection between any aspect of monastic discipline and the establishment of the Jesus Prayer. Its objective is rather to shine a new light upon the culture out of which the Jesus Prayer is believed to have emerged by focusing on one particular expression of monasticism, which up to now has not been strongly associated with the early development of this prayer. To this end, we will consider the relevance of Eastern monastic psalmody of the late fourth and early fifth centuries to the environment which, by general consensus, gave birth to the Christ-centred invocatory prayer which first appeared in its standard form in the *Peri tou Abba Philēmon*.

To this extent, we will be involved with the quest taken up by the orientalist, Irénée Hausherr. Born in Alsace in 1891, Hausherr entered the Jesuit order and was ordained to the priesthood. He went on to become a professor at the Oriental Institute in Rome, and is the author of a number

3 *Philokalia tōn Ierōn Nēptikōn, Vol. II*, 243–4; Palmer, Sherrard and Ware, *Philokalia, Vol. II*, 347.

of influential works, including *Noms du Christ et voies d'oraison*, published in 1960. In *Noms du Christ* Hausherr contends that the Jesus Prayer arose from a search for unceasing prayer in the life of the early Eastern monastics. The premise of this study is that the picture he offers is incomplete. Hausherr's concentration on the monastics' private asceticism has been at the expense of the broader picture of their liturgical life. The aim here is to correct this omission and to allow the monastic understanding of the psalms to make its own contribution to our comprehension of the culture out of which the Jesus Prayer developed.

Part One of the study begins with a critique of Hausherr's work, and goes on to explain the factors which justify the singling out of psalmody for this area of research. Part Two then explores the vital contribution made to this subject by Evagrius of Pontus, with particular reference to his understanding of the relationship between prayer and psalmody, and to his teaching on the manner in which and the extent to which the person of Christ is to be encountered in the Book of Psalms. From there it embarks, in Part Three, on an investigation into four key elements within the commentaries on the Septuagint Psalter, attributed to some of the leading authorities of this period, which were encouraging early Eastern monastics to understand psalmody in terms of a recurring invocation of the person of Christ.

The first of these elements is the recognition of Christ as the divine name (ὄνομα) of the Psalter, while the second consists of acknowledging him as the divine face or countenance (πρόσωπον). The third is the identification of Christ in the psalms as a partner in prayer for divine assistance, while the fourth consists of invoking him directly as a deliverer or indirectly as the agent of deliverance.[4] The analysis of the psalm-commentaries seeks to establish the meaning of these psalm-texts for those engaged in their habitual recitation. Following this analysis, the study, by way of a conclusion, makes an assessment of the contribution made by psalmody to the

4 See James F. Wellington, 'Encountering Christ in the Psalms: Antecedents of the Jesus Prayer in Eastern Monastic Psalmody c.350-c.450', in *SP* 52 (Leuven: Peeters Press, 2012), 19–26.

shaping of the early Eastern monastic culture which gave rise to the Jesus Prayer. It should be noted that, unless otherwise stated, the Greek texts of the Septuagint are taken from Henry Barclay Swete's edition.[5] Furthermore, translations of the Septuagint Psalter are based, in the main, on the work of Albert Pietersma.[6]

5 Henry Barclay Swete, ed., *The Old Testament in Greek according to the Septuagint, Vol. II, Pt. 1* (Cambridge: Cambridge University Press, 1891).

6 Albert Pietersma, trans., *A New English Translation of the Septuagint and other Greek translations traditionally included under that title, The Psalms* (Oxford and New York: Oxford University Press, 2000).

# PART ONE

# The Importance of Psalmody

CHAPTER ONE

# Updating an Alsatian

## I. *Noms du Christ et voies d'oraison*

### *1. Overview*

In Chapter 3 of *Noms du Christ*, Hausherr introduces the reader to what he understands to be the motivation behind the emergence of the Jesus Prayer. Quoting from the nineteenth-century Russian classic, *The Way of a Pilgrim*, he records the eponymous hero's question to his *staretz*: 'How is it possible to pray continually?' He continues:

> Many other men in preceding centuries had asked themselves the same question the Pilgrim asked. And the answers given have varied widely. It was from this very search for continual prayer that the Jesus Prayer was born. In order to understand and appreciate and situate this prayer we will have to accompany that search, discover its guiding principles and observe the results which it has produced.[1]

What follows is a Great Trek from the acts of prayer of the earliest Christian communities to Nicephorus and the Athonite teaching on the Jesus Prayer in the medieval period. For the purpose of this study our attention is focused on the third, fourth, and fifth chapters, which are the most relevant to our task. For in those chapters we are offered a detailed analysis of the elements within desert monasticism which, Hausherr claims, constitute the evolution whose end product was to be the invocation, 'Lord Jesus Christ, Son of God, have mercy on me'. Let us consider a brief résumé of those chapters.

1 Hausherr, *Noms du Christ*, 128; English translation by Charles Cummings, *The Name of Jesus*, Cistercian Studies Series 44 (Kalamazoo, Michigan: Cistercian Publications, 1978), 126.

## 2. *Résumé of the relevant chapters*

In the third chapter, Hausherr describes the patristic quest to understand the Pauline injunction to 'pray always',[2] and he recounts the various interpretations of those two words 'pray' and 'always'. He shows how this discussion moved on to the concept of κατάστασις νόος, a state of prayer, and how this concept was developed in the writings of Evagrius of Pontus to mean an intellectual state free from disturbance and distraction.

From here, Hausherr unpacks the patristic treatment of three key elements in the evolution of continual prayer: the remembrance of God (μνήμη Θεοῦ), the rule of life (πολιτεία), and the secret or inward meditation (κρυπτὴ μελέτη). He relates how μνήμη Θεοῦ was seen as a more attainable alternative to the Evagrian κατάστασις νόος, how scope for individuality in meeting the demands of asceticism was given through πολιτεία, and how the interior activity of κρυπτὴ μελέτη involved, among other things, the memorization of the New Testament and the Psalter, and the recitation of short prayers.

In the fourth chapter Hausherr turns his attention to these short prayers. He gives an account of the occurrence of such prayers in the Gospels, with particular reference to the invocations of Jesus as 'Lord' or 'Son of David', and notes the presence of the Jesus Prayer in the texts in fragmentary form.[3] He follows this up with a list of relevant texts from Acts, Romans, and Revelation. He observes how the Apostolic Fathers directed such prayers to Jesus and Mary. And he considers an array of diverse supplications from such monastic authorities as Cassian, Arsenius, Macarius, Sisoes, Nilus, and Poemen.

He goes on to explain how in the writing of Chrysostom and Pseudo-Chrysostom this diversity evolved towards the uniformity of a monologistic prayer. From here, he assesses the part played by Diadochus of Photice in the story of this development, and concludes that he is a 'witness to an intermediate stage in the evolution towards a fixed formula of prayer to Jesus'.[4]

2 1 Thessalonians 5.17.

3 Hausherr, *Noms du Christ*, 182.

4 Hausherr, *Noms du Christ*, 210; Cummings, *Name of Jesus*, 229.

In the fifth chapter Hausherr trains his sights on the place of the petition for mercy in this development. Here he draws on his earlier work, *Penthos: La doctrine de compunction dans l'Orient Chrétien*,[5] in which he accounts for the contribution of compunction, the mourning for sin, in early Eastern monastic formation.

Hausherr contrasts what he describes as two currents within monasticism, represented by two different formulae: the older, identified by Cassian and based on the use of βοήθησον, as a cry for help; and the other, based on the use of ἐλέησον, as a cry for forgiveness. He argues that with the rise of monasticism, a movement for which πένθος was of central importance, and, with the 'invasion ... of the *Kyrie eleison* style of prayer',[6] the latter formula gradually replaced the former in Christian usage.

Once more, he catalogues the various patristic authorities, this time on the subject of penitential prayer, and, with reference to Evagrius, concludes that these prayers both served to 'develop and maintain a desired psychic *state*', and 'gave to this state the value of prayer by means of a frequently renewed attitude of supplication, confidence and humility'.[7]

## 3. *Critique of Hausherr's methodology*

It will be clear from the above, albeit brief, résumé that Hausherr has set himself to explore a particular development in the history of early Eastern monasticism from a relatively narrow perspective. Whilst we are treated to an impressive array of patristic texts and quotations, these texts and quotations are set in isolation from the wider context of monastic formation. Working through the evidence offered in *Noms du Christ*, the reader could be forgiven for forgetting the crucial role played by liturgical prayer in the lives of the monks in question, whose mind-set and spirituality were forged

5 Irénée Hausherr, *Penthos: La doctrine de compunction dans l'Orient Chrétien*, OCA 132 (Rome: Pontificium Institutum Orientalium Studiorum, 1944).

6 Hausherr, *Noms du Christ*, 217; Cummings, *Name of Jesus*, 243.

7 Hausherr, *Noms du Christ*, 234; Cummings, *Name of Jesus*, 260.

to a greater or lesser extent by the hours which they spent in participating in the divine offices, either privately or communally.

Hausherr makes little or no attempt to engage with the liturgical aspect of monastic life. His examination of the various texts is therefore of limited value, in so far as the reader is being invited to assess the impact which such texts would have had upon the individuals and communities in question without being presented with an adequate picture of the context in which those texts are being received and understood.

## II. More recent publications

Since 1960 we have witnessed an impressive wealth of scholarship which has helped to shed a greater light upon this corporate aspect of monastic formation. What many of these publications highlight, in their different ways, is the role played by psalmody in the liturgical life of the Desert Fathers.

### *1. The influence of psalmody*

Douglas Burton-Christie, in his study of the use of Scripture by the Desert Fathers,[8] refers to three scholars[9] who have researched the biblical citations in Cotelier's Greek Edition of the *Apothegmata Patrum*,[10] and affirms

8 Douglas Burton-Christie, *The Word in the Desert: Scripture and the Quest for Holiness in Early Christian Monasticism* (Oxford and New York: Oxford University Press, 1993) 96.

9 Benedicta Ward, trans., *The Sayings of the Desert Fathers: The Alphabetical Collection*, Cistercian Studies Series 59 (Kalamazoo, Michigan: Cistercial Publications, 1975); Lucien Regnault, *Les sentences des pères du désert* (Sablé-sur-Sarthe: Solesmes, 1981); Luciana Mortari, *Vita e detti dei padri del deserto, Vols. I and II* (Rome: Città Nuova, 1971).

10 Jean Baptiste Cotelier, ed., *Ecclesiae Graecae monumenta, Vol. I* (Paris: Muguet, 1677). Reprinted in Jacques-Paul Migne, *Patrologiae cursus completus. Series Graeca,*

that 'All agree that the most frequently cited Old Testament texts are the Psalms'.[11]

He is also at pains to emphasize the importance of the meditation on and rumination of Scripture in the monastic formation of the Desert Fathers. He writes, 'Such an approach to Scripture involved the saying of the words of a particular text, mulling them over in the mind, chewing on and slowly digesting the words'.[12] For the monks these texts had a power 'for aiding them in their battle with the demons; for healing and encouragement; for helping them to draw disparate thoughts and energies into a contemplative union'.[13] All of this was true of psalmody.

The place of the meditation on and rumination of Scripture, and therefore of psalmody, is, according to Burton-Christie, particularly significant with regard to the struggle against the demons. He cites Amma Syncletica as a witness that 'in the fight against *accidie*, that kind of grief or deep sadness so common to the desert, the psalms are one of the main sources of healing'.[14] He also quotes Theodore of Enaton who affirms that 'If God reproaches us for carelessness in our prayers and distractions in our psalmody [αἰχμαλωσίας τᾶς ἐν ταῖς ψαλμῳδίαῖς], we cannot be saved'.[15]

Again, Burton-Christie highlights the place of psalmody in this process of meditation and rumination. Referring to the testimony of Abba Isaac, regarding the repetition of Psalm 69.2, in Cassian's *Conlationes* 10, he writes: 'He says that the mind will go on grasping this single verse of Scripture "until it can cast away the wealth and multiplicity of other thoughts, and restore itself to the poverty of a single verse". Thus the repetition of a Scripture was held to unify the mind, helping one to overcome the kind of dissipation and distraction which left one open to the diverse attacks of the demons'.[16]

---

*Vol. LXV*, 72–440 (Paris: 1864). Supplemented by Jean-Claude Guy in *Recherches sur la tradition grecque des Apophthegmata Patrum. Subsidia Hagiographica* 36 (Brussels: Société des Bollandistes, 1962).

11 Burton-Christie, *Word in the Desert*, 97.

12 Ibid., 122.

13 Ibid.

14 Ibid., 126.

15 Ibid., 127.

16 Ibid., 128.

The place of psalmody in the structure of the daily offices of the Desert Fathers has also been well documented. In 'Praise in the Desert: The Coptic Monastic Office Yesterday and Today',[17] Robert F. Taft describes an element of continuity between the early Egyptian monastic office and present-day Coptic monastic liturgicalpractice. In his seminal work, *The Liturgy of the Hours in East and West*,[18] he outlines the liturgical offices in Lower Egypt (Scetis) and Upper Egypt (Pachomian office) in the fourth century, and, in respect of the former location, reiterates the witness of Cassian in *De institutis coenobiorum et de octo principalium vitiorum remediis*, Books II and III, which purports to give a detailed description of Egyptian monastic practice at this time, a witness to which we will return.

Taft makes a distinction between the 'cathedral' office of the secular churches during the second half of the fourth century and the 'monastic' office of the communities which had sprung up in Egypt and elsewhere. While the purpose of the former was one of liturgical ceremony, the purpose of the latter was one of quiet meditation on Scripture. And it is clear from Taft's account[19] that the Scripture in question included the psalms.[20]

In his chapter on the fourth-century Egyptian monastic office he claims that there were only two daily offices, one at cockcrow and one in the evening whose structure was exactly the same. This structure, he says, consisted of two elements, psalmody and lessons. The psalmody involved twelve psalms, which were read by a soloist and interspersed with communal silent prayer, prostrations and a collect read by the president, while the lessons involved an Old Testament and a New Testament reading on

17 Robert F. Taft, 'Praise in the Desert: The Coptic Monastic Office Yesterday and Today', in *Worship* 56, No.2 (Collegeville, Minnesota: St John's Abbey, 1982), 513–36.

18 Robert F. Taft, *The Liturgy of the Hours in East and West: the origins of the Divine Office and its meaning for to-day* (Collegeville, Minnesota: Liturgical Press, 1986).

19 Taft, *Liturgy of the Hours*, 57–73.

20 See also Paul Bradshaw, *The Search for the Origins of Christian Worship: Sources and Methods for the Study of Early Liturgy* (Oxford and New York: Oxford University Press, 2002), 172–5.

weekdays, and a reading from the Epistles or Acts, and one from the Gospels on Saturdays, Sundays and in Paschaltide.[21]

In a work first published in 1966, and praised by Taft himself, Derwas Chitty provides a very comprehensive account of the development of early Eastern monasticism.[22] Chitty encourages the reader to feast upon a series vignettes from the primary sources, which are served up in a colourful and engaging display of monastic life in the places and times in question. A number of these vignettes reveal the significance of psalmody for these individuals and communities.

A more recent compendium of early Eastern monastic traditions has been produced by William Harmless.[23] Echoing Burton-Christie, Harmless acknowledges the role of Scripture and of psalmody in particular in the spiritual environment of the desert, and points out that the use of Scripture, including psalmody, had a practical rather than discursive or ceremonial value: 'While the desert fathers chanted, recited, and chewed on biblical texts, they saw scripture less as something to be talked about than as something to be done'.[24] The chanting of psalmody was clearly designed to advance the spiritual practice (πρακτική) of these early monks.

Finally, in this brief survey of works which, over the past fifty years, have highlighted the influence of psalmody on early Eastern monasticism, some acknowledgement must be given to the contribution made by Gregory W. Woolfenden. In a paper presented at the Eleventh International Conference on Patristic Studies held in Oxford in 1991, and entitled 'The Use of the Psalter in Early Monastic Communities', Woolfenden offers a concise account of the part played by the recitation of the Psalter in Desert

21 Taft, *Liturgy of the Hours*, 60–1.

22 Derwas J. Chitty, *The Desert a City: An Introduction to the Study of Egyptian and Palestinian Monasticism under the Christian Empire* (Crestwood, New York: St Vladimir's Seminary Press, 1995).

23 William Harmless, *Desert Christians: An Introduction to the Literature of Early Monasticism* (Oxford and New York: Oxford University Press, 2004).

24 Ibid., 245.

Monasticism.[25] Referring to the early Desert Fathers' quest not for liturgical excellence but for solitary prayer, and their understanding of Scripture as a source of material for meditation, he poses the question as to 'why the Psalter became the dominant source of this meditational material, rather than any other book of the Bible'.[26]

He finds the answer in the idea that the Psalter embraced all Scripture, an idea which, as we have seen, was put into writing in the sixth-century *Peri tou Abba Philēmon*.[27] He finds further justification for this conclusion in the Pachomian requirement for monks to learn by heart the New Testament and the Psalter, and the expectation in the late fifth-century *Regula Orientalis* that they should pray and recite psalms whilst at work or on a journey, and that they should memorize as many psalms as they were able.[28]

Then he calls upon Basil of Caesarea to underline this concept of the Psalter as an edifiying summary of the whole of Scripture. Here he cites Basil's *Homilia in Psalmum I*: '...but the Book of psalms encompasses the benefit of them all. It foretells what is to come and memorializes history; it legislates for life, gives advice on practical matters, and serves in general as a repository of good teachings, carefully searching out what is suitable for each individual'.[29]

Whilst placing greater emphasis on this concept of the Psalter in early monastic communities, Woolfenden also acknowledges briefly another concept, which will receive fuller treatment later in this study. Here he draws attention to the work of Marie-Josèphe Rondeau who identifies the importance of prosopological exegesis in the psalm-commentaries of some of the patristic authors, especially Origen and Athanasius.[30] As we will see, this is a way of interpreting the Psalter whereby the psalmist is deemed to be speaking from the *persona* (*prosōpon* in Greek) of another character, normally Christ.

25 Gregory W. Woolfenden, 'The Use of the Psalter by Early Monastic Communities', in *SP* 26 (Leuven: Peeters Press, 1993), 88–94.

26 Ibid., 91.

27 Ibid.

28 Woolfenden, 'The Use of the Psalter', 92.

29 Ibid., 92 note 44. See PG 29, 209D–213C.

30 Marie-Josèphe Rondeau, *Les Commentaires Patristiques du Psautier, IIIe-Ve siècles, Vol. II: Exégèse prosopologique et théologie*, OCA 220 (Rome: Pontificium Institutum Studiorum Orientalium, 1985).

In conclusion, he places the early monastic recitation of the Psalter in the context of the whole of monastic life as an 'eschatological sign, an attempt to live out the realities of the risen life not yet totally fulfilled'.[31] For these early monks, he says, the Psalter was both God's word to his people and their response to him.

## *2. The influence of Evagrius*

We shall now consider how our understanding of the contribution made by one significantly influential Desert Father, and specifically identified by Hausherr as such, has been transformed by other works published since the appearance of *Noms du Christ*. As has been noted above, Hausherr explores the contribution made by Evagrius to the monastic *milieu* within which the search for continual prayer was conducted. This exploration is, of necessity, uninformed by the fruits of a publication which appeared in the same year as *Noms du Christ et voies d'oraison*.

The condemnation of Evagrius at the Fifth Ecumenical Council in 553 resulted insome of his writings being passed off as the work of other Fathers. The existence of the Evagrian *Scholia ad psalmos* was first proposed by Hans Urs von Balthasar in 'Die Hiera des Evagrius Pontikus'.[32] Von Balthasar put forward the idea that sections of the *Selecta in psalmos*, appearing under the name of Origen, and edited by Charles de la Rue[33] and by Joannes Baptista Pitra,[34] may have come from the pen of Evagrius. In 1960 his observations were taken up and further developed by Rondeau, who, using a key based on the manuscript Vaticanus Graecus 754, reconstructed the Evagrian commentary from the *Selecta in psalmos*.[35]

31 Woolfenden, 'The Use of the Psalter', 93.

32 Hans Urs von Balthasar, 'Die Hiera des Evagrius Pontikus', in *Zeitschrift für katholische Theologie* 63 (Innsbruck: Theologische Fakultät, 1939), 86–106, 181–206.

33 Jacques-Paul Migne, ed., *Patrologiae cursus completus. Series Graeca, Vol. XII* (Paris: 1862).

34 Joannes Baptista Pitra, ed., 'Origenes in Psalmos', in *Analecta sacra spicilegio solesmensi parata, Vol. II* (Paris: Tusculum, 1884), and *Vol. III* (Venice: St Lazarus Monastery, 1883).

35 Marie-Josèphe Rondeau, 'Le commentaire sur les Psaumes d'Évagre le Pontique', in OCP 26 (Rome: Pontificium Institutum Orientalium Studiorum, 1960), 307–48.

The establishment of an Evagrian psalm-commentary, as yet no more than an idea when Hausherr was penning his account of the early development of the Jesus Prayer, and its subsequent acceptance by scholarly consensus, necessitates a re-evaluation of the contribution made by the Pontic monk to the monastic search for continual prayer, which lies at the heart of the second part of *Noms du Christ*. This is because those texts, now attributable to Evagrius, pose new questions regarding the interplay of psalmody and prayer in the Evagrian understanding of the spiritual journey of the monk. These new questions have been taken up by three scholars in the past forty years, Adalbert de Vogüé,[36] Gabriel Bunge[37] and Luke Dysinger.[38]

To each of these scholars we shall return in due course and with greater scrutiny. What is clear from the observations made above is that, given that Hausherr acknowledges the special contribution made by Evagrius to the subject under investigation, it is impossible to allow his thesis to remain untroubled by the questions unearthed in the discovery of the *Scholia ad psalmos*, and by the ensuing explorations of the aforementioned scholars.

## III. Summary

This fleeting glimpse of but a handful of the publications which have appeared since *Noms du Christ* provides ample evidence that, with regard to the landscape of scholarship relating to monastic studies, the scenery has shifted significantly. Since 1960 there has been a renewed focus on the early

36 Adalbert de Vogüé, *La Règle de saint Benoit, Vol. VII, Commentaire Doctrinal et Spirituel* (Paris: Les Éditions du Cerf, 1977).

37 Gabriel Bunge, *Das Geistgebet: Studien zum Traktat, De Oratione des Evagrios Pontikos* (Cologne: Luther-Verlag, 1987).

38 Luke Dysinger, *Psalmody and Prayer in the Writings of Evagrius Ponticus* (Oxford and New York: Oxford University Press, 2005).

liturgical developments within monasticism and their place both within the broader liturgical history of the Church, and within monastic life itself.

The works referred to above also place an enhanced emphasis on the role of psalmody in the monastic formation of the Desert Fathers. Given this enhanced emphasis, Hausherr's decision to offer a catalogue of relevant short prayers drawn from Scripture without including any entries from the Psalter is now unsustainable.

Similarly, the rapid expansion of Evagrian studies in the past fifty years has had an even greater impact upon the landscape in which Hausherr was working. The identification of the *Scholia ad psalmos* has forced scholars not only to take more seriously Evagrius' use of psalmody, but also to reconsider and re-evaluate his teaching on prayer.

In the light of these developments it would to-day be impossible to attempt, as Hausherr does, to give an adequate account of Evagrius' understanding of the part played by prayer in monastic progression without some serious acknowledgement of his view of its relationship to psalmody. It is therefore time to update this Alsatian, to correct his omissions in the light of more recent scholarship and to allow the role of psalmody, which receives scant attention in his work, to make its own contribution to our understanding of the monastic culture from which the Jesus Prayer arose.

CHAPTER TWO

# The Spirit and Practice of Monastic Psalmody

The monastic culture of fourth-century Lower Egypt in which Evagrius produced his ascetical writings, and in which the monastic quest for continual prayer was conducted, has been vividly portrayed in a wide range of primary sources, and has been the focus of attention of an impressive corpus of modern scholarship. Among the former are to be found the *Apothegmata patrum*, Athanasius' *Epistola ad Marcellinum*, John Cassian's *Conlationes* and *De institutis*, the *Historia monachorum in Aegypto*, Palladius' *Historia Lausiaca*, the *Pachomiana Latina* of Jerome and the *Vita Pachomii*. The latter are well represented by the works referredto in Chapter 1.

How much we know about the belief, life and practice of the early Egyptian monastic communities is therefore the subject of a vibrant and ongoing discussion. This discussion will be the focus of the present chapter, in the course of which we will be examining the *De institutits*, the *Historia Lausiaca*, and the *Pachomiana Latina*. By way of introduction, however, let us consider the fourth-century understanding of the spirit of monastic psalmody afforded to us in Athanasius' *Epistola ad Marcellinum*.

## I. *Epistola ad Marcellinum*

In terms of the critical background of the *Epistola*, Rondeau offers a summary, noting how the text figures in the Codex Alexandrinus of the early fifth century. Whilst reporting that the authenticity of the work has in the past been called into question, she dismisses any suggestion that it is not Athanasian. She goes on to provide this useful introduction to the text:

> The Epistola ad Marcellinum takes root in the monastic world. Addressed to a character who seems to be a monk, claiming to transmit the teachings of an old man, using a vocabulary which will become desert technique, challenging profane culture, being interested in the problems of the spiritual life in the light of Scripture, and representing this as a fight against the demons, it is without doubt the fruit of Athanasius' well-known connections with the world of the desert. It is significant that one recovers there a very clear echo of the same teaching in Cassian's Conference X.[1]

The wisdom emanating from the 'learned old man',[2] and bearing the authority of a bishop and theologian who exerted enormous influence in fourth-century monastic circles, will have contributed significantly to the Desert Fathers' understanding of psalmody and to the development of the general spiritual environment in which they flourished. Let us now examine some of the elements which constituted this wisdom, and with it the spirit of monastic psalmody in late fourth- and early fifth-century Egypt.

### *1. Garden*

The account of the old man's wisdom begins with a recognition of the value and inspiration of every book of the Bible, but he singles out the Psalter for special mention above the others: 'Yet the Book of Psalms is like a garden (παράδεισος) containing things of all these kinds, and it sets them to music, but also exhibits things of its own that it gives in song along with them'.[3]

1 Marie-Josèphe Rondeau, *Les Commentaires Patristiques du Psautier (IIIe-Ve siècles), Vol. I, Les Travaux des pères grecs et latins sur le psautier. Recherches et bilan*, OCA 219 (Rome: Pontificium Institutum Studiorum Orientalium, 1982), 79–80.

2 Τινι φιλοπόνῳ γέροντι: *Epist. Marcell.* 1, PG 27, 12A; Robert C. Gregg, trans., *Athanasius: The Life of Anthony and the Letter to Marcellinus* (Mahway, New Jersey: Paulist Press, 1980), 101.

3 Η δὲ γε βίβλος τῶν Ψαλμῶν ὡς παράδεισος τὰ ἐν αὐτῇ φέουσα μελῳσεῖ, καὶ τὰ ἴδια δὲ πάλιν μετ' αὐτῶν ψάλλουσα δείκυσι: *Epist. Marcell.* 2, PG 27, 12C; Gregg, *Letter to Marcellinus*, 102.

Παράδεισος is a powerful and well-used image in patristic literature. It is employed in relation to heaven, as a place of life after death, and as a metaphor for God, the Virgin Mary, the saints, the Church, a spiritual state, and, as in the *Epistola*, for Scripture.[4]

Underpinning much of this imagery is the text of Genesis 2.8, 'And God planted a garden eastward in Eden, and placed there the man whom he had formed'.[5] The Garden of Eden is the paradise which God has created for human habitation, and it is replete with every kind of fruit for the satisfaction of all human needs. Though Athanasius makes no direct connection between this text and his description of the Psalter, the association of the two would not have been lost on readers well-versed in the Scriptures.

The παράδεισος metaphor is employed to express the concept already identified, and in line with Basil of Caesarea's *Homilia in Psalmum I*, that the Psalter encompasses the whole of Scripture. The same imagery which is used at the commencement of the work also finds a place as the author moves towards his conclusion: 'Now, my son, it is necessary for each of the readers of that book to read it in its entirety, for truly the things in it are divinely inspired, but then to take benefits from these, as from the fruits of a garden on which he may cast his gaze when the need arises' (λαμβάνειν δὲ λοιπὸν ἀπ' αὐτῶν ὡς ἐκ παραδείσου καρπῶν ὠφελείας).[6]

The fact that παράδεισος is employed both to introduce and to advance towards a conclusion of the thesis reveals much about the nature of the intervening chapters. The capacity of this garden to supply all the fruit required for the needs of the monk is the dominant and underlying *motif* of this work. Indeed, the whole of the *Epistola* could be described as a catalogue of the various fruits which constitute the garden produce in this liturgical version of Eden.

4 See Geoffrey W. H. Lampe, *A Patristic Greek Lexicon*, Seventeenth Impression (Oxford: Oxford University Press, 2003), 1010–13.

5 Καὶ ἐφύτευσεν ὁ Θεὸς παράδεισον ἐν Ἐδὲμ κατὰ ἀνατολάς· καὶ ἔθετο ἐκεῖ τὸν ἄνθρωπον, ὃν ἔπλασε: Lancelot C. L. Brenton, ed., *The Septuagint with Apocrypha: Greek and English* (London: Samuel Bagster and Sons, 1851), 3.

6 *Epist. Marcell.* 30, PG 27, 41C; Gregg, *Letter to Marcellinus*, 126.

## 2. *Encounter with Christ*

In terms of the content and interpretation of the psalm, throughout the *Epistola*, Athanasius reports, the old man is insistent upon the all-pervading presence of Christ in the Psalter. The primary fruit available to the monk in this παράδεισος is a constant and recurring encounter with Christ. This Christological presence within the Psalter may be briefly summed up as taking two forms: firstly as a proclamation of prophecy about Christ, and secondly as a proclamation of the words of Christ himself.

This all-pervading presence in the form of prophecies about Christ is most neatly summed up in a passage which identifies a series of psalms as testimonies to Christ's pre-existence, his incarnation, passion, resurrection and ascension, as well as the trophies of his victory for his followers:

> When you desire, in private, to extol the events concerning the Savior, you find such things in nearly every psalm ("Οτε δὲ θέλῃς κατ' ἰδίαν τὰ περὶ τοῦ Σωτῆρος ψάλλειν, ἐν ἑκάστῳ μὲν σχεδὸν εὑρίσκεις ψαλμῷ τὰ τοιαῦτα), but you have particularly Psalms 44 and 109, which show forth his true generation from the Father and his incarnate appearance. There are Psalms 21 and 68, which foretell about the divine cross and what great treachery he submitted to on our behalf, and the number of things he suffered; and Psalms 2 and 108, which signal both the plotting and wickedness of the Jews and the betrayal of Judas Iscariot; and the twentieth, forty-ninth, and seventy-first, also making manifest his kingship, his power as judge and, again, his appearance in the flesh for us, and also the calling of the gentiles. Psalm 15 demonstrates his resurrection from the dead. The twenty-third and forty-sixth announce his ascent into heaven, and while reading Psalms 92, 95, 97 and 98 you should be able to contemplate the benefits won for us by the Savior through his sufferings.[7]

The author, however, wishes his readers to understand that in certain texts the words of the psalms are not merely prophetic, but also prosopological, not merely words ABOUT Christ, but words OF Christ: 'In the twenty-first it tells the manner of the death from the Savior's own lips (ἐκ προσώπου

7 *Epist. Marcell.* 26, PG 27, 37BC; Gregg, *Letter to Marcellinus*, 123.

τοῦ Σωτῆρος φησιν)... And it says again through his own lips (Καὶ φησιν ἐκ προσώπου πάλιν αὐτοῦ) in Psalm 87, *Your wrath has pressed heavily upon me*, and in Psalm 68, *Then I restored that which I did not take away*'.[8]

The words of the Psalter should therefore be regarded as the instruction of the pre-incarnate Christ to those who would later follow him:

> It was indeed for this reason that he made this resound in the Psalms before his sojourn in our midst, so that just as he provided the model of the earthly and heavenly man in his own person, so also from the Psalms he who wants to do so can learn the emotions and dispositions of the souls, finding in them also the therapy and correction for each emotion.

> If the point needs to be put more forcefully, let us say that the entire Holy Scripture is a teacher of virtues and of the truths of faith, while the Book of Psalms possesses somehow the perfect image for the souls' course of life (ἡ δὲ γε βίβλος τῶν Ψαλμῶν ἔχει καὶ τὴν εἰκόνα πως τῆς διαγωγῆς τῶν ψυχῶν).[9]

## *3. Pattern for living*

From here another fruit is disclosed. Since the 'Book of Psalms possesses somehow the perfect image of the souls' course of life', inasmuch as it is the mouthpiece of the Christ who provides instruction for his disciples, it follows that the psalms have an essential practical implication for monastic life, and are designed to offer the monk a pattern for disciplined living, derived from Christ himself. Here Athanasius stresses the need for intelligent reading of the Psalter, with recourse to the word *συνετῶς*: 'You too, practicing these things and reciting the Psalms intelligently in this way (Ταῦτα καὶ σὺ μελετῶν, καὶ συνετῶς ἐντυγχάνων), are able to comprehend the meaning in each, being guided by the Spirit. And the kind of life the holy, God-bearing men possessed who spoke these things – this life you also shall imitate' (Τοιοῦτον δὲ καὶ σῦ ζηλώσεις βίον).[10]

8 *Epist. Marcell.* 7, PG 27, 16CD; Gregg, *Letter to Marcellinus*, 105.

9 *Epist.Marcell.* 13–14, PG 27, 25BC; Gregg, *Letter to Marcellinus*, 112.

10 *Epist. Marcell.* 33, PG 27, 45C; Gregg, *Letter to Marcellinus*, 129.

This emphatic injunction further underscores the significance of psalmody. Indeed, the old man says, this is an important distinction between the Psalter and the other biblical books, for the former educates its readers not only in the 'what' but also in the 'how':

> Now there certainly are in the other books preventive words that forbid wickedness, but in this book is also prescribed how one must abstain. Of such a sort is the commandment to repent – for to repent is to cease from sin. Herein is prescribed also how to repent and what one must say in the circumstances of repentance (ἐνταῦθα δὲ καὶ πῶς μετανοεῖν, καὶ τί δεῖ λέγειν ἐπὶ τῇ μετανοίᾳ, τετόπωτος).[11]

## *4. Words for prayer*

In this way the Book of Psalms is depicted as a provider of words for all sorts of occasions. This particular garden fruit makes it possible for the monk to find words to be used in prayer. Here the old man details how prayers of thanksgiving, prayers of endurance under suffering, and prayers of blessing are supplied to the worshipper by this biblical book for all seasons:

> Furthermore, there is a command to give thanks in all circumstances, but the Psalms also teach what one must say when giving thanks. Then hearing from others that as many as wish to live a godly life will be persecuted, from these we are taught how one must call out while fleeing and what words must be offered to God while being persecuted and after being delivered subsequent to persecution. We are asked to bless the Lord, and to acknowledge him. But in the Psalms we are instructed how one must praise the Lord and by speaking what words we properly confess our faith in him. And in the case of each person one would find the divine hymns appointed for us and our emotions and equanimity (Καὶ ἐφ' ἑκάστου δὲ τις οὕτως ἂν εὕροι τὰς θείας ᾠδὰς, πρὸς ἡμᾶς καὶ ἡμῶν κινήσεις καὶ καταστάσεις κειμένας).[12]

11 *Epist. Marcell.* 10, PG 27, 20D–21A; Gregg, *Letter to Marcellinus*, 108.

12 *Epist. Marcell.* 10, PG 27, 21B; Gregg, *Letter to Marcellinus*, 108–9.

Similarly, the words of the psalms provide the monk with prayers to be used within the ascetic struggle, as a weapon of battle, in combat with the powers of evil. Such words are deemed to be particularly efficacious:

> Therefore, reciting even now the same words, let each person be confident, for God will pay heed quickly to those who make supplication through these. Whether one is afflicted at the time he recites these things, he will regard as great the encouragement that is in them; or whether he is tested and persecuted while chanting thus, he will be shown forth as more worthy, and will be protected by the Lord, who watched over the one who originally said these things. In these he will overthrow the devil, and he will drive away his demons (ἐν τούτοις τὸν μὲν διάβολον ἀνατρέψει, τοὺς δὲ δαίμονας αὐτοῦ σοβήσει).[13]

## 5. *Self-reflection*

Another fruit from the garden is the opportunity for self-reflection. The exceptional character of the Psalter also extends to the input of the Holy Spirit, whose special grace in the psalms enables the monk to learn about himself:

> Let there be such a common grace of the Spirit in all, and let it be found existing in each one, the same grace among all, whenever the need demands and the Spirit desires. The more and the less in this need do not differ, as each unstintingly accomplishes and completes its own service. But even so, the Book of Psalms thus has a certain grace of its own (καὶ οὕτως ἔχει τινὰ πάλιν χάριν ἰδίαν), and a distinctive exactitude of expression. For in addition to the other things in which it enjoys an affinity and fellowship with the other books, it possesses, beyond that, this marvel of its own – namely, that it contains even the emotions of each soul, and it has the changes and rectifications of these delineated and regulated in itself... For in the other books one hears only what one must do and what one must not do... But in the Book of Psalms, the one who hears, in addition to learning these things, also comprehends and is taught in the emotions of the soul, and, consequently, on the basis of that which affects him and by which he is constrained, he also is enabled by this book to possess the image deriving from the words (ἔτι καὶ τὰ κινήματα τῆς ἑαυτοῦ ψυχῆς ἐν αὐτῇ κατανοεῖ καὶ διδάσκεται).[14]

13 *Epist. Marcell.* 32, PG 27, 44B; Gregg, *Letter to Marcellinus*, 127.

14 *Epist. Marcell.* 10, PG 27, 20CD; Gregg, *Letter to Marcellinus*, 107–8.

Furthermore, the monk learns about himself in so far as the words of the psalms, as compared to the words of other biblical books, become his own words:

> Indeed, it is clear that one who reads the books utters them not as his own words, but as the words of the saints and those who are signified by them. But contrariwise, remarkably, after the prophecies about the Savior and the nations, he who recites the psalms is uttering the rest as his own words, and each sings them as if they were written concerning him (ὡς ἴδια ῥήματα λαλῶν ἐστι, καὶ ὡς περὶ αὐτοῦ γραφέντας αὐτοὺς ἕκαστος ψάλλει)[15]

The effect of singing the words of the psalms, in this way, as if in a mirror, is transformative both for the monk himself and for the community as a whole: 'And it seems to me that these words become like a mirror (ὥσπερ εἴσοπτρον) to the person singing them, so that he might perceive himself and the emotions of his soul, and thus affected, he might recite them'.[16]

### *6. Inner harmony*

Finally, the old man insists, the gift of inner harmony is also part of the garden produce. He says that the words relating to Christ, and indeed the words of the Psalter as a whole, need to be sung rather than said. This, he says, has nothing to do with the aesthetic beauty of music as such. It is more concerned with providing benefits to the soul, particularly with regard to the creation of harmony within the human person:

> It is important not to pass over the question of why words of this kind are chanted with melodies and strains (Διὰ τί δὲ μετὰ μέλους καὶ ᾠδῆς ψάλλονται οἱ τοιοῦτοι λόγοι). For some of the simple among us, although they believe indeed that the phrases are divinely inspired, imagine, however, on account of the sweetness of the sound, that also the psalms are rendered musically for the sake of the ear's delight. But this is not so. For Scripture did not seek out that which is pleasant and winning, but this also has been fashioned for the benefit of the soul, and for all number of reasons,

15 *Epist. Marcell.* 11, PG 27, 24A; Gregg, *Letter to Marcellinus*, 110.
16 *Epist. Marcell.* 12, PG 27, 24BC; Gregg, *Letter to Marcellinus*, 111.

> but especially on account of two. First, because it is fitting for the Divine Scripture to praise God not in compressed speech alone, but also in the voice that is richly broadened (μὴ μόνον τῇ συνεχείᾳ, ἀλλὰ καὶ τῇ κατὰ πλάτος φωνῇ τὸν Θεὸν ὑμνεῖν)... The second reason is that, just as harmony that unites flutes effects a single sound, so also, seeing that different movements appear in the soul – and in it is the power of reasoning, and eager appetite, and high-spirited passion, from the motion of which comes also the activity of the parts of the body – the reason intends man neither to be discordant in himself, nor to be at variance with himself (ὥσπερ ἁρμονία τοὺς αὐλοὺς συντιθεῖσα μίαν τὴν συμφωνίαν ἀποτελεῖ).[17]

The creation of this inner harmony, he continues, enables the psalms to be chanted both with greater understanding and with rhythm, as a 'sure sign of the harmony of the soul's reflections':

> But when they chant in the way mentioned earlier, so that the melody of the phrases is brought forth from the soul's good order and from the concord with the Spirit (ὥστε τὴν μελῳδίαν τῶν ῥημάτων ἐκ τοῦ ῥυθμοῦ τῆς ψυχῆς καὶ τῆς πρὸς τὸ πνεῦμα συμφωνίας προσφέρεσθαι) such people sing with the tongue, but singing also with the mind (καὶ τῷ νοΐ) they greatly benefit not only themselves but even those willing to hear them... Therefore the Psalms are not recited with melodies because of a desire for pleasant sounds. Rather, this is a sure sign of the harmony of the soul's reflections (ἀλλὰ τεκμήριον τῆς ἁρμονίας τῶν ἐν τῇ ψυχῇ λογισμῶν). Indeed, the melodic reading is a symbol of the mind's well-ordered and undisturbed condition.[18]

In terms of the context of the whole work, Paul R. Kolbet argues that the promotion of the use of the Psalter in the *Epistola* is part of Athanasius' programme to unite desert and urban manifestations of the Egyptian Church, and that Marcellinus is probably a Christian from one of the cities.[19] In relation to the issue of inner harmony, he offers this comment:

> The outer musical harmony not only expresses the inner concord of the soul, but also contributes to it. Athanasius says that the one 'beautifully singing praises brings rhythm' to the 'soul and leads it ... from disproportion to proportion.' The soul gains

17 *Epist. Marcell.* 27, PG 27, 37D–40A; Gregg, *Letter to Marcellinus*, 123–4.
18 *Epist. Marcell.* 29, PG 27, 40D–41C; Gregg, *Letter to Marcellinus*, 125.
19 Paul R. Kolbet, 'Athanasius, the Psalms, and the Reformation of the Self', in *HTR* 99 (Cambridge, Massachusetts: Harvard Divinity School, 2006), 85–101.

> 'its composure by singing the phrases' of the Psalter, 'rejoices' as it 'becomes forgetful of the passions,' and conceives the 'most excellent thoughts' while it 'sees in accordance with the mind of Christ'.[20]

The concept of psalmody as an introit into the contemplation of the things of Christ, and, consequently, into a deeper union with the divine, is of crucial significance to this study, and one to which we shall return. Having considered the spirit of monastic psalmody in the light of Athanasius' *Epistola ad Marcellinum*, we now turn to an investigation of the practice of that psalmody as portrayed by three works written during the period in question.

## II. *De institutis*

Evidence of the practice of monastic psalmody at Nitria and Kellia in Lower Egypt at the time of Evagrius is derived largely from the witness of John Cassian in *De institutis* (or, more accurately, *De institutis coenobiorum et de octo principalium vitiorum remediis*). Cassian was born around 360 and took up the monastic life in Bethelehem. Around 385 he and his friend Germanus went to Egypt where he became a disciple of Evagrius, remaining there until Evagrius' death in 399. After a period in Constantinople he travelled westwards, eventually founding monasteries in Gaul. The *De institutis* were written by Cassian around 417–25. They are according to Columba Stewart a 'foundational work designed to guide and instruct and thus are more than simply a collection of customs and rules'.[21]

20 Ibid., 100.

21 Columba Stewart, *Cassian the Monk* (Oxford and New York: Oxford University Press, 1998), 29.

### *1. Cassian's account*

Writing a quarter of a century after the end of his monastic life in Egypt, and for the purpose of promoting monastic practice in the very different context Cassian's description may not be totally trustworthy. Cassian himself says he no longer trusts his memory.[22] Furthermore, he also concedes that where he considers the Egyptian practice to be inappropriate for the Gallic context, on account of the 'harsh climate or difficulty or diversity of behavior', he will temper what he writes 'by recourse to the customs of the monasteries in Palestine and Mesopotamia'.[23] This, however, does not prevent him from describing in detail the practices which he claims to have observed at first hand.

These cautionary remarks in the *Praefatio* raise questions regarding the reliability of Cassian's witness to Egyptian monastic practice in *De institutis*. To what extent does his desire to make a claim for Egyptian authority within the context of competing notions of monasticism make his statements more definite than they should be? We will shortly consider this ongoing debate. First, however, let us examine Cassian's account of those practices which he claims to have observed.

Thus we learn from Cassian: 'And so, throughout Egypt and the Thebaid, where monasteries are not established at the whim of a single renunciant but remain through a succession of elders and their traditions even to the present day and are founded to stay, we see that the correct number of prayers is maintained in the evening gatherings and at the night vigils'.[24]

22 *minime iam possumus ad integrum retinere: De inst. Praefatio* 4; Jean-Claude Guy, *Jean Cassien Institutions Cénobitiques*, SC 109 (Paris: Les Éditions du Cerf, 1965), 26.

23 *institutis monasteriorum, quae per Palaestinam uel Mesoptamiam habentur, aliquatenus Temperem: De inst. Praefatio* 9; Guy, SC 109, 32; Boniface Ramsey, *John Cassian: The Institutes, translated and annotated* (New York and Mahwah, New Jersey: The Newman Press, 2000), 14.

24 *legitimum orationum modum in uespertinis conuentibus seu nocturnis uigilis uidimus Retentari: De inst.* II.3; Guy, SC 109, 60; Ramsey, *Institutes*, 37–38.

Again, he asserts: '...the number of twelve psalms is maintained throughout all of Egypt and the Thebaid in both the evening and the night-time services in such a way that, when they are finished, two readings follow, one from the Old and one from the New Testament'.[25]

In *De institutis* II.5 he continues his description:

> As they were getting ready to carry out the daily rites of prayer, someone in their midst arose to sing the psalms to the Lord. And when all were seated, as is still the custom throughout Egypt, and had fixed the full attention of their hearts upon the cantor's words (*in psallentis uerba omni cordis intentione defixis*), he sang eleven psalms that were separated by the interposition of prayers (*undecim psalmos orationum interiectione*), all the verses being pronounced in the same tone of voice. Having finished the twelfth with an Alleluia as a response, he suddenly withdrew from the eyes of all, thus concluding both the discussion and the ceremony.[26]

In *De institutis* II.7 he elaborates on the practice of prayer within Egyptian psalmody:

> They begin and end the aforementioned prayers, then, such that once the psalm is finished they do not immediately rush to kneel down, as some of us do in this region... Before they kneel they pray briefly, and while standing they pass the greater part of the time in supplication (*et stantes in supplicatione maiorem temporis partem expendunt*). After this they fall on the ground for a very short time (*puncto breuissimo*), as if only adoring the divine mercy. Then they get up very quickly and, erect once more with hands outstretched as they had been when they were standing in prayer before, they linger over their prayers (*suis precibus inmorantur*).[27]

With regard to the chanting of the psalms, in *De institutis* II.11, he notes how the division of some psalms into two or three sections, and these being interspersed with periods of prayer (*cum orationum interiectione*), was designed to enhance the mind's knowledge (*mentis intellegentia*).[28]

25 *De inst.* II.4; Guy, SC109, 64. This latter prescription is said to have angelic authority (*sed caelitus angeli magisterio patribus fuisse delatus*), *De inst.* II.4; Guy, SC 109, 64; Ramsey, *Institutes*, 39.

26 Guy, SC 109, 68; Ramsey, *Institutes*, 40–1.

27 Guy, 109, 70; Ramsey, *Institutes*, 41.

28 Guy, SC 109, 76.

Posture is considered in the following chapter,[29] where he recalls how monks were permitted to be seated during the chanting of the twelve psalms in order to facilitate the attentive listening (*cordis intentione*) which was required of them for spiritual engagement and progress.

Finally, in *De institutis* III.2 he places the Egyptian practice of monastic psalmody firmly within the overall goal of the quest for continual prayer:

> For they are constantly doing manual labour alone in their cells in such a way that they almost never omit meditating on the psalms and on other parts of Scripture (*ut psalmorum quoque, uel ceterarum Scripturarum meditatio numquam penitus omittatur*), and to this they add entreaties and prayers at every moment (*cui preces et orationes per singula momenta miscentes*), taking up the whole day in offices that we celebrate at fixed times.[30]

## 2. *The debate about Cassian's reliability*

The historical reliability of the *De institutis*, and also that of the *Historia Lausiaca*, was dismissed by Hermann Weingarten in *Der Ursprung des Mönchtums im nachconstantinischen Zeitalter*.[31] However, this extreme scepticism was challenged by Cuthbert Butler in the first of two volumes which he produced on Palladius' work.[32] In his study, Butler argues that the detailed contrasts which Cassian makes between the monastic liturgical practice in Egypt and that which held sway in Palestine includes information with regard to both regions which is verified by other sources.[33]

A more recent attack on the trustworthiness of Cassian's record was launched by Armand Veilleux in *La Liturgie dans le cénobitisme*

29 Ibid., 80.

30 Guy, SC 109, 92; Ramsey, *Institutes*, 59.

31 Hermann Weingarten, *Der Ursprung des Mönchtums im nachconstantinischen Zeitalter* (Gotha: F. A. Perthes, 1877), 62.

32 Cuthbert Butler, ed. and trans., *The Lausiac History of Palladius: a critical discussion together with notes on early Egyptian monachism, Vol. I* (Cambridge: Cambridge University Press, 1898).

33 Ibid., 205.

*pachômien au quatrième siècle*.[34] The thrust of Veilleux's attack is directed principally at Cassian's self-depiction as a reliable witness to the monastic practices of the Pachomian monasteries of the Thebaid in Upper Egypt, through his resort to such all-inclusive terms as 'throughout all Egypt and the Thebaid'.

Noting that Cassian never lived in Upper Egypt, and questioning the possible sources of his information, Veilleux argues throughout *La Liturgie* that Cassian bases his understanding of the practices of Pachomian cenobitic communities on those with which he was familiar in the semi-anchoritic environment of Nitria and Scetis. However, not content with having demolished Cassian as a reliable authority on monastic customs in Upper Egypt, Veilleux proceeds to seek to cast doubt on his value as a witness to liturgical life in Lower Egypt as well. For example, he implies that Cassian in *De institutis* II.6 invents the use of an Old and a New Testament reading at the office, which, he says, 'does not appear in any other Egyptian monastic document', and 'is also absent from the course of the Office in Palestine, in Antioch or in Cappadocia'.[35]

Similarly, he observes that Cassian 'says nothing about the prayer at the time of the meal, that is to say the ninth hour', which was known to have been the practice in Lower Egypt in his day. He surmises that this is because Cassian wishes to preserve what he considered to be the ideal form of prayer, which consisted of only two common offices, releasing the rest of the day for continual prayer.[36]

Notwithstanding these and other question marks which Veilleux places against the accuracy of Cassian's record with regard to the liturgical customs of Lower Egypt, the overall thrust of his argument would appear to strengthen rather than to diminish the case for such accuracy. Much of Veilleux's material would suggest that Cassian took the semi-anchoritic practices of Lower Egypt, with which he was personally acquainted, as

34 Armand Veilleux, *La Liturgie dans le cénobitisme pachômien au quatrième siècle*, Studia Anselmiana 57 (Rome: S. Anselmi de Urbe, 1968).

35 Veilleux, *Liturgie*, 337.

36 Ibid., 338.

his starting-point for assuming that these were shared by other Egyptians. Veilleux makes this argument particularly forcefully with regard to the so-called tradition of the twelve prayers or psalms.

Alexis van der Mensbrugghe claimed that the rule of twelve psalms per office, identified by Cassian in *De institutis* II.4 as the practice 'throughout all Egypt and the Thebaid', was found in the Pachomian office.[37] Veilleux emphatically refutes this claim, and goes on to argue that the tradition of the twelve prayers belongs to Nitria rather than to the Pachomian monasteries.[38]

Further on in his argument, Veilleux offers this comment: 'In certain circles, however, and more precisely at Nitria and Scetis, it seems that in the course of a later evolution, these prayers, henceforth accompanied by as many psalms, might have been gradually regrouped in two continuous series recited (in private as well as communally), one in the morning, the other in the evening. This is what we will find with Cassian…'.[39]

In other words, in spite of placing question-marks against certain aspects of Cassian's witness as to what he claims to have seen in Lower Egypt, and in spite of his regular and correct insistence that Cassian is not setting out to write a detailed account of liturgical practices in Nitria and Scetis, Veilleux is resting much of his case for Cassian's inaccuracy *viz-à-viz* monastic practice in Upper Egypt on the ground of his accuracy *viz-à-viz* monastic practice in Lower Egypt.

A more recent sceptic, Jean-Claude Guy, is, according to Columba Stewart, subject to the same kind of criticism as Veilleux. Notably, in *Les Apophtegmes des Pères. Collection systématique, Volume I*,[40] in 'Jean Cassien, historien du monachisme égytien?'[41] and also in 'Cassian St John', a

37 Alexis van der Mensbrugghe, 'Prayer-time in Egyptian Monasticism', in *SP* 2 (Leuven: Peeters Press, 1957), 435–54.

38 Veilleux, *Liturgie*, 280–2 and 298–300.

39 Ibid., 332.

40 Jean-Claude Guy, *Les Apophtegmes des Pères. Collection systématique, Vol. I*, SC 387 (Paris: Les Éditions du Cerf, 1993), 44.

41 Jean-Claude Guy, 'Jean Cassien, historien du monachisme égyptien?', in *SP* 8, Texte und Untersuchungen 93 (Berlin: Akademie Verlag, 1966), 363–72.

contribution to the *Coptic Encyclopedia, Volume II*,[42] Guy dismisses Cassian's testimony as 'fanciful'.

For example, in 'Jean Cassien historien du monachisme égyptien?' he says, 'In fact, Cassian has nothing of the historian about him. He is a theoretician of the spiritual life, and a theoretician of remarkable profundity'.[43] Again, in 'Cassian, St John' he says: 'Clearly Cassian has little concern for providing his readers with historical information, even about those personages who played a large part in his work'.[44] However, as Stewart claims, 'Guy ended up basing much of the prosopographical section of *Les Apophtegmes des Pères* (1:46–73) on the same "fanciful" evidence'.[45]

Stewart himself offers this conclusion to the debate on the trustworthiness of Cassian's record of monastic practice in Lower Egypt at the end of the fourth-century:

> In his monastic writings Cassian interweaves his direct knowledge with literary sources available to him. Much of the information contained in the *Institutes* and *Conferences* is unique to him and is based evidently on his own experiences. What he tells us about places and people can often be collated with other texts to indicate that by and large he is a useful, trustworthy and important witness to the late-fourth-century monastic scene in Lower Egypt.[46]

This summary concurs with the comments offered by de Vogüé in *De Saint Pachômien à Jean Cassien: Études littéraires et doctrinales sur le monachisme égyptien à ses débuts*,[47] a work dedicated to Veilleux. Having rendered a painstaking analysis of the sources of the first four books of the *De institutis*,

42 Jean-Claude Guy, 'Cassian, St John', in Aziz S. Atiya, ed., *Coptic Encyclopedia, Vol. II* (New York: Macmillan, 1991), 461–4.

43 Guy, *SP* 8, 372.

44 *Coptic Encyclopedia, Vol. II*, 463.

45 Stewart, *Cassian the Monk*, 144 note 49.

46 Ibid., 8.

47 Adalbert de Vogüé in *De Saint Pachômien à Jean Cassien: Études littéraires et doctrinales sur le monachisme égyptien à ses débuts*, Studia Anselmiana 120 (Rome: S. Anselmi de Urbe, 1996).

and having acknowledged the need for caution when assessing the historical input of Cassian, de Vogüé concludes:

> But often the Institutes also bring original information, drawn from the personal memories of Cassian, which corroborate, complete or qualify what other writings reveal to us. These precious pieces of information do not concern the cenobitism of the Thebaid (on the subject of which Cassian seems to depend entirely on the Pachomiana Latina, the Historia Monachorum, and the Historia Lausiaca), but the cenobitism of Palestine and Lower Egypt. Anyway, the coenobia of this latter region are not as different from those of Upper Egypt as certain recent authors believed to be the case. It is legitimate to speak simply, as Cassian sometimes does, of 'Egyptian' monasticism, showing throughout the various regions a certain unity.[48]

We shall consider the monastic practices of Upper Egypt later in this chapter. By way of concluding this section on the *De institutis*, it is worth pointing out that most scholars who have published works after Veilleux's observations were made in 1968, including Taft, de Vogüé, Stewart, Harmless and Woolfenden,[49] have endorsed, either explicitly or implicitly, the pattern of psalmody and prayer to which Cassian bears witness. Furthermore, as has been noted, the more sceptical conclusions of both Veilleux and Guy need to be qualified by the apparent willingness of both of those authors to indulge Cassian's veracity in some measure.

It therefore follows that, despite Cassian's confession that he did not trust his memory, and despite the fact that the *De institutis* is clearly written not primarily toconvey factual information but to promote a particular style of monastic order, the account of the practice of prayer and psalmody in monastic Lower Egypt at the time of Evagrius may be accepted as trustworthy. In particular, the oscillation of psalmody and prayer, according to Cassian's testimony in *De institutis* II.5–8, may, on this basis, be accepted as an accurate record of a pattern and a practice which he witnessed at first hand.

48 Ibid., 456.

49 Gregory W. Woolfenden, *Daily Liturgical Prayer: Origins and Theology* (Aldershot: Ashgate Publishing, 2004), 52–3, 171.

## III. *Historia Lausiaca*

We now turn our attention away from the work which provides evidence of the manner in which early Egyptian monastic psalmody was practised and towards that which, it is claimed, bears testimony to the way in which the discipline of prayer was carried out by one of the most influential fourth-century monastic authors on the subject, Evagrius of Pontus.

Palladius wrote the *Historia Lausiaca* around 419 or 420, interestingly coinciding with Cassian's production of the *De institutis*. Addressed to Lausus, the 'royal chamberlain', it is a collection of stories of male and female ascetics of the early monastic period, relating predominantly, though not exclusively, to Egyptian saints.

### *1. The debate about Palladius' reliability*

As has already been observed, Weingarten questioned the historical accuracy both of Cassian's *De institutis* and Palladius' *Historia Lausiaca*, and his challenge was refuted by Butler. With regard to Palladius' history, William Kemp Lowther Clarke affirmed Butler's refutation, and also defended *Historia Lausiaca* against the claim of Richard Reitzenstein[50] that the work was a collection of old literary motives formerly attached to pagan characters.[51]

Nonetheless, Veilleux notes that 'Modern criticism has hardly been kind to Palladius'.[52] He then proceeds to reel off a directory of scholars who have cast doubt on the historical accuracy of the *Historia Lausiaca*.[53] Since Veilleux's particular concern is with Chapters 32 to 34,

50 Richard Reitzenstein, *Hellenistichen Wundererzählungen* (Stuttgart: Teubner, 1906).
51 William Kemp Lowther Clarke, trans., *The Lausiac History of Palladius* (London: SPCK, 1918), 24–6.
52 Veilleux, *Liturgie*, 139.
53 Ibid., 139–44.

his detailed account is of limited value to this present study. Suffice it to say that the trustworthiness of the testimony of Palladius is subject to an even greater degree of uncertainty than that of Cassian, though it is of interest to note that Robert T. Meyer is prepared to endorse Palladius' reliability.[54]

## 2. *Palladius' account of Evagrius*

Meyer describes the *Historia Lausiaca* as being 'peopled with numerous personages who also appear in the anonymous *Historia monachorum in Aegypto* and in various collections of unknown authorship called the *Apothegmata patrum* or *Verba seniorum*'.[55] Among these 'numerous personages' is Evagrius, Palladius's mentor, to whom the author devotes the whole of Chapter 38.

What light, then, does Palladius throw upon the prayer life of Evagrius? At the beginning of Chapter 38 Palladius sets out his stall for what follows in his account of the monk from Pontus. His purpose is to describe how Evagrius practised asceticism worthily.[56] And he concludes his account with a tribute to the toil, the labour and the continual prayer which epitomized that asceticism.[57]

In the intervening section, however, precise information regarding Evagrius' mode of asceticism is in short supply. We are told that he used to eat a pound of bread, and that he got through a pint of oil in three months, that he endured nakedness in winter to combat the demon of fornication and that he abstained from lettuce, green vegetables, fruit, grapes, meat, and even bathing.[58] However, with regard to Evagrius' life of prayer there

54 Robert T. Meyer, trans., *Palladius: The Lausiac History* (London: Longmans, Greens and Co., 1965).

55 Ibid., 7.

56 ὅπως αὐτὸν ἐξασκήσας ἀξίως: Butler, *Lausiac History, Vol. II*, 116.

57 μετὰ τοσοῦτον βίον καὶ κόπον καὶ πόνον καὶ προσευχὴν ἀδιάλειπτον: ibid., 122–3.

58 Ibid., 120–2.

is only one reference, which reports that he 'made' one hundred prayers,[59] the meaning of which is highly contentious. To this particular debate we shall now turn.

Bunge has argued in favour of a translation of the text which attributes to Evagrius the recitation of one hundred prayers each day.[60] This is based on his reading of the words, ἐποίει δὲ εὐχὰς ἑκατόν,[61] which he interprets in the light of Palladius's account of the practice of Evagrius' mentor, Macarius of Alexandria, in Chapter 20. There, within the context of a discussion with Paul regarding the number of prayers which should be said each day, Macarius is recorded as saying, 'I am sixty years old and I say one hundred prayers (ἑκατὸν εὐχὰς ποιῶν) daily'.[62] Bunge thus equates ἐποίει with ποιῶν, in accordance with the usual translation of the verb when its direct object is εὐχὰς.

On the other hand, Robert T. Meyer prefers to translate ἐποίει δὲ εὐχὰς ἑκατόν as 'He composed one hundred prayers',[63] and within the context of this section of Chapter 38 this would appear to give a more accurate rendering of the text. For Palladius goes on to say immediately in the same sentence, γράφων τοῦ ἔτους τὴν τιμὴν μόνον ὧν ἤσθιεν, thus clearly laying his emphasis on Evagrius' practice of writing (γράφων) rather than of offering prayer.

Hence Bunge's attempt to reconstruct Evagrius's pattern of prayer in the form of a prayer being offered by the ascetic every ten minutes is based on a false premise. And, unfortunately for the purpose of this study, it has to be concluded that the only thing which the *Historia Lausiaca* contributes to our understanding of Evagrius'prayer life is that the practice of continual prayer was at its heart. We are therefore compelled to nod in agreement with the judgment of Robert E. Sinkewicz: 'Although Evagrius has a great deal to say about prayer, especially in his treatise on

59 ἐποίει δὲ εὐχὰς ἑκατόν: ibid., 120.
60 Bunge, *Geistgebet*, 31–2.
61 Butler, *Lausiac History Vol. II*, 120.
62 Ibid., 63; Meyer, *Lausiac History*, 71.
63 Meyer, *Lausiac History*, 113.

the subject, we ultimately know very little about the precise nature of his practice'.[64]

## IV. *Pachomiana Latina*

We turn now from the practice of monastic psalmody in the semi-anchoritic milieu of Lower Egypt to its working out in Tabennesi and the cenobitic Pachomian communities of Upper Egypt. Pachomius was born around 290. Once an army conscript, he was converted to Christianity and came under the tutelage of the hermit Paelemon. Around 320 he set up a monastery in Tabennesi, which spawned other foundations. To establish a disciplined framework for those who joined him in his monastic vocation, he drew up a series of rules, which evolved during his own life-time, and during the governance of his immediate successors after his death, which was in 346.

### *1. The rule of Pachomius*

The four series of regulations attributed to Pachomius were known for centuries only in a Latin translation, the *Pachomiana Latina*, written by Jerome from a Greek document in 404, and through some Greek fragments. They are now, in part, available in Coptic, the language of the original text, which generally serves to underline the fidelity of Jerome's translation.

The *Rule of Pachomius* is composed of four distinct books, of which the first, the *Praecepta*, is of relevance to our study. To what extent the text which was received by Jerome almost sixty years after Pachomius' death was the authentic work of the founder of cenobitism is both impossible

64 Robert E. Sinkewicz, *Evagrius of Pontus: the Greek Ascetic Corpus, Translated with Introduction and Commentary* (Oxford and New York: Oxford University Press, 2003), xxxii.

to determine, and also irrelevant to our purposes in this chapter. What is of essence here is to ascertain what this late fourth- or early fifth-century document can impart to us with regard to the practice of monastic psalmody at this time in Upper Egypt.

## *2. The place of psalmody in the Rule*

That psalmody was an essential part of monastic life in Tabennesi may be gleaned from Rule 140: '[One should learn by heart] at least the New Testament and the Psalter'.[65]

It is therefore somewhat surprising to find Veilleux effectively downplaying the role of psalmody in the liturgical life of the Pachomian community. In this section, Veilleux argues that the Pachomian office consists of an alternation of two elements, the one being of biblical texts recited by heart by a soloist, and the other being prayer in silence by the whole community. He insists that the biblical texts are taken from the whole of Scripture and are not restricted to the Psalter. In his view, psalmody appears only on Sunday and forms no part of the ferial office.[66]

In 'L'Office Pachômien: Psallere, Orare, Legere'[67] Frans Kok takes issue with this minimalist approach. 'Sensational discovery!' he exclaims. 'Psalmody, true speciality and dominant element of the monastic office, would have been almost absent from the birthplace of monasticism!'[68]

In essence, Kok argues that Veilleux's minimalism is based upon an argument from silence, misinterprets one of the key rules in question

65 *qui minimum usque ad nouum testamentum et psalterium*: Amand Boon, ed., *Pachomiana Latina, Règle et Épitres de S. Pachome, Épitre de S. Théodore et 'Liber' de S. Orsiesius, Texte latin de S. Jerome* (Louvain: Bureaux de la Revue, 1932), 50; Armand Veilleux, trans., *Pachomian Koinonia, Vol. II: Pachomian Chronicles and Rules*, Cistercian Studies Series 46 (Kalamazoo, Michigan: Cistercian Publications, 1981), 166.

66 Veilleux, *Liturgie*, 307–15.

67 Frans Kok, 'L'Office Pachômien: Psallere, Orare, Legere', in *Ecclesia Orans* 9 (Rome: Pontificio Istituto Liturgico, 1992), 69–95.

68 Ibid., 84.

(Rule 15) and ignores Rules 140, 141 and 142 which provide the core elements and, possibly, sequence of Pachomian liturgical practice. Dismissing Veilleux's argument from silence, Kok says: 'The Praecepta do not give a detailed description of the office, and the fact that they do not mention the recitations for Sunday or psalmody of the ferias does not signify, in itself, that these elements were missing from the one or the other of these days'.[69]

With regard to Rule 15, it is necessary to print the translation in full in order to appreciate Kok's argument:

> On Sunday (*die dominica*) or at the time of the Eucharist, none of the weekly servers (*ebdomadariis*) shall be absent from his seat on the *embrimium* and not responding to the psalmist. They are all [to be] from the same house that does the greater weekly service (*quae in maiori seruit ebdomade*) for there is another lesser weekly service performed in the individual houses by a smaller number. If a greater number is necessary, others from the same tribe shall be called by the housemaster (*praeposito domus*) doing the weekly service. Without his order shall no one come from another house of the same tribe to sing psalms (*ad psallendum ueniet*). Likewise, it shall not be permitted anyone at all to serve in the weekly service of a house other than his own, unless it be [a house] of the same tribe. They call a tribe a group of three or four houses – according to the population of the monastery – which we could designate as families or people of a single race.[70]

According to Kok, Rule 15 is not principally about regulations for Sunday, but rather is directed towards the conduct of the weekly servers. The reference to Sunday is introductory and incidental to the rule as a whole. Hence, Kok says, 'It seems therefore that the whole of the second part of Pr 15 does not concern the Sunday celebration, but the organization of the weekly service', which includes psalmody.[71]

Having stipulated in Rule 140 that every new recruit to the monastery should learn the Psalter off by heart, Pachomius, or the author of the rule, then states in Rule 141: 'No one shall find pretexts for himself for not going to the *synaxis*, the psalmody, and the prayer'.[72]

69 Ibid., 85.

70 Boon, *Pachomiana Latina*, 16–17; Veilleux, *Pachomian Koinonia, Vol. II*, 147–8.

71 Kok, 'Office Pachômien', 88.

72 *Ad collectam, et ad psallendum, et ad orandum, nullus sibi occasiones inueniat quibus quasi ire non possit*: Boon, *Pachomiana Latina*, 50; Veilleux, *Pachomian Koinonia, Vol. II*, 166.

The importance of both prayer and psalmody is further underlined in the Rule 142 following: 'One shall not neglect the times of prayer and psalmody (*orandi et psallendi tempora non praetermittet*), whether he is on a boat, in the monastery, in the fields, or on a journey, or fulfilling any service whatever'.[73]

The injunctions contained within these rules not only serve to underline the importance of regular commitment to psalmody and prayer, making it highly unlikely that Veilleux is correct in restricting psalmody to the Sunday office, but also, Kok argues, point towards a core within the Pachomian office itself, consisting of psalmodizing (*psallere*), praying (*orare*) and reading (*legere*), possibly in that sequence.

Kok appeals to Rule 8 in his defence of this speculation: 'These are the precepts of life handed down to us by the elders. If it happens that during the psalmody or the prayer or in the midst of a reading (*Si acciderit ut psallendi tempore, uel orandi aut in medio lectionis*) anyone speaks or laughs....'[74]

Whether or not Kok is correct in floating such a possibility, what is clear from his argument and from the texts in question is that the combination of psalmody and prayer played a much more significant part in the monastic life of Upper Egypt than is allowed by Veilleux in his *magnum opus*. We therefore arrive at the same point reached by de Vogüé in an observation already cited: 'It is legitimate to speak simply, as Cassian sometimes does, of "Egyptian" monasticism, showing throughout the various regions a certain unity'.[75] Whilst not wishing to minimize the differences in practice between the north and the south, there does appear to be some justification for asserting that in both regions where Egyptian monasticism flourished in the late fourth century the duality of psalmody and prayer proved to be key elements and a powerful combination in the development of monastic formation and in the blossoming of the spirituality of the Desert Fathers.

73 Boon, *Pachomiana Latina*, 50–1; Veilleux, *Pachomian Koinonia, Vol. II*, 166.

74 Boon, *Pachomiana Latina*, 15; Veilleux, *Pachomian Koinonia, Vol. II*, 146.

75 De Vogüé, *De Saint Pachômien à Jean Cassien*, 456.

# PART TWO

# The Influence of Evagrius

CHAPTER THREE

# The Relationship between Psalmody and Prayer

The purpose of this chapter is to explore the relationship between psalmody and prayer in the writings of Evagrius of Pontus. The three most relevant works under review here will be the *Scholia ad psalmos*, the *De oratione* and the *Antirrhētikos*, though some consideration will be given to *Ad monachos*, *Ad virginem*, *Kephalaia Gnostika*, *Peri Logismōn*, *Praktikos* and *Skemmata* (*Capita Cogniscitiva*).

Evagrius was born around 346, probably in Ibora in Pontus, in Asia Minor. A disciple of the Cappadocian Fathers, he was ordained deacon by Gregory of Nazianzus, whom he accompanied to the Second Ecumenical Council in 381. Following a brief stay in Jerusalem, he went to Egypt in 383 where he lived till his death in 399. Speculative teachings attributed to him led to his condemnation in 553, but his teaching on prayer and the practice of the monastic life ensured his continuing influence in monastic circles.

As has already been noted, the effective condemnation of Evagrius at the Fifth Ecumenical Council resulted in the secretion of some of his works within the offerings accredited to other authors, and often in different translations. Thus, his *Scholia ad psalmos* was successfully concealed within the psalm commentary attributed to Origen until the disclosures made by von Balthasar and Rondeau. Similarly, the *De oratione*, in the Greek *Philokalia*, is ascribed to Nilus, but, since the scrutiny of Hausherr,[1] its authorship has been recognized as Evagrian.[2]

1 Irénée Hausherr, 'Le Traité de l'Oraison d'Évagre le Pontique', in *Revue d'Ascétique et de Mystique, Vol. XV* (Brussels: Culture et Civilisation, 1934), 34–93, 113–70.

2 See also John Eudes Bamberger, *Evagrius Ponticus: The Praktikos & Chapters on Prayer, Translated with an introduction and notes*, Cistercian Studies Series 4 (Kalamazoo, Michigan: Cistercian Publications, 1981), xxiii–xxxv.

The *Antirrhētikos* is a work based on a Syriac text, the Greek and Latin versions having been lost or destroyed, possibly as a result of the anathema pronounced against Evagrius. It was written as a response to a request from a monk, Loukios, for a treatise which would assist him and others in spiritual conflict with the demonic powers.

This chapter will offer a brief résumé of the Evagrian ascetical context in which this exploration is being pursued. It will then examine the insights contributed to this area of study by the scholars, de Vogüé, Bunge and Dysinger. And finally, it will seek to draw together the various findings by way of a concluding summary.

## I. The ascetical context

Julia S. Konstantinovsky describes how the trilogy of *Praktikos*, *Gnostikos* and *Kephalaia Gnostika* is fundamental to an understanding of Evagrian thought. Whilst *Praktikos* concerns the more practical stage of the monastic struggle, *Gnostikos* deals with a more spiritual stage of knowledge and *Kephalaia Gnostika* marks a 'recapitulation of Evagrius's dogmatic and epistemic thought'.[3]

This element of spiritual progression is to some extent reflected in the gradations of spiritual life, which Evagrius describes in *Praktikos* 1: 'Christianity is the doctrine (δόγμα) of our Saviour Jesus Christ composed of practical virtue (πρακτικῆς), natural contemplation (φυσικῆς), and theology' (θεολογίας).[4]

These three levels are to be found elsewhere in Evagrius' works. For example, in *Ad Monachos* 118–20 he writes:

3 Julia S. Konstantinovsky, *Evagrius Ponticus: The Making of a Gnostic* (Farnham: Ashgate Publishing, 2009), 23.

4 Ibid., 30; see Sinkewicz, *Evagrius of Pontus*, 97; and also Bamberger, *Praktikos & Chapters on Prayer*, 15.

> Flesh of Christ: virtues of *praktikē*;
> he who eats it, passionless (ἀπαθής) shall he be.
>
> Blood of Christ: contemplation of created things (θεωρία τῶν γεγονότων);
> he who drinks it, by it becomes wise.
> Breast of the Lord: knowledge of God (γνῶσις θεοῦ);
> he who rests against it, a theologian (θεολόγος) shall he be.[5]

Jeremy Driscoll sums up the progressive aspect of this threefold succession as follows: 'Thus, as Evagrius consistently teaches, the virtues of *praktikē* lead to the contemplation of created things, and this contemplation leads to the knowledge of God. Passionlessness opens the way to wisdom, and this leads on to theology'.[6]

Konstantinovsky claims that these three ascending stages of the spiritual life sometimes find themselves compressed into two in the Evagrian corpus:

> Elsewhere Evagrius condenses the idea of the many levels of the spiritual life into an even more concise bi-partite schema subsuming practical life succeeded by the life of spiritual proficiency, or gnostic life (τοῦ βίου πρακτικοῦ καὶ τοῦ γνωστικοῦ). Clearly, the gnostic life in the bi-partite schema corresponds to the stages of natural contemplation and theology in the tri-partite model.[7]

The question arises as to where precisely psalmody and prayer and their relationship with one another fit into either schema. In order to provide an answer, we will now examine those works of Evagrius which are pertinent to how he understood this relationship by considering the insights offered by de Vogüé, Bunge and Dysinger.

5 Jeremy Driscoll, *Evagrius Ponticus: Ad Monachos, Translation and Commentary* (New York and Mahwah, New Jersey: The Newman Press, 2003), 62.

6 Ibid., 136.

7 Konstantinovsky, *Making of a Gnostic*, 30.

## II. Adalbert de Vogüé

In *La Règle de saint Benoit, Vol. VII*, de Vogüé's contribution to this investigation lies in the realm of scholarship relating to the general historical context of the subject matter, rather than to the specific works of Evagrius. Accepting both the authority and the accuracy of the evidence from the *De institutis*, he offers some interesting observations on the practice and purpose of Eastern monastic psalmody prior to what he describes as Cassian's 'revolution'.[8]

In the chapter entitled 'Psalmodie et Oraison', he insists that silent prayer occupied a considerable place within the office, not as short pauses in between psalms, but as prolonged interruptions, as an 'important element of the celebrations, in terms of duration'.[9] He continues; 'While the psalmody requires only a respectful bearing and an attentive mind, the prayer demands an intense effort of supplication. All the energies of the body are mobilized for this act'.[10] Prayer, then, requires the redoubling of effort after the psalms, rather than relaxation. He adds that the role of psalmody is to prepare the monk for prayer and to invite him to pray. The sequence is: man listens to the word of God in Scripture, that is the psalms, and then prays.[11]

Prayer is therefore a meditation on a scriptural text, and man's response to the word of God, part of a dialogue in which God always takes the initiative.[12] On the other hand, psalmody resounds as the word of God inviting prayer, but also guides the prayer which it has aroused: 'Thus the psalmody is both the scriptural preamble of prayer and the beginning of this prayer'.[13]

De Vogüé therefore, on the basis of the *De institutis*, affirms the interrelatedness of psalmody and prayer in the life of early Eastern monasticism,

8 De Vogüé, *Règle de saint Benoit, Vol. VII*, 218.

9 Ibid., 208; English translation by John Baptist Hasbrouk, *The rule of Saint Benedict, a doctrinal and spiritual commentary*, Cistercian Studies Series 54 (Kalamazoo, Michigan: Cistercian Publications, 1983), 141.

10 De Vogüé, *Règle de saint Benoit, Vol. VII*, 208–9; Hasbrouk, *rule of Saint Benedict*, 141.

11 De Vogüé, *Règle de saint Benoit, Vol. VII*, 211.

12 Ibid., 212.

13 Ibid., 213; Hasbrouk, *rule of Saint Benedict*, 144.

and the preparatory role of the former in respect to the latter. He makes explicit what appears to be barely implicit in Cassian's writings.

In describing psalmody as the 'beginning of prayer' he identifies a process, a 'revolution' initiated by Cassian, which begins to blur the distinction between the two, and which leads in the West to psalmody occupying the space once held by prayer, and becoming man's homage to God rather than God's message to man.[14] In all of this, de Vogüé underscores the eventuality of the mutual exchange of rhythms and thought processes: psalmody feeding into prayer, and prayer feeding into psalmody.

In the following chapter, entitled 'Précisions sur la prière continuelle et la prière commune', he defends his thesis, that in early Eastern monasticism the psalmody of the divine office was a form of preparation for continual prayer, against the denials of Irénée Hausherr,[15] Olivier du Roy[16] and Armand Veilleux.[17] His reflections provide a helpful summary of the relationship between these two aspects of the ascetic life at the time of Evagrius.

In a later article, 'Psalmodie n'est pas prier',[18] de Vogüé is buoyed up by Bunge's 'admirable little book', *Das Geistgebet*. Insisting on the importance of maintaining the clear Evagrian distinction between psalmody and prayer, he concludes by drawing out the insights derived from Bunge:

> For Evagrius, therefore, the explanation of the psalms does not aim to permit to 'pray' them, as one says to-day, but to extract from them the hidden meaning, to decipher symbols from them, to decode the 'spiritual teaching'. This is to what the *Scholia ad psalmos* is particularly connected. Any such word that the psalmist addresses to God is considered less like a prayer than as a 'prelude to prayer'. Whilst constantly taking psalmic verses as examples of formulated prayers, Evagrius thinks, when he speaks of prayer, of an action which is higher than the simple recitation of the same expressions. These intervene instead in the struggle against tempting thoughts. It is

14 De Vogüé, *Règle de saint Benoit, Vol. VII*, 218.

15 Irénée Hausherr, *Hésychasme et prière*, OCA 176 (Rome: Pontificium Institutum Orientalium Studiorum, 1966), 255–306.

16 Olivier du Roy, *Moines aujourd'hui: une experience de réforme institutionelle* (Paris: Épi Édition, 1972).

17 Veilleux, *Liturgie*.

18 Adalbert de Vogüé, 'Psalmodie n'est pas prier', in *Ecclesia Orans* 6 (Rome: Pontificio Istituto Liturgico, 1989), 7–32.

> thus in the *Antirrhētikos*, that the Psalter is used as a real arsenal, providing at any moment the appropriate weapon. Requests, intercessions, praises, all become there ejaculatory prayers to repulse the enemy.[19]

To that which inspired de Vogüé to write this piece we now turn our attention.

## III. Gabriel Bunge

In Chapter 1 of *Das Geistgebet* Bunge sets out his understanding of the relationship between psalmody and prayer in the Evagrian corpus. He outlines the background to this relationship in the *De institutis*[20] and, following de Vogüé, describes it as constituting a dialogue between God and humanity, whereby psalmody involves the divine speaking to the human, and prayer involves the human response to the divine initiative.[21]

Bunge underlines the Evagrian description of psalmody as 'spiritual teaching'.[22] The psalms are to be chanted 'with understanding',[23] in a well ordered and well-rhythmed way, which means to chant with the heart and not to move the tongue within the mouth,[24] and to chant without distraction, as in the presence of angels.[25]

According to Bunge, Evagrius in *Kephalia Gnostika* II.2 and III.1 associates the' wisdom of multiplicity' to be found in psalmody with Christ

19 Ibid., 9.

20 Bunge, *Geistgebet*, 13.

21 Ibid., 14.

22 Λάβετε διδασκαλίαν πνευματικὴν: *Scholion ad psalmum* 80.3, AS 3, 136; Bunge, *Geistgebet*, 14.

23 *Scholion* on *Psalm* 46.8, PG 12, 1437B; Bunge, *Geistgebet*, 15.

24 *Ad virginem*, 35; Bunge, *Geistgebet*, 15.

25 Ἐναντίον ἀγγέλων ψάλλειν ἐστι τὸ ἀπερισπαύστως ψάλλειν: *Scholion* on *Psalm* 137. 1, AS 3, 340; Bunge, *Geistgebet*, 15.

the God-Logos, where the created wisdom of God is reflected back in manifold ways through all created materiality.[26]

*De oratione* 83 is cited as evidence that Evagrius believes that the chanting of psalms, and the ensuing attentive listening to 'spiritual teaching' is an anti-dote to the passions,[27] and Bunge goes on to assert that the intellect itself becomes a psaltery, like David's harp.[28]

Psalmody, then, is the proper activity for human beings as they progress on their way from the assaults of passions to angelic knowledge.[29] And the chanting of psalms with understanding and without distraction is something more than the simple repetition of sacred texts. Psalmody is Spirit-inspired instruction concerning the mysterious actions of God. This Spirit-inspired knowledge, like David's psaltery, causes the intellect to ring out in hymn-prayer.[30]

As the 'Summa of the Old Testament', as in Athanasius' *Epistola ad Marcellinum*, the Psalter, when chanted, involves listening to every word which God directs to us, while prayer is the human response to God's speaking to us.[31] Prayer is the unmediated conversation between God and humans after the fashion of Moses at the burning bush.[32] The human requirement for this conversation is purification: as Moses took off his shoes, so must we detach ourselves from passionate thoughts.[33]

Prayer, then, is the laying aside of all thoughts.[34] The conversation with God must be face to face, as with Moses, without an intermediary, and

26 Bunge, *Geistgebet*, 16.

27 *Philokalia tōn Ierōn Nēptikōv, Vol. I* (Athens: Astir Publishing Company, 1957), 184; Bunge, *Geistgebet*, 17.

28 Τοῦ νοῦ μὲν σύμβολόν ἐστι τὸ ψαλτήριον: *Scholion* on *Psalm* 107.3, AS 3, 220; Bunge, *Geistgebet*, 17.

29 *Scholion* on *Psalm* 118.135, AS 3, 300; Bunge, *Geistgebet*, 18.

30 Bunge, *Geistgebet*, 19.

31 Ibid., 20.

32 *De oratione* 4, *Philokalia tōn Ierōn Nēptikōn, Vol. I*, 177; Bunge, *Geistgebet*, 20.

33 Προσευχὴ ἐστι κατάστασις νοῦ, φθαρτικὴ παντὸς ἐπιγείου νοήματος: *Skemmata* 26; Bunge, *Geistgebet*, 20–1.

34 Προσευχὴ γάρ ἐστιν, ἀπόθεσις νοημάτων: *De oratione* 71, *Philokalia tōn Ierōn Nēptikōn, Vol. I*, 182; Bunge, *Geistgebet*, 21.

this is to go 'immaterially into the immaterial'.[35] As psalmody is the prelude to prayer, so prayer, is the 'prelude to immaterial and non-multi-form knowledge'.[36]

According to Bunge, Evagrius sees both psalmody and prayer as divine charism, as different ways to do with the knowledge of God. Whereas psalmody belongs to the world of φυσική, the mediated knowledge of the multiform created wisdom of God that is reflected back in extant things, so prayer, by contrast, belongs to the world of θεωρητική, and is unmediated dialogue with God, the pure presence of the one to the other.[37]

For Evagrius, prayer is an increasingly dizzying process of ever-deepening interiority, as witnessed by his *Scholion* on Psalm 34.13 in which 'breast' in 'My prayer will return back to my breast…' is interpreted as intellect.[38]

Bunge goes on to repeat that, for Evagrius, psalmody is primarily not prayer, but a prelude to prayer. He cites the *Scholion* on Psalm 37.22, which contains the Blessed Trinity,[39] and in which prayer is a synonym for contemplation. Here, he says, 'All the petition and pleading, etc. of the Psalter leads on to contemplative prayer and precisely there has its true place'.[40] He goes on to say that the examples which Evagrius offers of formulated prayer are invariably short prayers drawn from the psalms, and in Chapter 2, note 33 he cites a number of these (see below).

Having listed the three Evagrian categories of prayer as supplication (δέησις), vow (εὐχή) and intercession (ἔντευξις), Bunge notes that Evagrius draws on all three forms from the psalms. This, he says, is the fruit of the ascetic's ongoing meditative reading of the psalms, but it is not prayer

35 ἀλλ' ἀύλως τῷ ἀύλῳ προσίσθι, καὶ συνήσεις: *De oratione* 67, *Philokalia tōn Ierōn Nēptikōn, Vol. I*, 182; Bunge, *Geistgebet*, 21.

36 *De oratione* 85; Bunge, *Geistgebet*, 21.

37 Bunge, *Geistgebet*, 22–3.

38 Κόλπον νῦν τὸν νοῦν ὀνομάζει: PG 12, 1312D–1313A; Bunge, *Geistgebet*, 23–4.

39 Ἔχεις γὰρ ἐν αὐτῷ καὶ τὴν ἁγίαν Τριάδα: AS 3, 27–28; Bunge, *Geistgebet*, 24–5.

40 Bunge, *Geistgebet*, 25; English translation by Luke Dysinger, *Spiritual Prayer*, accessed on 25 August, 2010 at <http://ldysinger.stjohnsem.edu@texts2/1985_bunge/01_GGB-pref_ch1.htm>.

in its highest sense.[41] He then proceeds to earth these observations on Evagrian psalmody and prayer in the monastic practice in Egypt at that time, which, he says, consisted of two offices, Vespers and Vigils, each with twelve psalms, with each psalm followed by 'prayer' as the human answer to the appeal by God in the text.[42] Here we see how he adopts de Vogüé's endorsement of the historical accuracy of the *De institutis*, and its direct relevance to Evagrius' own practice.

In summary, Bunge says that, for Evagrius, psalmody and prayer are not in opposition to one another, but are inseparably related to one another 'just like the indirect and direct knowledge of God reflected in them'.[43] He proceeds to show how this analysis fits in with Evagrius's description of three salvific paths of πρακτική, φυσική and θεωρητική. The intellect is elevated to the knowledge of God most of all in the mirror of his creation. And finally, he adds: 'The medium and expression of this knowledge is psalmody. From it proceeds the unmediated-personal encounter with God himself that comes to pass, according to Evagrius, in the "state of prayer"'.[44]

Like de Vogüé, Bunge follows up these insights with a chapter devoted to the subject of continual prayer, though, unlike the former, with a much greater emphasis on its relationship with psalmody. Repeating his point that for early Eastern monastics prayers followed the psalmody at intervals, he quotes a number of examples of such prayers, drawn directly from psalm-verses in the works of Evagrius.[45] These include Psalm 22.4 in *De oratione* 97, Psalm 90.10–11 in *De oratione* 96, Psalm 17.38ff in *De oratione* 135, and Psalm 102.2–4 in *De Diversis Malignis Cogitationibus* 22, *Recensio longior*.[46]

41 *Geistgebet*, 25.

42 Ibid., 26.

43 Ibid., 27; Dysinger, *Spiritual Prayer*.

44 Bunge, *Geistgebet*, 28; Dysinger, *Spiritual Prayer*.

45 Bunge, *Geistgebet*, 36 note 33; Dysinger, *Spiritual Prayer*.

46 For this last reference see Joseph Muyldermans, ed., *A travers la tradition manuscrite d'Évagre le Pontique: essai sur les manuscrits grecs conservés à la Bibliothèque Nationale de Paris*, Bibliothèque du Muséon 3 (Louvain: Bureaux du Muséon, 1932), 47–8.

Thus, Bunge claims, psalmody becomes a 'school of prayer', wherein the one who prays elaborates a wealth of images and concepts, and finds 'spiritual teaching' which relates to the 'knowledge of Christ'. He also finds Christ through everything, for, as Bunge says, the '"knowledge of Christ" (γνῶσις Χριστοῦ) is the *key* to every verse of the Old Testament, most particularly, the Psalter'.[47] Therefore, he insists, the memorization and recitation of the psalms have no goal other than prayer, prayer as a 'dialogue of the intellect with God'.

Bunge goes on to say that several elements flow to God from this single *élan*. Firstly, the prayers which accompany the twelve psalms at Vespers and Vigils have the effect of Christianizing the psalms for the cantor or listener, who makes them his own. Secondly, the use of psalmody and prayer together in daily work, as well as in church, has the effect of developing a personal rule for the monk in which manual labour is accompanied or punctuated by short prayers. Thirdly, the constant meditation on God's word is not interrupted by manual labour but rather accompanies it, the meditation not being concerned with the acquisition of new information but with encountering God.[48]

In this way, Bunge understands that psalmody is a form of preparation not only for prayer but for 'unceasing prayer'. He interprets this in the light of what he describes as Evagrius' understanding of two methods of prayer: πρακτική, relating to the quantitative aspect of prayer, and θεωρητική, possessing a qualitative term of reference.

Bunge insists that for Evagrius 'unceasing prayer' is concerned with the first of these two methods, and belongs to the realm of the 'practical methods of prayer'. In his view, therefore, continual prayer is for Evagrius an indispensible preliminary step towards θεωρητική, rather than itself being the highest form of prayer, prayer as a 'state of the intellect'.[49]

47 Bunge, *Geistgebet*, 37; Dysinger, *Spiritual Prayer*.
48 Bunge, *Geistgebet*, 37–8.
49 Ibid., 40.

## IV. Luke Dysinger

Dysinger's substantial work, *Psalmody and Prayer in the Writings of Evagrius Ponticus*, has been generally well received by the academic community, though not without criticism. With regard to its consideration of the relationship between these two elements of monastic life in the work of the Pontic monk, it provides a significant and essential contribution to Evagrian studies.

Building on the insights of de Vogüé and Bunge, Dysinger examines in detail the practice of Egyptian monastic psalmody as recorded by Cassian in *De institutis*.[50] He notes how Cassian in II.11 and II.12 recalls how the attentive listening (*cordis intentio*) of the monks to the words of the Psalter was to some extent facilitated by a period of refreshment (*refectio*), an interval of silent prayer, which concluded with a collect sung by the cantor, and by posture.

He goes on to describe an intimate relationship between psalmody and prayer in the work of Evagrius, and bases this description, in part, on a detailed analysis of *De oratione* 82, 83, 85 and 87.[51] For example, in Chapter 82, Evagrius says that prayer is to be offered gently and calmly (ἐπιεικῶς καὶ ἀταράχως), while psalms are to be sung intelligently and rhythmically (συνετῶς καὶ εὐρύθμως).[52] Dysinger notes that the adverb συνετῶς suggests an attentiveness to the meaning of the text being sung, and, in company with Athanasius' usage in *Epistola ad Marcellinum*,[53] implies a dynamic harmony between the different faculties of the soul.

Following his detailed analysis of the texts, he offers this summary:

> Evagrius' discussion of prayer and psalmody in *De oratione* 82 and 83 presupposes and mirrors the monastic practice of psalmody. He depicts the two practices as intertwining, each supporting the other, with psalmody serving a preparatory and

50 Dysinger, *Psalmody and Prayer*, 54–7.

51 Ibid., 70–103.

52 *Philokalia tōn Ierōn Nēptikōn Vol. I*, 184.

53 PG 27, 40D.

> subordinate role to prayer... Psalmody therefore serves the purpose of preparing the entire person, body, soul, and *nous*, for prayer.[54]

Dysinger then proceeds to flesh out the forms which this preparation takes, in three chapters, headed 'Psalmody as Spiritual Remedy', 'The Psalter as Spiritual Weapon' and 'The Psalter as Contemplative Vision'.

### *1. Psalmody as spiritual remedy*

In Chapter 4, he asserts that in *De Oratione* 83 Evagrius shows how the psalms serve as a spiritual remedy, calming the passions and rectifying the body's disharmony, and this is because it is Jesus who is encountered in the psalms.[55] He frequently employs medical images to describe the spiritual life. Ascetic practices are medical remedies, φάρμακα,[56] by which Jesus treats, purges and shrivels the passions.

For Evagrius, psalms have power to calm misdirected or excessive anger or indignation, θυμός. Θυμός plays an important role in the spiritual life but can be misdirected. The struggle with anger lasts till death, unlike the passions of the body, such as gluttony and lust. The chanting of psalms helps to calm the inner boiling of θυμός.[57] The 'indignations of the one singing the psalms are quieted'.[58] Elsewhere, Evagrius cites the example of David's psaltery calming the passion of Saul, in this regard.[59]

54 Dysinger, *Psalmody and Prayer*, 102–3.

55 Ibid., 104–30.

56 *Praktikos* 38; Antoine and Claire Guillaumont, ed. and trans., *Évagre le Pontique: Traité Pratique ou Le Moine*, SC 171 (Paris: Les Éditions du Cerf, 1971), 586.

57 *Praktikos* 71, 15; Guillaumont, SC 171, 658.

58 Ψάλλοντος ἡσυχάζει θυμὸς: *Ad Monachos* 98; Hugo Gressmann, ed., *Nonnensspiegel und Mönchsspiegel des Evagrios Pontikos*, Texte und Untersuchungen 39.4 (Leipzig: Hinrich, 1913), 161; see also *Peri Logismōn* 26, Paul Géhin, ed. and trans., *Évagre le Pontique Sur Les Pensées*, SC 438 (Paris: Les Éditions du Cerf, 1998), 248–50.

59 *Antirrhētikos* IV.2, Wilhelm Frankenberg, ed., *Evagrius Ponticus, Abhandlungen der königlichen Gesellschaft der Wissenschaften zu Göttingen*, Phil.-hist. Klasse, Neue Folge, 13.2 (Berlin: Weidmannche Buchhandlung, 1912), 505.

Singing the psalms, in Evagrius' understanding, Dysinger claims, changes κρᾶσις, the balance of humours thought to be responsible for health and fitness. And Dysinger argues that in *Praktikos* 69–71 Evagrius suggests that undistracted psalmody helps to create a new κρᾶσις or ἀνάκρασις, which is a complete blending of the self with the virtues.

Therefore psalmody, for Evagrius, is a spiritual remedy, and θυμός is an essential weapon in the spiritual arsenal, but must be controlled and employed against the enemy. While θυμός is against nature when it is used against humans, it is in accordance with nature when it is used against demons. This leads on to ἀντίρρησις, the rebuttal of demons.

## 2. *The Psalter as spiritual weapon*

In Chapter 5 Dysinger argues that the soul, according to Evagrius, in line with the whole monastic tradition, is in a continuous state of spiritual warfare. Victory consists of the attainment of virtues and of pure prayer.[60] The Psalter is a weapon in this conflict, and King David is a useful symbol for Evagrius. He describes the importance of the Psalter in his introduction to the *Antirrhētikos*. It is the means by which the Holy Spirit taught David πρακτική. It involves the memorizing of texts for use in the contest, the refutation of the enemies, and the contradiction of particular thoughts (λογισμοί) with particular texts.

With regard to the *Antirrhētikos*, Dysinger points out that ἀντίρρησις also appears in other works, such as *Praktikos*, where Evagrius emphasizes the need to rebut offending thoughts before proceeding to prayer. For him, the Psalter occupies a central place in the practice of ἀντίρρησις.[61] David is the symbol of a mature Gnostic (γνωστικός) who knows demonic assaults and how to withstand them. The Psalter is a record of the demons' accusations and how David countered them, a practice which is rooted in Jesus' temptations. In this conflict, ἀντίρρησις must be practised immediately.

60 Dysinger, *Psalmody and Prayer*, 131–49.

61 *Epistola* 11, Frankenberg, *Evagrius Ponticus*, 575.

Dysinger describes how the *Antirrhētikos* is divided into eight books, each based on one λογισμός. He claims that it contains 492 biblical texts, which are usually understood literally, 91 of which are taken from the Psalter, and 60 from *Proverbs*, though it should be noted that David Brakke disputes these figures.[62]

The *Antirrhētikos*, then, according to Dysinger, is an arsenal of texts to be used at the moment of temptation, while the *Scholia ad psalmos* is intended to enhance the experience of the γνωστικός of meditative reading (ἀνάγνωσις). He cites Paul Géhin's study of Evagrius' *Scholia ad proverbia*,[63] a work which lists six different categories of *scholia*, including antirrhetic *scholia* which Evagrius recommends for use against specific categories of demons. Dysinger agrees with Géhin that this type of *scholion* is also found in the psalms, but offers a number of qualifications to this eneral application.

Dysinger concludes that progression can be seen from the *Antirrhētikos* to the *Scholia ad psalmos*. The preoccupation with one's own spiritual improvement becomes a broader concern for others. The spiritual practioner (πρακτικός) employs the weapons of the *Antirrhētikos* on the battlefield of his own soul. The *Scholia* gives the γνωστικός healing texts which may be of help to him and others.

### *3. The Psalter as contemplative vision*

In Chapter 6 Dysinger states that Evagrius believed that the Psalter can serve as a training ground for the Christian contemplative, whereby the γνωστικός learns to perceive the divine principles (λόγοι) in the salvation events recounted in the psalms.[64]

62 David Brakke, *Talking Back: a monastic handbook for combating demons*, Cistercian Studies Series 229 (Collegeville, Minnesota: Liturgical Press, 2009), 15 note 30.

63 Paul Géhin, *Évagre le Pontique Scholies aux Proverbes*, SC 340 (Paris: Les Éditions du Cerf, 1987), 18.

64 Dysinger, *Psalmody and Prayer*, 150–95. See *Peri Logismōn* 17, Paul Géhin, *Évagre le Pontique Sur Les Pensées*, SC 438 (Paris: Les Éditions du Cerf, 1998), 212–14.

Evagrius places the psalms at the mid-point of the movement from the ascetic struggle to contemplative knowledge and back to the ascetic practice. There is a 'conversation with the psalter' (τῷ ψαλτηρίῳ προσομιλήσομεν), Dysinger claims,[65] which suggests an alternating and oscillating rhythm of attention to the biblical text followed by intervals of prayer. And in *Scholion* 1 on Psalm 80.3, Evagrius describes the psalter as 'spiritual teaching'.[66] There is a dynamic relationship between πρακτική and θεωρητική, and a reciprocal relationship between spiritual progress and biblical exegesis.

Evagrius refers to Jesus in 107 out of 149 psalms in the *Scholia*, and, in Dysinger's reckoning, such a reference is often implicit in the remaining forty-two psalms. The title Χριστός is used in 159 psalmodic *scholia*, and that of Κύριος in 130, the majority of which, Dysinger insists, relate to Christ. It should be noted here, however, that in his on-line selection and translation of the *Scholia ad psalmos* Dysinger catalogues eighty-nine *scholia* in which Κύριος appears, only twenty-two of which have a clear Christological reference.[67]

Dysinger claims that Evagrius has a different approach to Jesus and the psalms from other patristic writers. The person or sayings of Jesus explicate the inner meaning of the psalms, to which Jesus is the exegetical key. Here again, it should be noted, however, that in the *Scholia ad psalmos* Evagrius shows very little interest in the Christological concerns which occupy the writers of other psalm-commentaries of this period.[68]

Similarly, Evagrius in his psalm-commentary generally demurs from identifying Christ as the recipient of the psalm-prayer. There is nothing to suggest that the Κύριος, who is the recipient of the twenty-five psalm-prayers in the *Antirrhētikos*, is to be identified with the Second rather than with the First Person of the Trinity. Neither does he associate Christ with references to the divine name or face in the relevant psalm-texts.

65 Dysinger, *Psalmody and Prayer*, 151.

66 διδσακαλίαν πνευματικὴν: AS 3, 136; see Bunge, *Das Geistgebet*, 14 note 2.

67 *Selected Scholia on the Psalms*, translated by Luke Dysinger, Greek Text based on Migne [PG], Pitra [AS] and the collation of M.-J. Rondeau, accessed on 20 December, 2010 at <http://www.ldysinger.com/Evagrius/08_Psalms/00a_start.htm>).

68 Dysinger, *Psalmody and Prayer*, 154.

With regard to ascetical progression, in *Scholion* 2 on Psalm 126.1,[69] Dysinger shows how Evagrius marries up his Christology with his threefold categorization.[70] He says that Christ is the 'Master of the house' at the level of πρακτική. At the level of φυσική, with which most of the *Scholia ad psalmos* are concerned, Christ is the 'Enthroned King', while a few *scholia* pertain to θεολογία, the 'summit of Evagrius' model of spiritual progress'.

A large number of texts attest to the centrality of Jesus in Evagrius' theology. The formula of Jesus the 'Lord who with God the Word has dwelt among us' is used. This was cited as heretical by Antoine Guillaumont, as evidence of an Origenistic Christology condemned by Justinian.[71] According to Guillaumont, the Evagrian Jesus is not truly an incarnation of the Λόγος but an enfleshed 'Christ-nous'. Dysinger observes that this view has been challenged by Bunge and others, and goes on to defend their refutation. In this defence, he cites evidence from the following: *Scholion* 7 on Psalm 44.3, *Scholion* 10 on Psalm 104.15, *Scholion* 4 on Psalm88.7 (2), *Scholion* 2 on Psalm 118.3, *Scholion* 5 on Psalm 131.7, and *Scholion* 4 on Psalm 22.5 (1).[72]

Again, as his treatment of *Scholion* 2 on Psalm 126.1 would indicate, Dysinger is content to locate the Evagrian Christ in the whole movement from πρακτική to θεωρητική, arguing that 'Evagrius undoubtedly intends his reader to interpret the "knowledge of mysteries" shared at the "table" of Christ as essential knowledge, that *gnosis* of the Father which Christ alone can share with others'.[73] And he concludes this section with the following assertion:

> Whereas in the *Scholia on Psalms* and in the practice of psalmody Evagrius emphasizes the perception of Christ in the 'richly diverse wisdom' of salvation history and creation, in *De oratione* and during the interval for prayer which follows each psalm

69 PG 12, 1641C-1644A.

70 Dysinger, *Psalmody and Prayer*, 155.

71 Antoine Guillaumnot, *Les 'Kephalaia Gnostica', d'Évagre le Pontique et l'histoire de l'Origénisme chez les Grecs et chez les Syriens*, Patristica Sorbonensia 5 (Paris: Editions du Seuil, 1962), 133–70.

72 Dysinger, *Psalmody and Prayer*, 158–71.

73 Ibid., 170.

> Evagrius encourages the laying aside of images and words in order to enjoy that 'immaterial and uniform' wisdom which is Christ's gift of knowledge of the Father.[74]

While the debate about Evagrian Christology lies largely, though not entirely, outside the remit of this present study, it should be noted here that in *Evagrius Ponticus: The Making of a Gnostic*, Konstantinovsky argues forcefully that, despite some errors in his account, there is substance to Guillaumont's case against Evagrian orthodoxy.[75] She interprets Evagrius as implying that Christ is 'numerically and ontologically distinct from the Logos', and that it is therefore problematic to conceive of the Evagrian Christ as the Word made flesh. In her assessment, then, Christ, as distinct from the Λόγος in the thought of Evagrius, belongs to the world of the 'multiplicity and materiality'. His function is to reveal spiritual knowledge, and his domain is a 'spiritual realm that precedes the higher natural contemplation, being lower than it'.[76]

To return to Dysinger, there follows a lengthy consideration of the λογοί of judgment and providence in the *Scholia ad psalmos*. Dysinger brings the chapter to an end by stating that these λογοί reveal the person and purposes of Christ within the text of the Psalter. However, they are not the final end of contemplation, but are rather healing remedies. He concludes: 'Psalmody and all it affords serves therefore as a preparation for that "pure prayer" which is akin to *theologia*, during which the *nous* peers beyond the diversity of creation to behold something of the Blessed Trinity'.[77]

Dysinger proceeds to summarize the findings of his study in his final chapter.[78] He states that Evagrius' admonitions to lay aside thoughts and images in prayer presuppose a monastic culture steeped in the rich language and imagery of the Scriptures, especially the psalms. His 'time of prayer' refers to the interval between each chanted psalm or reading at the offices. The prayers which followed each psalm are not protracted.

74 Ibid., 170–1.
75 Konstantinovsky, *Making of a Gnostic*. See especially 148–9.
76 Ibid., 148.
77 Dysinger, *Psalmody and Prayer*, 195.
78 Ibid., 196–8.

Evagrius, according to Dysinger, assumes that wordless or imageless prayer takes place in an oscillating, dynamic relationship with the word-filled, image-filled psalms and biblical readings. There is a background rhythm of alternating psalm and prayer. The psalms make prayer possible by calming the passions. The alternating rhythm of psalmody and prayer stores in memory and brings to consciousness an arsenal of spiritual weapons against the demons.

For Dysinger, Evagrius sees the oscillating rhythm of psalmody and prayer as a training ground for the Christian contemplative. The movement between the diverse wisdom of the psalms and the simple wisdom of prayer helps the monk to learn to perceive the divine λογοὶ in salvation-history and in his own temptations.

Dysinger concludes that the underlying rhythm of spiritual progress consists in movement between the poles of πρακτική, φυσική and θεολογική. This is reflected in the monastic discipline of psalmody. There is an analogous movement in the relationship between psalmody and prayer: the monk sees in the mirror of the psalms his need for reform, and regularly arises from chanting the 'manifold wisdom' of Jesus in the psalms to rest in undistracted, wordless conversations with the Father.

## V. Assessing de Vogüé, Bunge and Dysinger

As we have seen in the previous chapter, Evagrius himself says virtually nothing about the actual practice of prayer and psalmody and prefers to devote himself to an examination of their relationship by way of theological and spiritual categories. For that reason, it may be wise to counsel a little more caution than that displayed by either Bunge or Dysinger when seeking to correlate so closely reflections found in *De oratione*, the *Antirrhētikos*, and the *Scholia ad psalmos* with the framework revealed in the testimony of *De institutis*. Both scholars are convinced that what Evagrius writes about prayer can be identified with the slot, comprising of both the 'greater part of time' (*maiorem temporis partem*) and the 'very short time' (*puncto brevissimo*), as attested in *De institutis* II.7, which separates the end of the recitation of one psalm in the divine office from the beginning of the next one.

However, Evagrius himself never makes such a clear-cut identification. His interest lies entirely with the theology behind the practice (πρᾶξις) rather than with the details of the practice itself. Indeed, his theologizing on the relationship between psalmody and prayer presupposes the overall context of ascetic practice, which includes private monastic devotion in the cell, and the accompaniment provided by psalmody and prayer to manual labour, as well as the corporate worship (σύναξις).

Nevertheless, while the degree of precision asserted by Bunge and Dysinger in this regard may go beyond the available evidence, the drift of the Evagrian writings examined in this study points firmly in the direction of a close interconnectedness between psalmody and prayer, in which the one nourishes and feeds upon the other.

We now turn our attention to the ascetical context and the nature of the relationship which was forged between them. There is, as we have seen, considerable justification for linking psalmody and prayer together as dialogue, as complementary engines for different stages of spiritual progression, and as co-facilitators of an encounter with Christ, in the works of Evagrius. To each of these subjects we shall now turn.

### *1. Psalmody and prayer as dialogue*

Conversation, communion, or intercourse is for Evagrius a feature of both psalmody and prayer. Each of these words may be used to translate the Greek text of *De oratione* 3, where prayer is said to be ὁμιλία of the intellect with God, a word which, following Herodotus and Xenophon in classical Greek, conveys the sense of intimacy.[79]

Again, as Dysinger points out, in the quest for spiritual growth, Evagrius encourages his readers to combat listlessness by engaging in a

79 See reference A.2.a with regard to ὁμιλία: Lampe, *Patristic Greek Lexicon*, 951.

conversation with the Psalter, where the verb προσομιλήσωμεν can carry with it a similar sense of conjugality, according to Epiphanius.[80] Not only are psalmody and prayer inseparable aspects of a divine-human dialogue, but they also give testimony to the bonding and unitive character of the relationship in which such communication takes place.

Evagrius emphatically describes psalmody as 'spiritual teaching' (διδασκαλίαν πνευματικὴν) in *Scholion* 1 on Psalm 80.3. This makes explicit that which is implicit in all his didactic works: the assumption that all Scripture is divine teaching,[81] the word of God to humanity. As part of Scripture, the psalms are used by Jesus to educate the soul in the art of πρακτική,[82] and as divine communication they must be received appropriately in order to be effective as such.[83] The manner of such receptivity, for the majority of monks, is akin to their hearing of the word of God proclaimed in the Bible readings, since, as listeners rather than cantors, they maintain a similarly passive mode.

Hence we see how Evagrius picks up the tenor of Athanasius' *Epistola ad Marcellinum* in insisting that the Psalter be recited 'with understanding and rhythm' (συνετῶς καὶ εὐρύθμως), so that the cantor and those listening may ascend to the heights like a young eagle, having understood the divine inner meanings of what has been chanted. Here we see a link with Cassian's 'mind's knowledge' (*mentis intelligentia*) of *De institutis* II.11, and his 'attentive listening' (*cordis intentione*) of *De institutis* II.12.

It is worth noting at this point that Evagrius' insistence on συνετῶς is an implicit encouragement to his readers to deepen their appreciation of the Psalter through the study of his own works which relate to the Book of Psalms (*Scholia ad psalmos*, *Antirrhētikos*) and also through the study of works which cover the same area, written by other Fathers, such as Athanasius, who like him were renowned teachers of the faith. And if psalmody is the divine initiative in this encounter, then prayer is the human

80 See reference 2. with regard to προσομιλέω: ibid., 1180.

81 Konstantinovsky, *Making of a Gnostic*, 56.

82 Ibid., 114.

83 *De oratione* 82.

response, seeking to go 'immaterially into the immaterial',[84] in pursuit of the unmediated conversation enjoyed by Moses with God at the burning bush,[85] as free from distractions as the liberator was free from sandals.

## *2. Psalmody and prayer as spiritual progression*

It is abundantly clear from the evidence of his works that Evagrius understood the relationship between psalmody and prayer within the wider context of a monk's spiritual progression, within the ongoing process of the 'making of a Gnostic'. The conversation or communion to which the intellect aspires in prayer is possible only after purification. The θεωρητική of *De oratione* 3 is dependent upon the πρακτική of *De oratione* 4.

The role of psalmody is bound up with the setting aside of passionate thoughts and distracting images, a clearing of the decks in order to make way for prayer. It achieves this through embracing and gathering together the multiplicity of images in the manifold wisdom of God, and thence, following a process of meditation or rumination, making it possible for the monk to move towards a simple knowledge of the divine.[86]

In this preparatory role, psalmody also calms the passions,[87] and quietens inner disharmony.[88] It leads the monk away from passionate thoughts and towards angelic knowledge.[89] As a spiritual remedy it heals the monk from the disorders caused by the passions, and as a spiritual weapon it defends him from the assaults inflicted by the demons.

In all of this, psalmody is not only a preparation for prayer, but also the beginning of prayer. The psalm-verses recommended in the *Antirrhētikos* to thwart the wiles of the demons include a series of short prayers, which constitute the beginning of a conversation or communion of the intellect

84 Ibid., 67.
85 Ibid., 4.
86 Ibid., 85.
87 Ibid., 83.
88 Burton-Christie, *Word in the Desert*, 122–7.
89 *Scholion* on *Psalm* 118.135.

with God. These are supplemented by antirrhetic *scholia* in the *Scholia ad psalmos*.[90] Also, Evagrius makes it clear in *Scholion* 1 on Psalm 137.1 (3) that the chanting of psalms before angels, the 'undistracted psalmody', is to be equated with contemplative prayer.

As psalmody is a prelude to prayer, so prayer itself is a prelude to the immaterial and simple knowledge of God.[91] Indeed, as we have seen, prayer enables the monk to go 'immaterially into the immaterial'. There appears, therefore, to be something of a continuum in Evagrius' conception of the relationship of psalmody and prayer, whereby psalmody is the beginning of prayer, even continual prayer, and prayer is the beginning of 'pure prayer', a 'state of the intellect', that is, the unmediated knowledge of the immaterial God.

This helps us to consider how the relationship between psalmody and prayer fits in with Evagrius' three gradations of spiritual progress, as outlined in *Praktikos* 1: πρακτική, φυσική and θεολογία. Outwardly, as interconnected, constituent elements of monastic discipline, both psalmody and prayer are concerned with πρακτική, in so far as they relate to the practice of asceticism (ἄσκησις). Inwardly, in so far as they both relate to the inner development of the Gnostic life (γνωστική) of the monk, the position is less straightforward.

It is tempting to make the generalization that, for Evagrius, whereas psalmody is related to φυσική, prayer, on the other hand, is related to θεολογία, and that, while psalmody concerns the indirect knowledge of God to be gained by contemplating him in the natural world, and in the 'wisdom of multiplicity', prayer, on the other hand, concerns the direct knowledge of God to be gained by contemplating him, as the One, without any intermediary.

Broadly speaking, as the evidence unearthed indicates, this is a valid interpretation of Evagrian thought. However, as with other aspects of Evagriana, it does not furnish us with the whole picture of a complex spiritual teaching which defies any easy analysis.

90 Dysinger, *Psalmody and Prayer*, 142–9.

91 *De oratione* 85.

As we have seen, with regard to *Scholion* 1 on Psalm 137.1 (3), while Evagrius is generally disposed towards locating the thrust of psalmody in the world of φυσική, this does not prevent him from flirting with elements which would at least come close to placing the chanting of psalms in the realm of θεολογία. The same thing is evident from *Scholion* 13 on Psalm 37.22, and also the *Scholion* on Psalm 34.13. It should be further noted that each of these *scholia* provide examples of how Evagrius' practice of prayer impacts on his understanding of psalmody, thus underlining the mutualism at the heart of the relationship between the two aspects of monastic discipline.

And given that the concept of prayer enjoys a certain degree of elasticity in Evagrius' writings, and that psalmody itself is conceived as being the beginning of prayer, it would not appear to be out of the question to identify elements of prayer, with psalmody, in the world of φυσική, whilst acknowledging that, for Evagrius, the main purpose of prayer is to move the one who prays into the realm of θεολογία.

This much arises as a consequence of interpreting Evagrius' conceptualization of psalmody and prayer, on the one hand, and πρακτική, φυσική and θεολογία, on the other, in terms of a continuum rather than in terms of a neatly defined categorization. Given the sheer complexity of Evagrius' thought, such an approach would appear to do greater justice to the evidence.

### *3. Psalmody and prayer as encounter with Christ*

Due attention has been paid to the prominence afforded to the person of Christ in Evagrius' exegesis of the psalms, and Dysinger does not exaggerate when he describes Jesus as the Evagrian exegetical key in the *Scholia ad psalmos*. The statement in *Scholion* 4 on Psalm 9.12 that the one who has Christ within himself sings psalms bears witness to Evagrius' conviction that the practice of psalmody is an ongoing encounter with Jesus.

The spiritual progression identified above, the movement from πρακτική to φυσική, and then on to θεολογία, and back and forth, is deliberately explicated by Evagrius in Christological terms. *Scholion* 2 on Psalm

126.1 places Christ at the centre of Evagrius' understanding of this tripartite division. Here and elsewhere Christ is the exegetical key who unlocks the inner meanings of the psalm-texts.

Similarly, behind his use of therapeutic and combative metaphors to unpack the meaning of the Psalter, there lies, barely hidden from view, the figure of Christ the Great Physician who heals the wounds brought about by the passions, and Christ the resister of Satan in the wilderness, who deflects and defeats the attacks of the demons by the potency of his word.

Whether or not Χριστός is, in Evagrius' writings, identical with Λόγος, as Dysinger and Bunge claim, or whether, as Konstantinovsky asserts, Christ is 'numerically and ontologically distinct from the Logos', is, strictly speaking, of secondary rather than primary importance to this particular study. Acknowledging the sheer complexity of Evagrius' thought, it may be necessary to accept a degree of inconsistency in the works, with the exegetical Evagrius pointing in one direction, and the speculative and esoteric Evagrius suggesting another.[92]

However, it is clear that, whether or not Christ is the one to be encountered as the final goal of spiritual progression in Evagrius' thought, he is the one who meets and is met by the monk in the course of his journey through psalmody to prayer. As we shall see, as distinct from the works ascribed to Origen, Eusebius of Caesarea, Athanasius, or Didymus the Blind, Christ is not met to any significant extent in the *Scholia ad psalmos*, or in any other Evagrian work, as the offeror or recipient of psalm-prayer, or as the divine name or face of the relevant psalm-texts. His, however, is the presence which accompanies the monk as he moves from the 'wisdom of multiplicity' of the Psalter to the simple knowledge of prayer.

92 See, however, the argument advanced by Augustine Casiday in *Reconstructing the Theology of Evagrius Ponticus: Beyond Heresy* (Cambridge: Cambridge University Press, 2012) that the version of the *Kephalaia Gnostika* upon which the case for Evagrius' heterodoxy rests may not have been written by Evagrius himself.

## VI. Summary

Having considered, in some depth, the various insights provided by the scholarship of de Vogüé, Bunge and Dysinger, we may now conclude that the relationship between psalmody and prayer in the Evagrian works reviewed can be summarized in terms of the three dynamic elements of encounter, dialogue and progression.

Firstly, for Evagrius, the relationship originates within an encounter between the monk and the person of Christ. For Evagrius, the monk encounters Christ in the psalms as the key to the inner meanings of the psalm-verses, as the one who instructs, and who also heals and defends the suppliant soul. Whatever view is taken with regard to the orthodoxy or heresy of Evagrius' Christology, it is clear that as far as the exegetical Evagrius, as opposed to the speculative Evagrius, is concerned, Christ encounters the monk through the chanting of psalmody, and does so recurrently, throughout most of the Psalter, though rarely in ways suggested by other fourth-century Eastern exegetes.

Secondly, the monk's encounter with Christ gives rise to a divine-human dialogue, in which, as we have seen, psalmody is the word of divinity to humanity, as 'spiritual teaching', and prayer is the human response, as the engagement with the divine. Here psalmody is not only the prelude to prayer, and indeed to continual prayer, but is also the beginning of prayer, and it is to be more faithful to the evidence to understand the relationship between the two not so much in terms of a clear-cut categorization, but more in terms of a continuum, befitting a partnership in which the one both nourishes and is nourished by the other.

To this extent, Dysinger's use of the phrase of 'oscillating rhythm' to highlight the nature of the relationship between psalmody and prayer in Evagrian works is not altogether adequate. It is more accurate to describe the association of the two in terms of a partnership or *symbiōsis*, wherein the interconnectedness of the two aspects of monastic discipline is characterized by a mutualism which ensures the exchange of spiritual impulses from each to the other.

Thirdly, the encounter with Christ and the ensuing divine-human dialogue facilitate spiritual progression. In the journey of the monk towards Gnostic maturity, through πρακτική and φυσική and towards θεολογία, psalmody has been shown to have played, on the whole, a preparatory and subordinate role to prayer, purifying the intellect, calming the passions, thwarting the distractions, and enabling the soul to be ready to go 'immaterially into the immaterial'.

It has been shown that there is substance to the broad generalization that whereas psalmody pertains to φυσική, prayer is concerned with θεολογία. Nevertheless, it is also clear that, once again, a too neatly drawn categorization will fail to do justice to the complexity of the evidence unearthed.

In summarizing the thrust of her book, Konstantinovsky describes Evagrius' writings as his own 'spiritual autobiography'.[93] In his works, Evagrius seeks to impart to his readers and listeners a pathway to monastic progress which he himself has trodden. The symbiotic partnership of psalmody and prayer is a key element in the construction of that pathway, both for him and for those influenced by his teachings.

The progress produced by such a partnership is always of a gradual rather than a rapid nature, the product of years spent on the training ground for the Christian contemplative. Let Konstantinovsky have the last, concluding word on this Evagrian ascent:

> By advancing in contemplation gradually rather than abruptly, the mind conforms to the realities it contemplates more gently, adjusting to the change at its own pace. Its healing is thus more complete. That the ascent is gradual is itself anagogic: there is always more of God's perfections to be known which enchants the seeker to press on, in fulfilment of 1 Cor. 13.10: 'But when that which is perfect is come, then that which is in part shall be done away'.[94]

93 Konstantinovsky, *Making of a Gnostic*, 3.

94 Ibid., 180.

CHAPTER FOUR

# Encountering *Christos* in the *Scholia ad Psalmos*

Having considered at some length the relationship between psalmody and prayer in the works of Evagrius, and having identified the encounter with Christ as one of the key elements in that relationship, we will now explore more deeply the nature of that encounter as it is revealed in the *Scholia ad psalmos*.

Dysinger writes: 'The theme encountered most frequently in Evagrius' *Scholia on Psalms* is Jesus Christ'.[1] As has been noted in the previous chapter, he goes on to state that the title Χριστός is 'explained or employed in 159 scholia', and in a footnote he lists each of these references.

The purpose of this chapter is to examine the various ways in which this title is employed in the *Scholia ad psalmos*, in order to attain a fuller picture of how Evagrius sought to explain his understanding of the encounter with the person of Christ, which he believed that he and his fellow monks experienced in the reading of, chanting of, or listening to monastic psalmody of the late fourth century.

It should be noted from the outset that in the absence of a published edition of the *Scholia ad psalmos* such a task has proved to be far from easy. Dysinger offers only a selection of such psalm-texts in his on-line edition and translation,[2] and of the 159 *scholia* recorded by him only 151 have been located by the present author. This edition and translation follows the collation proposed by Marie-Josèphe Rondeau, which is itself based on

1 Dysinger, *Psalmody and Prayer*, 152.

2 Dysinger, *Selected Scholia*.

the editions of Charles de La Rue,[3] Joannes Baptista Pitra[4] and Bernard de Montfaucon.[5]

Nevertheless, within this limitation, it has been possible to glean sufficient evidence from the available material to offer some sort of answer to the question of how this celebrated teacher of πρακτική, φυσική and θεολογία was encouraging those who looked to him for monastic wisdom to conceptualize the presence of Jesus Christ in the Psalter.

The 151 *scholia* containing the title Χριστός, located by this study, are spread out in79 psalms. Of these, the most well-populated is Psalm 88 wherein eight such *scholia* are to be found, followed by Psalm 118 in which there are seven. Psalms 17 and 44 account for six each. Five Χριστός-bearing *scholia* are located in Psalm 5, while there are four in each of Psalms 9, 21, 43, 47, 67, 71, 76 and 134. Psalms 49, 93, 94 and 119 each account for three *scholia*, while each of Psalms 15, 18, 26, 32, 34, 35, 39, 68, 90, 97, 104, 109, 117 and 136 contain two. Finally, a single Χριστός-bearing *scholion* is harboured by each of Psalms 14, 19, 20, 22, 24, 25, 27, 28, 30, 33, 36, 37, 42, 46, 53, 56, 60, 61, 63, 64, 69, 70, 73, 77, 84, 85, 87, 89, 91, 98, 101, 105, 106, 107, 108, 111, 113, 114, 126, 132, 134, 135, 138, 139, 140, 142 and 150.

The importance which Evagrius attached to biblical cross-referencing is also noteworthy. There are at least fifty direct Scriptural quotations within the *Scholia ad psalmos*, as well as numerous textual allusions. Thirteen of these are taken from John, and the same number from 1 and 2 Corinthians. The Book of Psalms, and the Letters to the Romans and the Philippians each account for three more, while Mark and Hebrews each provide a pair. Finally, a single reference is drawn from each of the First Book of Samuel, Proverbs, Matthew, Luke, the Acts of the Apostles, Galatians, Ephesians, Colossians and 1 Peter.

Let us now turn to a comprehensive categorization of the contents of the 151 *scholia* which form the basis of this analysis. For the sake of

3 Migne, PG 12.

4 Pitra, AS 2 and 3.

5 Jacques-Paul Migne, ed., *Patrologiae cursus completus, Series Graeca, Vol. XXVII* (Paris: 1857).

convenience, and with full acknowledgement of the imprecise and highly generalized nature of the exercise, this categorization will place each *scholion* under one of the headings of *Christos* as Divine Being, *Christos* as Divine Activity, *Christos* as Assumed Humanity and *Christos* in Other Texts, with some inevitable overlapping.

## I. *Christos* as divine being

### *1. Christos as God*

Evagrius' liberal use of the title Χριστός includes eight passages in which Christ is emphatically and unequivocally identified with Θεός. His offerings on Psalm 49 are effusive in their proclamation of the God-ness of Χριστός, as he makes the same point in three separate *scholia*. The manifest arrival of God as prophesied in verse 2 is seen to have been fulfilled in the incarnation of Christ, according to *Scholion* 1 on Psalm 49.2 (2): 'For if God came conspicuously, and Christ is God, then 'conspicuously' refers to the flesh'.[6]

Again in *Scholion* 2 on Psalm 49.3 (2–3) he says: 'Our God came conspicuously. Christ is our God. Christ came conspicuously. Christ has come in the flesh. Therefore "conspicuously" refers to the flesh. For the flesh of Christ was perceptible to the senses'.[7]

The easy equation of Χριστός with Θεός is rounded off in *Scholion* 4 on Psalm 49.6 (2), this time with the intrusion into the text of another person of the Godhead. In interpreting 'The heavens will declare his righteousness for God is judge', he writes: 'Here clearly he means Christ is God.

6 Εἰ γὰρ ὁ Θεὸς ἐμφανῶς ἥξει ὁ δὲ Χριστὸς Θεός ἐστι, τὸ, ἐμφανῶς, ἄρα τὴν σάρκα δηλοῖ: PG 27, 229D–232A.

7 Ὁ Θεὸς ἡμῶν ἐμφανῶς ἥξει· Θεὸς δὲ ἡμῶν ὁ Χριστός ἐστι· Χριστὸς ἐμφανῶς ἥξει. Χριστὸς ἐλήλυθεν ἐν σαρκί. Τὸ <ἐμφανῶς> ἄρα τὴν σάρκα δηλοῖ· αἰσθητὴ γὰρ ἦν ἡ σὰρξ τοῦ Χριστοῦ: PG 12, 1449BC; cf. PG 23, 436B.

For the "Father has given all judgment to the Son"'.[8] He makes a similar identification of Χριστός with Θεός in five other *scholia*.[9]

## 2. *Christos as divine anatomy*

As well as identifying Christ as God pure and simple, Evagrius also, in a number of passages, equates Christ with certain parts of the divine anatomy. In these passages, Χριστός is designated as the right hand, the right arm, the arm and the face of Θεός.[10]

Thus, in the context of the psalm-verse, 'With your strong arm you redeemed your people, the descendants of Jacob and Joseph', Evagrius has no difficulty in discerning the presence of Χριστός. In *Scholion* 11 on Psalm 76.16 he says: 'Christ is the right arm of God (Βραχίων τοῦ Θεοῦ ὁ Χριστὸς), by whom he effects the good things in him, the things which come into being according to his desire'.[11]

## 3. *Christos as divine attribute*

In a number of passages Evagrius introduces the title Χριστός in relation to his explanation of a particular attribute or property of God which appears in the relevant psalm-text. These attributes include wisdom (σοφία), truth (ἀλήθεια), righteousness (δικαιοσύνη), salvation (σωτήριος), power (δύναμις) and life (ζωή).

In *Scholion* 8 on Psalm 21.19 (1) he identifies Χριστός as the σοφία, ἀλήθεια and δικαιοσύνη of God: 'While the Jews serve the written law, the perceptible clothing of the Word is divided. And we who keep the spirit of the word divide the noetic garments of our Saviour, having been

8 Ἐνταῦθα προδήλως τὸν Χριστὸν λέγει Θεόν. <Πᾶσαν> γὰρ <τὴν κρίσιν ἔδωκεν ὁ Πατὴρ τῷ Υἱῷ.>: PG 12, 1452A; cf. PG 27, 233C.

9 PG 12, 1185D; PG 12, 1429CD; PG 12, 1441B; AS 3, 181; PG 12, 1641D.

10 PG 12, 1440D; AS 3, 99; PG 12, 1521BC; PG 12, 1544B.

11 AS 3, 108.

baptized into Christ, and having put him on as wisdom and truth and righteousness'.[12]

In this passage it is also worthy of note that Evagrius is content, through an obvious allusion to the passion, to make a clear equation between Λόγος and Χριστός, rather than giving the impression of there being some element of distinction between the two, as he does in other references.

In further passages he identifies Christ as the divine σοφία in the psalm text.[13] And in *Scholion* 10 on Psalm 76.15 he follows Paul in 1 Corinthians 1.24 with the emphatic statement, equating Christ with the divine δύναμις as well as with σοφία: 'This is the Christ; for Christ is the power and wisdom of God'.[14] And he repeats the commentary in *Scholion* 2 on Psalm 79.3 (1): 'Christ is the power of God and the wisdom of God'.[15]

Texts associating Christ with the divine truth (ἀλήθεια) are also very much in evidence.[16] Predictably making use of John 14.6, Evagrius explains 'Guide me by your way, O Lord, and I shall walk in your truth' in *Scholion* 7 on Psalm 85.11 as follows: '"I am the way", says the Christ; and again, "I am the truth". So he prays first to be in him, because Christ is the way, that is, virtue; then afterwards like truth, which pertains to contemplation'.[17]

Christ is defined as righteousness (δικαιοσύνη) in *Scholion* 1 on Psalm 30.2 (2). Here, again with recourse to 1 Corinthians 1.30, Evagrius offers this comment on 'in your justice deliver me and rescue me': 'Or more

12 Ἰουδαῖοι μὲν τὸν γραπτὸν νόμον τηροῦντες καὶ τὰ αἰσθητὰ ἱμάτια τοῦ Λόγου διαμερίζονται· ἡμεῖς δὲ τὸ πνεῦμα τοῦ λογοῦ φυλάσσοντες, τὰ νοητὰ ἱμάτια τοῦ Σωτῆρος ἡμῶν διαμεριζόμεθα, εἰς Χριστὸν βαπτιζόμενοι, καὶ αὐτὸν ἐνδυόμενοι ὡς σοφίαν καὶ ἀλήθειαν καὶ δικαιοσύνην: PG 12, 1257B.

13 PG 12, 1313B; AS 3, 147; PG 12, 1553C; PG 12, 1588CD; AS 3, 329.

14 Τουτέστι τὸν Χριστόν· Χριστὸς γὰρ δύναμις καὶ Θεοῦ σοφία: PG 12, 1540C; Dysinger, *Selected Scholia*.

15 Χριστὸς Θεοῦ δύναμις καὶ Θεοῦ σοφία: PG 12, 1544B.

16 AS 2, 455; PG 12, 1273B; AS 3, 55; AS 3, 61; AS 3, 308.

17 ...Εὔχεται τοίνυν πρῶτον μὲν ἐν αὐτῷ γενέσθαι, ὡς ὁδὸν τὸν Χριστὸν, τουτέστιν ὡς ἀρετὴν, ἔπειτα δε ὡς ἀλήθειαν, ὅπερ ἐστι τῆς θεωρίας: AS 3, 149.

likely, justice means Christ. For he "became our wisdom from God, and our justice, and sanctification, and redemption"'.[18]

Divine salvation (σωτήριος) is also seen to be embodied in Χριστός. In *Scholion* 4 on Psalm 69.5, commenting on 'Let those who love your salvation say evermore, "Let God be magnified!"', Evagrius boldly proclaims: 'Christ is the salvation of God the Father'.[19]

In a single text Evagrius identifies Χριστός with the divine life (ζωή). In *Scholion* 5 on Psalm 35.10 (1) he offers this interpretation of 'For in you is life's fountain, and in your light shall we see light': 'If the fountain is the life, and the life is Christ, then the fountain is Christ'.[20]

In addition to his propensity for affirming the divinity of Christ by identifying Χριστός with a series of divine attributes, Evagrius also proclaims the eternity of Christ in a striking exegesis of 'To-day if you would hear his voice, do not harden your hearts'. In *Scholion* 1 on Psalm 94.8, quoting two verses from Hebrews 13.8 and 3.13, he is eager to assert the relevance of the dimension of 'forever' (εἰς τοὺς αἰῶνας' in relation to the 'to-day' (σήμερον) of Χριστός: '"To-day" signifies this life. For it says, "Jesus Christ yesterday, to-day and forever" And again, "As long as it is called to-day"'.[21]

## *4. Christos and the divine Word*

The precise relationship between Χριστός and Λόγος in the *Scholia ad psalmos* is somewhat ambiguous. In at least one passage there is a clear identity between the two, whereas in others Evagrius gives the impression of drawing some kind of distinction between them. Whatever the intended relationship, in a number of passages Evagrius uses the two titles in tandem.

18 Ἢ τάχα δικαιοσύνη λέγει τὸν Χριστόν· αὐτὸς γὰρ <ἐγενήθη ἡμῖν σοφία ἀπὸ Θεοῦ, δικαιοσύνη τε καὶ ἁγιασμὸς καὶ ἀπολύτρωσις>: PG 12, 1297D–1300A.

19 Σωτήριον τοῦ Θεοῦ καὶ Πατρός ἐστιν ὁ Χριστὸς: AS 3, 88; see also PG 12, 1552C.

20 Εἰ ἡ πηγή ἐστιν ἡ ζωὴ, ἡ ζωὴ δὲ ἐστιν ὁ Χριστὸς, ἡ πηγὴ ἐστιν ὁ Χριστός: PG 12, 1316B.

21 Τὸ σήμερον τὸν βίον τοῦτον σημαίνει· < Ἰησοῦς γὰρ, φησὶ, Χριστὸς χθὲς, καὶ σήμερον καὶ εἰς τοὺς αἰῶνας· > καὶ πάλιν· <Ἄχρις οὗ τὸ σήμερον καλεῖται.>: PG 12, 1556A; cf. AS 3, 181; see also PG 12, 1549B.

In *Scholion* 1 on Psalm 47.3 (1), referring to Psalm 31.7, he comments on '[God] being well rooted in the enjoyment of all the earth': 'Christ is well rooted in exaltation. For, he says, "You are my enjoyment, redeem me from those who encircle me". And God the Word who is in him is his root.'[22] This *scholion* again reaffirms Evagrius' attestation of the divinity of Χριστός. He is the Θεός referred to in the psalm-text. But he is also said to be rooted in Θεὸς Λόγος who is in him. And the presence of God the Word in Christ is reiterated in further passages.

Commenting on 'Your way, O God, is in the sanctuary; what god is so great as our God?', he writes in *Scholion* 9 on Psalm 76.14 (1): 'Either: in every holy place is the way of God; or, in the Christ is his Word.'[23]

Similarly, he writes in *Scholion* 2 on Psalm 98.5, in interpreting 'Extol the Lord our God; worship at the footstool of his feet, because he is holy!': 'Some say that the footstool is the flesh of Christ, which is worshipped on account of Christ. But Christ is worshipped because of the Word of God in him.'[24]

In five passages, in contrast with *Scholion* 8 on Psalm 21.19, Evagrius' use of the phrase μετὰ τοῦ Θεοῦ Λόγου might appear to place some distinction between Χριστός and Λόγος, though Dysinger resolutely defends the 'famous deacon's' Christological orthodoxy in each case.[25]

It is not the purpose of this chapter to appraise this debate, already noted in the previous chapter, as far as it concerns the whole Evagrian corpus. It is, however, of interest to observe that Konstantinovsky criticizes Dysinger for evaluating the entire corpus in the light of what Evagrius

22 Εὔριζον ἀγαλλίαμά ἐστιν ὁ Χριστός. <Τὸ ἀγαλλίαμα γάρ μου, φησὶν, λύτρωσαί με ἀπὸ τῶν κυκλωσάντων με.> Ῥίζα δὲ αὐτοῦ ὁ Θεὸς Λόγος ὁ ἐν αὐτῷ: PG 12, 1440A; cf. AS 3, 46.

23 Ἤτοι ἐν παντὶ ἁγιῷ ἡ ὁδὸς τοῦ Θεοῦ, ἢ ἐν τῷ Χριστῷ ὁ λόγος αὐτοῦ: PG 12, 1540B; Dysinger, *Selected Scholia*.

24 Τὸ ὑποπόδιον τῶν ποδῶν εἶπόν τινες εἶναι τὴν σάρκα τὴν τοῦ Χριστοῦ, ἥτις διὰ τὸν Χριστόν ἐστι προκυνητή· ὁ δὲ Χριστὸς προκυνητὸς διὰ τὸν ἐν αὐτῷ Λόγον Θεοῦ: PG 12, 1557B.

25 *Scholion* 7 on Psalm 44.3; *Scholion 10* on Psalm 104.15; *Scholion* 4 on Psalm 88.7 (2); Scholion 2 on Psalm 118.3; *Scholion* 5 on Psalm 131.7; Dysinger, *Psalmody and Prayer*, 158–71.

says in the *Scholia ad psalmos*,[26] without acknowledging that there is a corresponding danger of interpreting the *Scholia ad psalmos* in the light of such works as the *Kephalaia Gnostika*. The purpose of this chapter is to evaluate the Evagrian use of the title Χριστός in the psalm-commentary, rather than in the Evagrian corpus as a whole, and so the first port of call for such a consideration must be the evidence gleaned from the *Scholia ad psalmos* itself. Therefore while the debate concerning the orthodoxy or otherwise of Evagrius' Christology is of vital importance to Evagrian studies as such, it can shed little light upon the issue which is immediately before us.

## 5. *Christos as divine object*

Throughout the *Scholia ad psalmos* Christ is defined in terms of a series of objects which in varied ways mediate the being and presence of God. These include the rock, the sun, the mountain, the throne, the temple, the tabernacle, the crown and the ark.

With regard to the rock (πέτρα), reference or allusion is constantly made to 1 Corinthians 10.4, where Paul boldly writes, concerning the water-and life-giving rock of Horeb in Exodus 17.6, 'And the rock was Christ' (ἡ πέτρα δὲ ἦν ὁ Χριστός).[27] Thus Evagrius offers this commentary in *Scholion* 2 on Psalm 39.3 (3): '"And he set my feet upon a rock". The rock is the faith of Christ. "And he directed my steps", through *praktike* and true teaching'.[28]

Evagrius also equates Christ with the sun (ἥλιος).[29] Summoning into action the texts of John 14.10 and 2 Corinthians 5.19, he records this reflection on 'He set his tent in the sun', in *Scholion* 1 on Psalm 18.5: 'Our Lord

26 Ibid., 9.

27 See AS 3, 69; AS 3, 115; PG 12, 1573A.

28 <Καὶ ἔστησεν ἐπὶ πέτραν τοὺς πόδας μου.> Πέτρα ἐστι πίστις Χριστοῦ. <Καὶ κατεύθυνε τὰ διαβήματὰ μου·> διὰ τῆς πρακτικῆς καὶ τῶν ἀληθινῶν δογμάτων: PG 12, 1409BC.

29 PG 12, 1584B; PG 12, 1664A.

is the sun of justice, in whom the Father dwells, according to this: "I in the Father, and the Father in me". And again, "The Father who abides in me performs the works". And the Apostle says, "God was in Christ reconciling the world to himself"'.[30]

Evagrius is explicit in his treatment of 'they led me and brought me to your holy mountain and to your tents', in *Scholion* 2 on Psalm 42.3 (2): 'The holy mountain is the Christ of God: his tabernacles are the holy powers in which he dwells'.[31] Χριστός as the holy mountain (ὄρος ἅγιόν) features in three other *scholia*.[32]

The words, 'You sat on the throne, you who give righteous judgments' prompts Evagrius to make an emphatic identification of Χριστός with the seat of divine power (θρόνος), while at the same time offer an observation with regard to the latter's *cathedra*. In *Scholion* 2 on Psalm 9.5 (2) he writes: 'For the throne of God is Christ; but the throne of Christ is the incorporeal nature'.[33]

An equally emphatic identification is made in response to 'God is seated on his holy throne', in *Scholion* 5 on *Psalm* 46.9 (2): 'Christ is the throne of God, and the nature of Christ is endowed with reason'.[34] Other less emphatic identifications of Χριστός with θρόνος are found in two other *scholia*.[35]

In *Scholia* 4 and 5 on Psalm 5.8 (1–2), commenting on 'I will bow down towards your holy temple in awe of you', Evagrius makes an explicit identification of Christ with the temple of God, utilizing 2 Corinthians 5.19 and John 2.19 in the process, and making it clear that Christ is an object of worship and not just a place of worship: '*Holy temple* is the Christ of

30 Ὁ Κύριος ἡμῶν ὁ ἥλιος τῆς δικαιοσύνης ἐστὶν… PG 12, 1241D.

31 Ὄρος ἅγιόν ἐστι Θεοῦ ὁ Χριστός· σκηνώματα δὲ αὐτοῦ, αἱ ἅγιαι δυνάμεις ἐν αἷς κατοικεῖ: PG 12, 1421B; Dysinger, *Selected Scholia*.

32 PG 12, 1208C; AS 3, 46; PG 12, 1548D.

33 Θρόνος μὲν Θεοῦ ὁ Χριστὸς, θρόνος δὲ Χριστοῦ ἡ ἀσώματος φύσις: PG 12, 1188C; Dysinger, *Selected Scholia*.

34 Θρόνος μὲν Θεοῦ ὁ Χριστός· Χριστοῦ δὲ ἡ φύσις λογική: PG 12, 1437B.

35 AS 3, 158; PG 12, 1553D.

God, for *God was in Christ reconciling the world to himself. In the fear of God all turn away from vice*: so, *in the fear* of the Lord [all] worship the temple which is Christ; for he says, *destroy this temple and in three days I will raise it up*'.[36]

Similar identifications of Χριστός as the temple of God (ναὸς Θεοῦ) follow in *Scholion* 4 on Psalm 17.7 (3) and in *Scholion* 2 on Psalm 27.2 (2).[37]

With the help of Psalm 18.6, Evagrius defines Christ as the tabernacle (σκηνή) of God in *Scholion* 4 on Psalm 26.5 (1–2), with reference to 'He hid me in the tabernacle in the day of troubles; he sheltered me in the secret spot of his tabernacle; he set me high on a rock'. In the course of this, he also brings into play explicitly Christ's identification with the sun, and implicitly his association with the rock: 'He calls Christ a tabernacle in whom God was dwelling. For he says, "In the sun did he place his tabernacle". And the Lord is the Sun of Righteousness'.[38]

'You set a crown of precious stone on his head' presents Evagrius with the opportunity of depicting Χριστός as a crown (στέφανος) in *Scholion* 1 on Psalm 20.4 (1): 'For God is the crown of Christ, and Christ is the crown of the rational nature'.[39]

Once more Evagrius summons up one of his most employed New Testament texts (2Corinthians 5.19) in seeking to give explanation to the psalm-verse, 'Rise up, O Lord, and go into your rest, you and the ark of your sanctity'. This ark (κιβωτός) he unequivocally identifies as Χριστός as the ark in *Scholion* 6 on Psalm 131.8: 'For the flesh is the ark of the Lord, and Christ is the ark of God, if indeed God was in Christ reconciling the world to himself".[40]

36 Ναὸς ἅγιός ἐστι τοῦ Θεοῦ Χριστὸς ... ἐν φόβῳ δὲ Κυρίου προσκυνεῖ τὸν ναὸν, ὅς ἐστι Χριστός: AS 2, 455; Dysinger, *Selected Scholia*.

37 PG 12, 1225D–1228A and PG 12, 1285A.

38 Σκηνὴν τὸν Χριστὸν ὀνομάζει ἐν ᾧ καὶ κατεσκήνωσεν ὁ Θεός· <Ἐν τῷ ἡλίῳ> γὰρ, φησὶν, <ἔθετο τὸ σκήνωμα αὐτοῦ.> Ἥλιος δὲ δικαιοσύνης ὁ Κύριος: PG 12, 1280D–1281A.

39 Στέφανος μὲν Χριστοῦ ὁ Θεὸς, Χριστὸς δὲ τῆς λογικῆς φύσεως: PG 12, 1249A.

40 Ἡ σὰρξ μέν ἐστι κιβωτὸς τοῦ Κυρίου· κιβωτὸς δὲ Θεοῦ ὁ Χριστὸς, εἴπερ ὁ Θεὸς ἦν ἐν Χριστῷ κόσμον καταλλάσσων ἑαυτῷ: AS 3, 330.

## II. *Christos* as divine activity

### *1. Christos as divine creativity*

In two passages Evagrius uses the word 'maker' (δημιουργός) in relation to Χριστός, thus placing himself within the tradition represented by Diognetus, Tatian, Clement of Alexandria, Origen, Athanasius, and later Cyril of Alexandria in assigning this title to the Second Person of the Trinity.

In *Scholion* 2 on Psalm 89.4 he states quite bluntly: 'And our Lord Jesus Christ is the maker of our bodies'.[41] And he is equally explicit in his commentary in *Scholion* 4 on Psalm 135.23: 'Except that this must be known, that these concepts are predicated on contemplation of things that have come into being, and this contemplation sets forth Christ as maker'.[42] The theme of new creation through the agency of Christ is highlighted in two further *scholia*.[43]

### *2. Christos as divine warrior*

As well as identifying Χριστός with δημιουργός, Evagrius is also at pains to associate the person of Christ with other specific roles assigned to God within the Psalter. Of these the most frequently addressed is that of Divine Warrior.

The background to the concept of Divine Warrior in ancient near-eastern literature has been the subject of a considerable body of scholarship over the years, and has given rise to an extensive and growing bibliography. It is certainly beyond the remit of the present study to survey this in any great detail. However, it would be of some assistance to our quest to highlight just two of the many publications *en passant*.

41 σωμάτων δὲ δημιουργός ἐστι ὁ Κύριος ἡμῶν Ἰησοῦς Χριστός: AS 3, 167.

42 πλὴν τοῦτο ἰστέον, ὅτιπερ αὗται αἱ ἐπίνοιαι κατὰ τῆς τῶν γεγονότων θεωρίας κατηγοροῦνται, ἥτις ὡς δημιουργὸν παρίστησι τὸν Χριστόν: PG 12, 1657B.

43 AS 3, 196; PG 12, 1429A.

Harold Wayne Ballard Jr.'s *The Divine Warrior Motif in the Psalms* provides a brief, useful guide to the various elements of the concept which may be found in the Hebrew Psalter.[44] According to him, the recurrent themes of Yahweh as judge, king, protector and peacemaker are all elements which contribute to this *motif*. In *The Divine Warrior: The New Testament Use of an Old Testament Motif*, Tremper Longman III charts how Christ is interpreted in the light of this concept in the Revelation of John, in the Gospel resurrection narratives and in some of the Epistles.[45]

There is no doubt that Evagrius, as many other Fathers, was eager to make use of the hermeneutical key of Ephesians 6.12 in order to interpret the martial language of the Psalter in terms of inner warfare. In this interpretation Χριστός becomes the Θεός of the psalm-verse, as the Divine Warrior who struggles against the enemy forces of evil and chaos.

Such a *motif* is prevalent throughout the *Scholia ad psalmos*, which itself presents the Psalter as a weapon against spiritual foes.[46] Indeed in the commentaries on Psalms 44.6 and 73.11 this concept is very much to the fore. Let us now consider other passages from the *Scholia ad psalmos* where Χριστός is portrayed as assuming this divine role.

Evagrius understands the psalmist's call, 'Take up circular shield and oblong shield, and rise up to help me', as a call to Christ, in the light of Christ's claim in John 16.33 to have overcome the world. He says in *Scholion* 2 on Psalm 34.2: 'If the one who has overcome in war reduces the warriors to servitude, and if Christ has overcome the world as he said: "Take courage; I have overcome the world" [John 16.33], then Christ reduced the world to servitude, so that all may become servants of Christ'.[47]

44 Harold Wayne Ballard, Jr., *The Divine Warrior Motif in the Psalms*, BIBAL Dissertation Series 6 (North Richland Hills, Texas: BIBAL Press, 1999).

45 Tremper Longman III, 'The Divine Warrior: The New Testament Use of an Old Testament Motif', in *Westminster Theological Journal* 44 (Philadelphia: Westminster Theological Seminary, 1982), 209–307.

46 Dysinger, *Psalmody and Prayer*, 131–49.

47 Χριστὸς ἄρα τὸν κόσμον κατεδουλώσατο, ἵνα γένωνται πάντες δοῦλοι Χριστοῦ: PG 12, 1312A; Dysinger, *Selected Scholia*.

In a psalm which Ballard specifically identifies as exemplary of the Divine Warrior *motif*, we find Evagrius portraying Christ as a redeemer from sin rather than from political captivity. In a sense, he contradicts the outcry of the psalmist against the national champion, 'You sold your people without price, and there was no abundance in their exchange'. Instead, he asserts that the captivity is self-inflicted, and he proclaims Christ as the faithful warrior who stands up for his people, in *Scholion 8* on Psalm 43.13: 'For we were sold to sins, from which Christ redeemed us'.[48]

*Scholion* 1 on Psalm 63.2 (2) focuses on the psalmist's prayer, 'Deliver my life from the fear of the enemy'. Here again Evagrius, making use of Mark 6.50, invokes the combative role of Christ, who, like a military commander, exhorts his troops with words of encouragement: 'The enemy is fear, or what comes to us from fear, or the opposite of confidence in Christ. For, he says, "Take courage, don't fear, it is I"'.[49]

Ephesians 4.8 provides him with inspiration for his exegesis in *Scholion* 13 *bis* on Psalm 67.19. Like a conquering general returning home with his human booty, Χριστός is depicted both by Paul and by Evagrius as leading the humiliated and vanquished captivity of sin and death into captivity itself in his triumphal procession to heaven: 'Paul says concerning Christ: *Having ascended on high he led captive captives, and he gave gifts to men* [Eph. 4.8]. I call gifts the gifts of the Holy Spirit'.[50]

Psalm 88 furnishes Evagrius with copious material for Christological reflection. In *Scholion* 12 on Psalm 88.23 (1) the battle between Christ the Divine Warrior and his enemies is once more to the fore, as he offers this interpretation of 'An enemy shall not profit by him; a son of lawlessness shall not continue to harm him': 'If, whenever we sin, we help our enemies, and Christ has not sinned, Christ did not help his enemies'.[51]

48 Ταῖς γὰρ ἁμαρτίαις ἐπράθημεν, ἀφ' ὧν ἡμᾶς Χριστὸς ἐξηγόρασεν: PG 12, 1425AB.

49 Ἐχθρὸς φόβος ἐστὶν ἤτοι ὁ παρὰ τοῦ ἐχθροῦ ἡμῖν ἐγγινόμενος, ἢ ὁ ἐναντίος τῷ τοῦ Χριστοῦ θάρσει. <Θαρσεῖτε γὰρ, φησὶν, ἐγώ εἰμι· μὴ φοβεῖσθε>: PG 12, 1492A.

50 PG 12, 1508D.

51 Εἰ, ὅταν ἁμαρτάνωμεν, τοὺς ἐχθροὺς ἡμῶν ὠφελοῦμεν, Χριστὸς δὲ οὐχ ἥμαρτεν· ἄρα τοὺς ἐχθροὺς αὐτοῦ οὐκ ὠφέλησεν ὁ Χριστός: PG 12, 1549A.

In one of the psalms which Ballard singles out for special treatment in his study, Evagrius, in *Scholion* 7 on Psalm 104.11 (1), associates the Canaanites of the psalm-verse with the spiritual powers which formerly occupied the soul, and Christ with the one who evicts them by force: 'Before the coming of Christ the Canaanites possessed our souls, not permitting us to bear spiritual fruit'.[52]

Christ's battle with Satan for the human soul is the background for his exegesis of the text, 'Let it be like a coat that he wraps around himself, like a belt that he always wears'. Thus in *Scholion* 15 on Psalm 108.19 (2) he writes: 'And as Satan through wickedness strips those who put on Christ, so Christ clothes with the virtues those who have stripped off the curse'.[53]

With some assistance from Galatians 4.26 and Isaiah 59.20 he interprets 'I will acknowledge you with an upright heart, when I have learnt your righteous judgments' as a prophecy of the coming of Christ as the Deliverer from Zion. In *Scholion* 5 on Psalm 118.7 he writes:

> He glorifies God in uprightness of heart – the one who has learned from the Lord the *logoi* concerning judgment ... and what 'Jerusalem above' is [Gal. 4.26]; and what its Zion is, from which its Christ is said to come (ἀφ' ἧς λέγεται ἔρχεσθαι ὁ Χριστὸς); for it says 'there shall come from Zion the Deliverer (ἐκ Σιὼν ὁ ῥυόμενος), and he will turn back impiety from Jacob' [Isa. 59.20].[54]

In *Scholion* 2 on Psalm 134.6 Evagrius turns to the theme of the deep waters representing 'subterranean demons'. Here he makes use of the story of the Gadarene swine in Matthew 8.31 to distinguish them from the 'terrestrial demons' exorcised by Christ in this miracle: '...So also in the allegorically-interpreted depths there are the subterranean demons (οἱ καταχθόνοι δαίμονες), to which the terrestrial demons (οἱ ἐπίγειοι δαίμονες) pleaded that Christ would not send them in the Gospels [Matt. 8.31]. The more

52 Πρὸ τῆς ἐπιδημίας Χριστοῦ οἱ Χαναναῖοι κατεῖχον ἡμῶν τὰς ψυχὰς, μὴ ἐῶντες ἡμᾶς καρποὺς ἐκφέρειν πνευματικούς: PG 12, 1564C.

53 Ὥσπερ τοὺς Χριστὸν ἐνδυσαμένους διὰ τῶν κακῶν ἐκδύει ὁ Σατανᾶς, οὕτως καὶ τοὺς κατάραν ἐκδυσαμένους διὰ τῶν ἀρετῶν ἐνδύε, ὁ Χριστός: AS 3, 225.

54 AS 3, 254–5; Dysinger, *Selected Scholia*.

accurate knowledge of their worlds and their various bodies is stored up in the *logoi* concerning judgment'.[55]

So prolific is Evagrius' equation of Χριστός with the Divine Warrior that this title is used in relation to this role in a further twelve passages in the psalm-commentary.[56]

### *3. Christos as divine peacemaker*

Strongly connected to the Divine Warrior *motif*, as noted by Ballard, is the role of the Divine Peacemaker, who establishes his *pax* by way of subduing his foes. Here again, we find Evagrius portraying Χριστός as the one who brings tranquillity to the prevailing scene of turbulence.

In another psalm which features prominently in Ballard's study, Evagrius grapples with the text in which the psalmist endeavours to arouse the apparently sleeping Divine Warrior: 'Wake up! Why do you sleep, O Lord? Arise and do not reject us totally!' Thus in *Scholion* 15 on Psalm 43.24 he writes: 'At some time Christ was sleeping in the disciples' boat, but when the storm came the disciples roused him'.[57]

Here he clearly interprets the psalm-text against the background of Christ's stilling of the storm in Matthew 8.23–7, Mark 4.35–41, and Luke 8.22–5. The expectation of the psalmist that the warrior God of Israel will arouse himself to defeat the nation's enemies is identified with the disciples' expectation that Christ, their champion, will arise to save them from the forces of nature.

The same story provides Evagrius with his exegesis of 'He rebuked the Red Sea and it became dry' in *Scholion* 5 on Psalm 105.9 (1). The Christ who brings tranquillity (γαλήνη) to the Sea of Galilee is equated with the God of Israel who imposes his *pax* on the waters in the story of the

55 Dysinger, *Selected Scholia*; cf. AS 3, 334.

56 AS 2, 455; PG 12, 1232B; PG 12, 1248C; PG 12, 1292A; PG 12, 1317D; PG 12, 1429C; PG 12, 1540C; PG 12, 1552B; AS 3, 188; AS 3, 275; PG 12, 1629C; PG 12, 1657D.

57 Ἐκάθευδέ ποτε ἐν τῷ πλοίῳ τῶν μαθητῶν ὁ Χριστὸς, ἀλλὰ γενομένου χειμῶνος ἐξήγειραν αὐτὸν οἱ μαθηταί…: PG 12, 1428B.

Exodus: 'And in the Gospels Christ rebuked the wind and the sea, and there was a great calm'.[58]

In *Scholion* 1 on Psalm 106.3 he addresses the psalm-text, 'He gathered them in from the lands, from the east and the west, and the north and the sea'. Here he relates this generally to the progress of the spiritual life in which Χριστός calms the unruly waters of unsound doctrine: 'And if anyone has been delivered from the north wind and the sea, and this person is grounded in true doctrine, they are no longer cast about by every wind of teaching, nor are they shipwrecked in their faith, for they possess divine steering through the grace of Christ'.[59]

## 4. *Christos as divine teacher*

Throughout the Psalter God is portrayed as a teacher of spiritual truth and wisdom. In a number of *scholia* Evagrius identifies Χριστός with this didactic role. By implication, his exposition of 'I shall be blameless before him, and I shall keep myself from lawlessness' points in this direction. Christ in John 14.6 teaches his disciples that he himself is the way of God. Thus Evagrius, with some additional help from Psalm 17.31, writes in *Scholion* 13 on Psalm 17.24 (2): 'He is blameless who has within himself the way of God, the Christ. For he says, "I am the way". And David himself calls this way blameless, saying, "O my God, your way is blameless"'.[60]

In *Scholion* 2 on Psalm 91.4, a text reproduced in the commentary on Psalms 32.2[61] and 150.3,[62] Evagrius offers this explanation of the meaning

58 Καὶ ἐν τοῖς εὐαγγελίοις ὁ Χριστὸς ἐπετίμησεν τῷ ἀνέμῳ καὶ τῇ θαλάσσῃ, καὶ ἐγένετο γαλήνη μεγάλη: AS 3, 212.

59 Εἰ δέ τις τοῦ βοῤῥᾶ καὶ τῆς θαλάσσης ἀπήλλακται, οὗτος ἐν ἀληθέσι δόγμασιν ὢν, οὐκέτι περιφέρεται παντὶ ἀνέμῳ διδασκαλίας, οὐδὲ περὶ τὴν πίστιν ναυαγεῖ, κυβέρνησιν θείαν κτησάμενος διὰ τῆς χάριτος τοῦ Χριστοῦ: AS 3, 215.

60 Ἄμωμός ἐστιν ὁ ἔχων ἐν ἑαυτῷ τὴν ὁδὸν τοῦ Θεοῦ, τὸν Χριστόν. <Ἐγὼ γὰρ, φησὶν, εἰμὶ ἡ ὁδός.> Ἄμωμον δὲ ταύτην τὴν ὁδὸν καὶ αὐτὸς ὁ Δαυῒδ ἔφη λέγων· <Ὁ Θεός μου, ἄμωμος ἡ ὁδός σου>: PG 12, 1233AB.

61 *Psalmody and Prayer*, 151 note 9; cf. PG 12, 1304BC.

62 PG 12, 1684C.

of 'on the ten-stringed harp with an ode on the cithara': 'And a cithara is a *praktike* soul, moved by the commandments of Christ'.[63]

To the psalm-text, 'The stone which the builders rejected has become the chief cornerstone', he applies an exegesis which amplifies Christ's teaching role, in *Scholion* 6 on Psalm 117.22 (2): 'The corner is the teaching of our Saviour Jesus Christ, who brings peace in heaven and on earth'.[64]

Again resorting to a Divine Warrior *motif*, Evagrius highlights the didactic work of Χριστός in relation to spiritual warfare, in his treatment of 'I was for peace; when I would speak to them, they would fight me without reason'. Thus in *Scholion* 4 on Psalm 119.7 he writes: 'Then the attacks of the demons become even more severe, whenever anyone responds to their tempting thoughts. And Christ who himself was tempted teaches us to do this'.[65] Χριστός is identified as the Divine Teacher in three other passages.[66]

## *5. Christos in other divine roles*

Evagrius assigns to Χριστός the roles of ruler, shepherd and helper. To the text 'All kings shall worship him, and all nations do him service', Evagrius, with reference to Philippians 2.10, attributes the following meaning in *Scholion* 7 on Psalm 71.11 (2): 'If this is so, then every rational nature shall serve Christ. And this is the saying of Paul, that every knee shall bow to him'.[67] Four other *scholia* also affirm this sovereignty.[68]

Predictably, Evagrius identifies the 'shepherd' of Psalm 22 with Χριστός, while at the same time, with recourse to John 15.4, marking the transition

63 κιθάρα δέ ἐστι ψυχὴ πρακτικὴ ὑπὸ τῶν ἐντολῶν τοῦ Χριστοῦ κινουμένη: PG 12, 1552D.

64 Γωνία ἐστι διδασκαλία τοῦ Σωτῆρος ἡμῶν Ἰησοῦ Χριστοῦ, τὰ ἐν οὐρανοῖς καὶ ἐπὶ γῆς εἰρηνεύοντος: AS 3, 243.

65 Τότε μάλιστα χαλεπώτεροι γίνονται πολεμοῦντες οἱ δαίμονες, ὅταν τις αὐτοῖς πρὸς τοὺς λογισμοὺς ἀποκρίνηται· καὶ διδάσκει ἡμᾶς τοῦτο ποιεῖν ὁ Χριστὸς πειραζόμενος: AS 3, 318.

66 AS 3, 37; PG 12, 1548B; PG 12, 1660A.

67 Εἰ δὲ τοῦτο, πᾶσα ἄρα φύσις λογικὴ δουλεύσει τῷ Χριστῷ· καὶ τοῦτό ἐστι τὸ παρὰ τῷ Παύλῳ εἰρημένον, ὅτι αὐτῷ κάμψει πᾶν γόνυ: PG 12, 1524D.

68 PG 12, 1429B; PG 12, 1484C; PG 12, 1549B; AS 3, 298.

of the divinity from pastor to friend in the progress of the soul, in *Scholion* 4 on Psalm 22.5 (1):

> At first as a *shepherd* Christ *shepherds* the *sheep*; but now henceforth as a friend he calls [his] friends to the *table* (πρότερον μὲν ὡς ποιμὴν ὁ Χριστὸς ποιμαίνει τὰ πρόβατα· νῦνὶ δὲ λοιπὸν ὡς φίλος καλεῖ τοὺς φίλους ἐπὶ τὴν τράπεζαν). 'For I no longer call you servants', says the saviour, 'but friends' (John 15.4). For the fear of God produces a servant; while knowledge of mysteries [produces] a friends (καὶ δοῦλον μὲν ποιεῖ φόβος θεοῦ, φίλον δὲ γνῶσις μυστηρίων).[69]

Again, predictably, Evagrius makes use of John 10.11 in his interpretation of 'For he is our God, and we are the people of his pasture and the sheep of his hand', in *Scholion* 4 on Psalm 94.7 (1): '"I am", says Christ, "the good shepherd"'.[70] Like the 'Lord' of much psalmody Christ is depicted as a helper. In *Scholion* 9 on Psalm 93.18, with reference to the text 'If I were to say, "My foot has been shaken," your steadfast love, O Lord would help me', Evagrius identifies Χριστός with the Κύριος whose help is summoned.[71]

## III. *Christos* as assumed humanity

In contrast to the extensive employment of Χριστός to identify some aspect of the divinity of Christ in the meaning of the Psalter, Evagrius uses the same title very sparingly throughout his *Scholia ad psalmos* in relation to reflections on his humanity. Nevertheless, for the sake of completeness, it behoves us to note those texts in which some rumination on the incarnation is coupled with the appearance of Χριστός in the commentary.

69 Dysinger, *Psalmody and Prayer*, 169–70; cf. PG 12, 1264C.
70 AS 3, 181.
71 PG 12, 1553CD; PG 27, 412A.

## *1. Christos as human flesh*

In several passages Evagrius introduces the flesh of Christ into his exegesis. In a fragment preserved only in Latin, he employs Χριστός (*Christus*) in his interpretation of 'moreover my flesh shall dwell in hope'. In *Scholion* 7 on Psalm 15.9 (3) he highlights the consequence of Christ's ascension into heaven: 'Whoever wants to be offended by our address, let them be offended, but I shall affirm with all confidence that just as Christ was the first-born from the dead, so he first carried flesh up to heaven'.[72]

In a similar spirit to *Scholion* 4 on Psalm 26.5 (1–2) he defines the flesh of Christ as a tabernacle. In *Scholia* 7–8 on Psalm 17.12 (1–2), making use of 2 Corinthians 5.16, he offers this exposition of 'around him was his tabernacle, dark waters in airy clouds': 'He named as his tabernacle the flesh in which Christ was seated; and further he shows the tabernacle because of the transcience of the incarnation. "For", he says, "we once knew Christ according to the flesh, but we no longer know him in that way"'.[73]

In *Scholion* 2 on Psalm 49.3 (2–3), as we have seen, in his interpretation of 'God will come conspicuously, our God – and he will not pass by in silence', he writes about the perceptibility of the flesh of Christ: 'Our God came conspicuously. Christ is our God. Christ comes conspicuously. Christ came in flesh. Therefore the "conspicuously" refers to the flesh. For the flesh of Christ was perceptible to the senses'.[74] Three other *scholia* also relate directly or indirectly to the flesh of Χριστός.[75]

72 *Offendatur qui vult ex nostro sermone: ego autem cum omni fiducia assevero, quia sicut primogenitus ex mortuis est Christus, ita primus carnem evexit ad coelum*: PG 12, 1215–1216C note 36: "*Exstat hoc fragmentum in Apologia Pamphili martyris pro Origene*".

73 Σκηνὴν δὲ αὐτοῦ τὴν σάρκα ὠνόμασεν, ἐν ᾗ Χριστὸς ἐκαθέζετο· ἔτι δὲ καὶ τὸ φάνει σκηνὴν διὰ τὸ πρόσκαιρον τῆς σαρκώσεως. <Εἰ γὰρ ἐγνώκαμεν, φησὶ, Χριστὸν κατὰ σάρκα, ἀλλὰ νῦν οὐκέτι γινώσκομεν>: PG 12, 1229A.

74 Ὁ Θεὸς ἡμῶν ἐμφανῶς ἥξει· Θεὸς δὲ ἡμῶν ὁ Χριστός ἐστι· Χριστὸς ἐμφανῶς ἥξει. Χριστὸς ἐλήλυθεν ἐν σαρκί. Τὸ <ἐμφανῶς> ἄρα τὴν σάρκα δηλοῖ· αἰσθητὴ γὰρ ἦν ἡ σὰρξ τοῦ Χριστοῦ: PG12, 1449BC; cf. PG 23, 436B.

75 PG 12, 1229A; PG 12, 1256AB; PG 12, 1568B.

## 2. *Christos as humiliated humanity*

In a passage, in which he makes a call on Ezekiel 31.9, Evagrius emphasizes the depths of Christ's humiliation by likening him to the worm in 'But I am a worm and not human', in a psalm associated more strongly with the passion by other contemporary Fathers. Thus he writes in *Scholion* 3 on Psalm 21.7 (1): 'And if even rational natures are called trees – for it says, "all the trees of paradise drove you out" – and Christ was such as to be born among these rational natures of wisdom and justice, then Christ is rightly called a worm when in such trees'.[76]

In one *scholion* Christ is designated as High Priest, in line with Hebrews 4.14, but the thrust of the exegesis would appear to be rather more on his state of humiliation than on his office. In *Scholion* 11 on Psalm 68.20 (2), another psalm more heavily linked by other Fathers to the passion, Evagrius thus renders this interpretation of 'For you know the reproach I receive, and my shame and embarrassment': 'For our High Priest was dishonoured on our account. He is Christ, who passed through the heavens, who was reproached by the hostile spirits'.[77]

## 3. *Christos as perfected humanity*

In contrast to these two *scholia*, Evagrius utilizes Ephesians 4.13 in his interpretation of 'It is like perfume on the head which descends upon the beard', which identifies Christ not with humiliation but with perfect manhood. He writes in *Scholion* 3 on Psalm 132.2 (3): 'This is the beard worn by him who has attained perfect manhood, growing "into the measure of the full stature of Christ"'.[78]

76 Εἰ δὲ ξύλα καὶ αἱ λογικαὶ ὀνομάζονται φύσεις· <Σὲ> γὰρ, φησὶν, <ἐξήλωσαν πάντα τὰ ξύλα τοῦ παραδείσου.> ἐν δὲ ταύταις πέφυκε γεννᾶσθαι Χριστὸς ὡς σοφία, καὶ δικαιοσύνη· καλῶς ὁ Χριστὸς ὀνομάζεται σκώληξ ἐν τοῖς τοιούτοις ξύλοις γενόμενος: PG 12, 1253BC.

77 Αἰσχύνεται δὲ ἐφ' ἡμῖν ὁ ἀρχιερεὺς ἡμῶν, ὅς ἐστι Χριστὸς ὁ διεληλυθὼς τοὺς οὐρανοὺς, ὀνειδιζόμενος ὑπὸ τῶν ἐναντίων πνευμάτων: PG 12, 1516AB.

78 Τοῦτον τὸν πώγωνα φέρει ὁ καταντήσας εἰς ἄνδρα τέλειον, εἰς μέτρον ἡλικίας τοῦ πληρώματος τοῦ Χριστοῦ: AS 3, 333.

Christ's perfection of manhood is further underlined in Evagrius' exegesis of 'I held my life in my hands continually, but I did not forget your law'. Here he invokes the sinlessness of Christ, with reference to 1 Peter 2.22, in *Scholion* 48 on Psalm 118.109: 'That is to be in the hands of God. For Christ alone had righteousness in thought. He committed no sin, that is in activity, and no deceit was found in his mouth'.[79]

## 4. *Christos as son of David*

Almost as an afterthought, he proclaims the Davidic sonship of Christ, from Matthew 1.1, in his exposition of the opening verse of the royal Psalm 71, a theme which is conspicuous largely by its absence from much of the *Scholia ad psalmos*. Thus he comments on 'Regarding Solomon' in *Scholion* 1 on Psalm 71.1: 'For Solomon the son of David: "The book of genealogy of Jesus Christ the son of David" [Matt. 1.1]. For Solomon is interpreted as meaning "peaceful"; for he is our peace'.[80]

## 5. *Christos as eucharist*

Two *scholia* find Evagrius focusing on the flesh of Christ in a eucharistic context. In *Scholion* 1 on Psalm 26.2 he relies on John 6.55 for this exegesis of 'When evildoers would approach me to devour my flesh ... they became weak and fell': 'If we eat the flesh of Christ – for he says, "Whoever eats my flesh and drinks my blood" – and the demons eat our flesh, perhaps the demons also eat the flesh of Christ in their eagerness to destroy the virtues and the true teachings which are in us'.[81]

79 ὅπερ ἐστι τὸ εἶναι ἐν ταῖς χερσὶ τοῦ Θεοῦ· ἡ γὰρ κατὰ διάνοιαν δικαιοπραγία μόνῳ προσῆν τῷ Χριστῷ, ὅς ἁμαρτίαν οὐκ ἐποίησε, δηλονότι κατ' ἐνέργειαν, καὶ οὐχ εὑρέθη δόλος ἐν τῷ στόματι αὐτοῦ: PG 12, 1609C.

80 PG 12, 1521D; Dysinger, *Selected Scholia*.

81 Εἰ ἡμεῖς τὰς τοῦ Χριστοῦ σάρκας ἐσθίομεν, < Ὁ τρώγων> γάρ <μου,> φησὶ, <τὴν σάρκα, καὶ πίνων μοῦ τὸ αἶμα·> τὰς δὲ ἡμετέρας οἱ δαίμονες· μήποτε καὶ τὰς τοῦ Χριστοῦ

Again, in *Scholion* 15 on Psalm 67.24 (1), another psalm highlighted by Ballard for its treatment of the Divine Warrior theme, he gives this explanation of 'so that your foot may be dipped in blood, the tongues of your dogs in that of the enemies': 'The foot of Christ, a human being, born of Mary, through suffering was dipped in blood. This very blood the enemies prevent us from drinking, always wanting us to be dogs, and not to come to an understanding of the truth. For they see that those who eat Christ's flesh and drink his blood abide in him, and he in them'.[82]

### *6. Christos as incarnation*

In two further passages Evagrius uses the word 'incarnation' (ἐνανθρώπησις) in association with the title Χριστός. Commenting on 'Rule is yours on the day of your power among the splendour of the holy ones; from the womb before the morning star I brought you forth', and making use of John 16.32 to convey the unity of Christ with the Father, he identifies the 'day of power' with either the cross or the incarnation, in *Scholion* 1 on Psalm 109.3 (1): 'If the beginning of the son is the father, while the beginning was with Christ (Εἰ ἀρχὴ τοῦ Υἱοῦ ὁ Πατὴρ, ἡ δὲ ἀρχὴ ἦν μετὰ τοῦ Χριστοῦ); then it is well said in the Gospels: "Not I alone, but I and the Father who sent me". Day of power means the day of the cross or the day of the incarnation' (Ἡμέραν δὲ δυνάμεως εἶπε τὴν ἡμέραν τοῦ σταυροῦ, ἡ τῆς ἐνανθρωπήσεως).[83]

Again, in *Scholion* 8 on Psalm 139.13, commenting on 'I knew that the Lord would maintain the cause of the poor and would maintain justice for the needy', he associates the psalm-verse with a prophesy of the incarnation: 'He knew by the prophetic spirit about the incarnation of Christ'.[84]

---

ἄρα σάρκας οἱ δαίμονες ἐσθίουσι, τὰς ἐν ἡμῖν ἀρετὰς καὶ τὰ ἀληθῆ δόγματα διαφθείρειν σπουδάζοντες: PG 12, 1277A.

82 Ποῦς Χριστοῦ, ὁ ἐκ Μαρίας ἄνθρωπος, ὅστις διὰ τοῦ πάθους ἐβάφη τῷ αἵματι· ὅπερ αἷμα κωλύουσιν ἡμᾶς οἱ ἐχθροὶ πίνειν, κύνας ἡμᾶς ἀεὶ βουλόμενοι εἶναι, καὶ μηδέποτε εἰς ἐπίγνωσιν ἀληθείας ἐλθεῖν. Οἴδασιν γὰρ ὅτι οἱ τρώγοντες τοῦ Χριστοῦ τὰς σάρκας καὶ πίνοντες αὐτοῦ τὸ αἷμα ἐν αὐτῷ μένουσιν, καὶ αὐτὸς ἐν αὐτοῖς: AS 3, 84.

83 PG 12, 1569A; Dysinger, *Selected Scholia*.

84 Ἔγνω τῷ προφητικῷ πνεύματι τὰ περὶ τῆς ἐνανθρωπήσεως τοῦ Χριστοῦ: AS 3, 348.

## *7. Christos as church*

In several *scholia* Evagrius pursues the theme of Χριστός as assumed humanity in an ecclesiological context. He employs the imagery of Christ and the Church being united as one in holy matrimony in his interpretation of 'And he like a bridegroom, going out from his bride's chamber, will rejoice like a giant to run his course'. Thus he writes, with reference to John 3.29, in *Scholion* 2 on Psalm 18.6: 'Christ is as the bridegroom; for he says, "The bridegroom is he who has the bride"'[85]

Marital imagery comes to the fore once more in the royal Psalm 44. In response to 'at your right hand stands the queen in woven-gold clothing, decked out in many colours', Evagrius again employs the symbolism of the Bride of Christ, this time in order to portray the female monarch as his Church. Thus he writes in *Scholion* 8 on Psalm 44.10: 'And all these souls, united in faith and virtue, constitute the one queen who is standing at the right of God's Christ'.[86]

In *Scholion* 4 on Psalm 111.5 Evagrius understands 'He who has compassion and lends is a kind man; he will manage his words with discretion' in the light of Paul's words in 1 Corinthians 4.1, regarding the ministerial order of Christ's Church: 'The saying is to be directed towards those who thoughtlessly disclose the mysteries of the sacred Scriptures indiscriminately; and so Paul says, "Let a man thus account us as ministers of Christ and stewards of the mysteries of God"' [1 Cor. 4.1].[87]

The classical Vespers psalm-text, 'Let my prayer arise as incense before you, and the lifting up of my hands as an evening sacrifice', is also given ecclesiological treatment. With reference to 2 Corinthians 2.15, Evagrius gives this text a deliberately corporate spin in *Scholion* 1 on Psalm 140.2

85 Ὡς νυμφίος ἐστὶν ὁ Χριστός· Ὁ γὰρ ἔχων, φησὶ, τὴν νύμφην νυμφίος ἐστί: PG 12, 1244A.

86 Πᾶσαι δὲ αὗται αἱ ψυχαὶ, κατὰ τὴν πίστιν καὶ τὴν ἀρετὴν ἑνούμεναι, μίαν ἀπεργάζονται βασιλίδα παρεστῶσαν ἐκ δεξιῶν Χριστοῦ τοῦ Θεοῦ: PG 12, 1432A.

87 Χρηστέον τῷ ῥητῷ πρὸς τοὺς ἀπερισκέπτως ἐκφέροντας τὰ θεία μυστήρια τῆς θείας Γραφῆς, καὶ ἀδιακρίτως· καὶ γὰρ ὁ Παῦλός φησιν· < Οὕτως ἡμᾶς λογιζέσθω ἄνθρωπος ὡς ὑπηρέτας Χριστοῦ καὶ οἰκονόμους τῶν μυστηρίων Θεοῦ >: PG12, 1572A; cf. AS 3, 231; Dysinger, *Selected Scholia*.

(1): 'His prayer rises straight up like incense who is able to say: we are the fragrance of Christ to God among those who are being saved and among those who are perishing' [2 Cor. 2.15].[88] Ecclesiology figures in six other Χριστός texts.[89]

## IV. *Christos* in other texts

In the previous two sections we have examined those texts from the *Scholia ad psalmos*, which serve to emphasize either the divinity or the humanity of Χριστός. In this section we will explore other passages which also contain the Christological title, but which do not so easily lend themselves to such a categorization.

### *1. Gnōsis and theōria*

Of the remaining texts, a significant number associate Χριστός with some form of teaching on knowledge (γνῶσις) and contemplation (θεωρία). Both subjects are evident in Evagrius' treatment of 'For with you is life's fountain, and in your light shall we see light'. Thus he writes in *Scholion* 6 on Psalm 35.10 (2): '"In your light shall we see light". In the contemplation of things that have been brought into being we shall see Christ, or in the knowledge of Christ we see God'.[90]

In response to the psalm-verse, 'The river of God was filled with water; you prepared the nourishment it gives, for so is your preparation', he observes, with a clear allusion to John 7.38, in *Scholion* 7 on Psalm 64.10:

88 Τούτου κατευθύνεται ἡ προσευχὴ ὡς θυμίαμα, τοῦ δυναμένου εἰπεῖν· < Χριστοῦ εὐωδία ἐσμὲν ἐν τοῖς σωζομένοις καὶ ἐν τοῖς ἀπολλυμένοις>: PG12, 1665A; AS3, 348.

89 PG 12, 1229D; PG 12, 1272C; PG 12, 1525A; PG 12, 1525B; AS 3, 298; AS 3, 350.

90 <Ἐν τῷ φωτί σου ὀψόμεθα φῶς.> Ἐν τῇ θεωρίᾳ τῶν γεγονότων ὀψόμεθα τὸν Χριστὸν, ἢ ἐν τῇ γνώσει τῇ τοῦ Χριστοῦ ὀψόμεθα τὸν Θεόν: PG 12, 1316B.

'The knowledge of God is filled with rational natures, if indeed rivers of water flow from the belly of the one who believes in Christ'.[91]

Again, γνῶσις features strongly in his interpretation of 'If you lie down among the allotments – a dove's wings covered with silver, its back feathers with golden greenness'. He also introduces πρᾶξις and θεωρία into his explanation, in *Scholion* 10 on Psalm 67.14 (1–2): 'Some call the allotments and the doves' wings the Old and New Testaments. Others call them practice and contemplation. Others call them knowledge of the corporeal and incorporeal. And still others call them knowledge of God, and of Christ who has been sent by him'.[92]

And finally, θεωρία once more comes into play as he grapples with 'Of the fruit of your body I will set upon your throne' in *Scholion* 10 on Psalm 131.11 (2): 'While the reasoning nature is the throne of God, the contemplation of the ages which have been and are yet to be is the throne of Christ'.[93] Three other passages relate Χριστός to γνῶσις.[94]

## 2. *Anapausis*

Evagrius identifies Χριστός as a source of rest and refreshment (ἀνάπαυσις) in a small number of *scholia*. In response to 'For my acts of lawlessness went over my head; they weighed on me like a heavy burden' he offers Jesus' invitation in Matthew 11.28, in *Scholion* 2 on Psalm 37.5b: '"Come all of you", says the Christ, "who are heavy laden, and I will give you rest"' [Matt. 11.28].[95]

Similarly, his exegesis of 'Return, O my soul, to your rest' (Ἐπίστρεψον, ψυχή μου, εἰς τὴν ἀναπαυσίν σου) relies on Paul's yearning to be at rest

91 Ἡ γνῶσις τοῦ Θεοῦ ἐπληρώθη φύσεων λογικῶν, εἴπερ ποταμοὶ ῥέουσιν ὕδατος ἐκ τῆς κοιλίας πιστεύσαντος Χριστῷ: AS 3, 75.

92 Τοὺς κλήρους καὶ τὰς πτέρυγας οἱ μὲν εἰρήκασι Παλαιὰν καὶ Καινὴν Διαθήκην· οἱ δὲ πρᾶξιν καὶ θεωρίαν· ἄλλοι δὲ γνῶσιν σωμάτων καὶ ἀσωμάτων· ἕτεροι δὲ γνῶσιν Θεοῦ, καὶ τοῦ ἀποσταλέντος ὑπ' αὐτοῦ Χριστοῦ: PG 12, 1508BC.

93 Θρόνος μέν ἐστι τοῦ Θεοῦ ἡ φύσις ἡ λογική· θρόνος δὲ Χριστοῦ ἡ θεωρία τῶν γεγονότων καὶ γενησομένων αἰώνων: AS 3, 331.

94 PG 12, 1213A; PG 12, 1508C; AS 3, 165.

95 κἀγὼ ἀναπαύσω ὑμᾶς: PG 12, 1368B; Dysinger, *Selected Scholia*.

with Christ in Philippians 1.23. He writes in *Scholion* 3 on Psalm 114.7 (1): 'And the apostle says this in this way: "I want to be set free and to be with Christ"'.[96] Two further *scholia* take up the same theme.[97]

### 3. *Miscellanea*

In a text which offers itself as a summary of his approach to the psalms, Evagrius acclaims the power of the indwelling Christ to inspire the believer to psalmody, in his treatment of 'Make music to the Lord who resides in Zion', in *Scholion* 4 on Psalm 9.12 (1): 'Whoever who has Christ within them sings psalms'.[98]

A play on the words χρηστός and Χριστός is, according to a text submitted by Dysinger, the key to understanding Evagrius' interpretation of 'O taste and see that the Lord is kind', in *Scholion* 7 on Psalm 33.9 (1): 'If the Lord is tasted, he is tasted through faith; and if he is kind, he is Christ through knowledge'.[99] Χριστός references are to be found in eight other passages.[100]

## V. Assessment of *Christos*

Within the material which has been uncovered in this investigation, it is possible to single out three key motors which propel Evagrius to present Χριστός as the one who is so constantly encountered in psalmody. Let us consider each one in turn.

96 ...Θέλω ἀναλῦσαι καὶ σὺν Χριστῷ εἶναι: AS 3, 235.
97 PG 12, 1427A; PG 12, 1632A.
98 Ἐκεῖνος ψάλλει ὁ ἔχων ἐν ἑαυτῷ τὸν Χριστόν: PG 12, 1189A.
99 εἰ γευστός ἐστιν ὁ κύριος, διὰ τῆς πίστεώς ἐστι γευστός· καὶ εἰ χρηστὸς, διὰ τῆς γνώσεώς ἐστι Χριστός: Dysinger, *Psalmody and Prayer*, 162 note 57; cf. PG 12, 1308C; cf. AS 3, 7.
100 A 2, 454; PG 12, 1192A; PG 12, 1425B; PG 12, 1516C; PG 27, 389C; A 3, 166–7; AS 3, 187; AS 3, 229.

## *1. Christos as meeting-place*

Without doubt, the thrust of Evagrius' presentation of Χριστός in the *Scholia ad psalmos* is to identify Christ with the God of the Psalter. Whilst it would be wrong to overlook those passages which are designed to speak of the unity of Jesus with the human race, and most certainly inaccurate to associate Evagrius with any form of Gnosticism which denies the humanity of Christ, nonetheless, it is clear from the above analysis that, at least at first glance, Evagrius' emphasis is on the formula Χριστός = Θεός rather more than on Χριστός = ἄνθρωπος.

It should be observed, for example, that there is nothing in the *Scholia ad psalmos* resembling Athanasius' Christological exposition of the Psalter. For the latter, as we shall see in Part Three, Christ lives, prays, suffers, dies and rises again 'on behalf of humanity' (ἐκ προσώπου τῆς ἀνθρωπότητος), a phrase encapsulating the Christological, soteriological and ecclesiological thrusts of his understanding of the texts. For Evagrius, on the other hand, a prosopological concern for the humanity of Christ is conspicuous by its absence.

Nevertheless, it is equally true that in Evagrius' usage of Χριστός in his psalm-commentary the manhood of Christ is in evidence in a way which is less forceful and more subtle than it is in the work accredited to Athanasius, but which is no less significant with regard to its Christological content. For whereas the Athanasian usage could be described as 'incarnational' in terms of its emphasis on embodiment, the Evagrian usage, on the other hand, could be described as 'epiphanic' in terms of its stress on manifestation.

The Evagrian equation of Χριστός and Θεός, as we have seen, finds its core expression in that collection of texts in which the writer states unreservedly, 'Christ is God' (Χριστός ἐστιν ὁ Θεὸς), and its variations. It takes further shape as Evagrius seizes upon anthropomorphic imagery within the psalm-verses to press home his insistence that to encounter Χριστός in the Psalter is to encounter Θεός. To affirm Χριστός to be the right hand, arm and face of God, against the background of the collection of texts referred to above, is to highlight his essential divinity.

However, this emphasis needs to be qualified by what Evagrius has to say about Χριστός in relation both to the divine attributes and to the divine objects, previously cited. With regard to each of these aspects, he appears to move away from the simplicity of Χριστός ἐστιν ὁ Θεὸς, and towards a more nuanced understanding of the role of Χριστός in the Psalter, in which Christ is not merely God, but rather the God-man making himself accessible to human beings, the God-man opening up and allowing himself to be a meeting-place for divinity and humanity.

For the attributes of wisdom, truth, righteousness, power, life and salvation relate not only to Christ as divine being, but also to Christ as human being. Indeed, Evagrius is happy to describe Χριστός as 'our wisdom', thereby acknowledging his solidarity with the human race as well as his membership of the Godhead. In particular, wisdom and righteousness are affirmed as qualities which mortals are privileged to share with the immortal. These qualities, then, cease to be solely indicators of divinity. Instead they become a place of meeting for the divine and the human, the manifestation of a location for divine-human engagement.

A similar picture emerges from a reflection on the series of objects to which Χριστός is compared. Here it is the created order which is summoned into service for the Evagrian insistence that the Psalter must be read in terms of Χριστός, the God-man, making himself accessible to the human race.

This is particularly evident in Evagrius' selection of holy mountain, temple and tabernacle as manifestations of Χριστός. Each of these words and concepts, throughout the biblical tradition, represents a place where the divine creator chooses to meet and to engage with the human creature. This selection is Evagrius' way of associating Christ with the meeting-point for God and humanity, with the *rendez-vous* between heaven and earth.

In terms of holy mountain, Evagrius would have been aware of his readers' knowledge of Scriptures which set forth the various sagas of God's engagements with his people on Moriah, Sinai and Gilboa, for example, in the Old Testament. He would have assumed also their familiarity with such New Testament stories of divine-human encounters on the location of the Sermon on the Mount, Tabor, Calvary and the Mount of Olives.

Similarly, he would have tapped into their understanding of the texts in the Old Testament which describe the temple as the habitation of the divine name and the place where faithful worshippers could, at least to some degree, come into the presence of God. He would have also taken for granted their acquaintance with those New Testament texts in which Jesus defines himself as the temple of God, the place of association for creator and creature, the place, as Evagrius himself is at pains to point out, where God is reconciling the world to himself.

Again, he would have expected that they would have remembered the stories about the erection of the tabernacle during the wandering in the wilderness, and the creation of the holy place in which the God of Israel was pleased to dwell for the sake of his people. He would also have counted upon them to recall the reference to the incarnation in John 1.14, 'and the Word was made flesh and tabernacled among us' (καὶ ὁ λόγος σὰρξ ἐγένετο καὶ ἐσκήνωσεν ἐν ἡμῖν), where Jesus is identified as that holy place where God and humanity meet together.

## 2. *Christos as deliverer*

As has been evident from the material assembled in the course of this study, the understanding of Χριστός which lies at the root of the *Scholia ad psalmos* is not for Evagrius, in this work, a matter of abstract speculation, but an issue of dynamic presentation, relating not merely to divine-human being but more particularly to divine-human activity.

If the main thrust of Evagrius' presentation of Χριστός in the *Scholia ad psalmos* is to identify Christ with the God of the Psalter, one of the chief purposes of such a presentation is to instill in his readers the understanding that this is a God who has 'overcome the world' (ἐγὼ νενίκηκα τὸν κόσμον), and who is the 'Deliverer from Zion' (ἐκ Σιὼν ὁ ῥυόμενος), who will lead them to victory in their own spiritual warfare.

We have seen how the study of the psalms by Ballard served to highlight the prevalence of the Divine Warrior *motif* in the Psalter. It is therefore no coincidence that this should prove to be the leading role attributed to Χριστός in Evagrius' psalm-commentary. In this attribution, he mobilizes a number of passages from Scripture to support his contention that Christ is encountered in the psalms as the one in whom and through whom his readers are to triumph in their ascetic struggles.

Both the works and the teachings of Christ are conscripted to this cause. As well as John 16.33, other Gospel texts are eagerly employed in order to identify Χριστός as the liberating Θεός who regularly confronts and reassures those who read, sing or listen to the psalmody.

Pauline authority is also invoked in order to impress upon the audience the truth that the God encountered in so much of the Psalter is Christ the Divine Warrior. Thus, Χριστός is the one who has 'led captivity captive', who has made a public spectacle of the rulers and authorities, and who will similarly disarm their noetic enemies. Χριστός is the one who clothes his followers with himself, and who will also kit them out for spiritual combat. Χριστός is the one who will ensure that, like Paul, they will have fought the good fight, and will have finished the race.

Indeed, in the *Scholia ad psalmos* we see a much greater use of the military metaphor in relation to the role of Χριστός than that which is indicated by Dysinger. Dysinger's concern is to explore how Evagrius depicts the Psalter as a spiritual weapon, and in so doing he concentrates his focus on the *Antirrhētikos*, and on those elements within the psalm-commentary with antirrhetic connotations.

His tendency, however, is to overlook the image of Χριστός which lies behind so much of the *Scholia ad psalmos*. This is Χριστός as the 'Deliverer from Zion', who extinguishes the fiery arrows of the enemies, who saves the soul from Canaanite occupation, and who thwarts the various wiles of the subterranean demons. This is the Χριστός who emerges in other roles, such as peacemaker, king, judge and shepherd, as the divine deliverer of the people of God.

For Evagrius the Psalter is not merely a testimony to the divinity of Christ, but is rather a proclamation of the deliverance, liberation and victory which Christ as God achieves on behalf of those who seek him in prayer and psalmody. For him, *Christus Victor* strides triumphantly through the various psalms, humiliating his enemies and exalting his friends.

Again, however, as we have already observed, it is important to acknowledge that, with respect to Christ's role as deliverer, Χριστός = Θεός is not the only show in town. The Divine Warrior is also a human warrior, and *Christus Victor* strides forth not simply as God, but as the God-man. This much is particularly evident from *Scholion* 5 on Psalm 118.7, where

Evagrius makes use of the quotation from Isaiah 59.20: 'for it says "there shall come from Zion the Deliverer (ἐκ Σιὼν ὁ ῥυόμενος), and he will turn back impiety from Jacob"'.

The choice of the words ὁ ῥυόμενος is of great significance for the point at issue. The verbal noun carries with it a middle sense, meaning not only one who delivers, but also, at the same time, one who is delivered. Hence, for Evagrius, the Χριστός who delivers the soul or the people of God from exile, is at the same time some one who is himself liberated from captivity.

This being the case, it is not only Christ the divine deliverer who is at work in this role, standing over and above his people, defeating their foes for them. It is also Christ the human deliverer, standing among his people, and subject like them to the captivity of death, who brings freedom for himself as well as for them through his resurrection. Christ conquers his and humanity's enemies from within humanity, rather than purely from outside it. Once more, in his preferred *sotto voce* manner, we find Evagrius affirming Χριστός as the one in whom the divine and the human come together.

### *3. Christos as pathway*

As well as presenting Χριστός as the God-man who provides a meeting-point for divinity and humanity, and who brings deliverance from hostile powers, Evagrius, in the *Scholia ad psalmos*, also provides a good deal of material which portrays him as the one who is himself the pathway to the deeper things of Θεός.

Two *scholia* specifically identify Χριστός with the ὁδός of God. In *Scholion* 13 on Psalm 17.24 (1) he writes: 'Blameless is the one who has within himself Christ, the pathway of God'. And again, in *Scholion* 7 on Psalm 85.11, he comments: '"I am the way", says the Christ; and again, "I am truth" [John 14.6]. He prays therefore that God may first become for him like a way, which is to say like virtue; then afterwards like truth, which pertains to contemplation'.

That Χριστός is understood to be both the God-man and the pathway or way of God (ὁδός τοῦ Θεοῦ) in the psalm-commentary is evident from *Scholion* 2 on Psalm 126.1, where, in his characteristic categorization of spiritual advancement, Evagrius refers to Christ as the soul's master in relation to πρακτική, his king in relation to φυσική and his God in relation to θεολογία.

It should be observed in passing that Konstantinovsky's judgment that in this *scholion* Evagrius is saying that 'while Christ performs the *function* of God, he is not God in the true sense of the appellation',[101] is not entirely convincing. It is the product both of a debateable interpretation of ὡς θεὸν ὑπάρχοντα (Christ 'existing as God'), and also of succumbing to the temptation, already noted, of reading the *Scholia ad psalmos* in the light of the *Kephalaia Gnostika*.

Throughout the commentary Χριστός is presented as the one through whom a deeper θεωρία and a more extensive γνῶσις of the divine mysteries is attained. To this extent, it is unsurprising that, after that of Divine Warrior, the role which Evagrius ascribes most often to Χριστός is Divine Teacher, whereby the one who is the truth leads the soul into greater truth.

The manner in which this teaching is given again underscores the Evagrian implication that in Χριστός we encounter not God, pure and simple, but the God-man, who teaches as he delivers, from within rather than from outside humanity. Thus *Scholion* 4 on Psalm 119.7 reveals Χριστός not as a detached divine oracle, but as one who provides instruction on spiritual warfare through practical experience and by personal example.

At the level of πρακτική, it is the 'true teaching', the 'spiritual teaching' and the 'commandments' of Χριστός which bring peace to heaven and earth, and which enable the soul to withstand the demons, and to progress inwardly. At the level of φυσική, the throne of Χριστός is the contemplation of ages that have been and of those which are yet to be. Again, Χριστός may be discerned as the creator of things which have come into being through the contemplation of the natural world. Such contemplation is also described as ἡ γνῶσις τοῦ Χριστοῦ. Indeed, γνῶσις is used recurrently throughout the *Scholia ad psalmos* in relation to Χριστός. It is described both as a weapon, and as the inheritance of Χριστός. Χριστός alone is exalted in the γνῶσις of the Father, and it is in such γνῶσις that we see Χριστός.

101 Konstantinovsky, *Making of a Gnostic*, 137.

It is through γνῶσις that Χριστός is tasted, and it is through γνῶσις μυστηρίων Θεοῦ that Χριστός is transformed from a master into a friend. Ἡ γνῶσις τοῦ Θεοῦ is associated with the waters which flow from the belly of one who believes in Χριστός, while the farms and doves' wings of the psalm-verse are equated with the γνῶσις of both Θεός and Χριστός. Finally, the captivity of Christ (Αἰχμαλωσία...Χριστοῦ) is defined as the rising up of reasoning natures from vices and ignorance to virtue and γνῶσις.

In the *Scholia ad psalmos* there is no firewall separating Χριστός from γνῶσις, any more than there is one separating Χριστός from Θεός, or Χριστός from Λόγος. Throughout this particular work, in contrast to his more esoteric texts, Evagrius is at pains to present Christ as the manifestation of God or the God-man. For him, he is also a revelation of the Word, and is both the route towards and the manifestation of the spiritual knowledge to which he summons his readers.

As has been noted already, it is not the purpose of this study to engage in the ongoing debate surrounding the orthodoxy or otherwise of Evagrius' Christology. Nonetheless, whatever conclusions may be drawn from an analysis of the *Kephalaia Gnostika*, the present study has revealed a presentation of Χριστός in the *Scholia ad psalmos* which is markedly different from the Evagrian Christology summarized by Konstantinovsky. In the *Scholia*, at least, there is a far greater fluidity in Evagrius' gradations of spiritual progress than may be apparent from other works of his. As *Scholion* 2 on Psalm 126.1 makes clear, Christ is not confined to πρακτική and φυσική in the soul's spiritual advancement, but finds himself trespassing into the realm of θεολογία AS GOD! This is in keeping with the main thrust of the work. Dysinger sums up this position admirably in his comment on *Scholion* 4 on Psalm 22.5 (1):

> The movement from *praktiké* to *gnostiké*, from 'fear of God' to 'knowledge of mysteries', is here presented as ascent from the status of servant or slave to that of friend. Christ's gift of knowledge is depicted as an ennobling invitation to share with a new-found friend at table. Evagrius undoubtedly intends his reader to interpret the 'knowledge of mysteries' shared at the 'table' of Christ as essential knowledge, that *gnosis* of the Father which Christ alone can share with others, and which is the subject of the Christological scholia *on Psalms* 44 and 104.[102]

102 Dysinger, *Psalmody and Prayer*, 170.

## VI. Summary

As we have seen from the evidence, for Evagrius the Psalter is a meeting-place between the monastic and the Christ, who is himself a meeting-place between God and humanity. More precisely, in line with Evagrius' dictum in *De oratione* 85, Christ, like the psalmody which encapsulates him, pertains to the manifold wisdom of God, which is itself a prelude to immaterial and simple knowledge.

Hence Christ appears in the texts in a multiplicity of images and veneers. As a wide variety of attributes and objects, Χριστός is the manifestation of the presence of Θεός, into which human beings are invited and drawn. As deliverer and teacher, Χριστός is the God-man who stands in the midst of humanity in order to bring salvation and enlightenment. As the pathway, he is both the one who personifies the true γνῶσις, and also the one who is the route towards the true γνῶσις, the goal for the faithful monastic.

What Evagrius Ponticus bequeathed to his contemporaries and their successors in the monasteries of Egypt and elsewhere was an understanding of the Psalter as a holy place, a dwelling-place of Christ, wherein Χριστός could be encountered consistently and recurrently, in many forms, as the power and presence of God.

We shall now consider one avenue along which the Evagrian legacy was developed in the work of a fifth-century author, whose prominence in the emergence of the Jesus Prayer has been highlighted by Hausherr in *Noms du Christ et voies d'oraison*.

CHAPTER FIVE

# The Development by Diadochus of Photice

The purpose of this chapter is to deal with the question as to whether those passages relating to the invocation of Jesus in the *Capita centum de perfectione spirituali* by Diadochus of Photice owe anything to the legacy of Evagrius of Pontus. In particular, the investigation will explore the linkage between those passages and Evagrius' understanding of the role of psalmody, as described in Dysinger's *Psalmody and Prayer in the Writings of Evagrius of Pontus.*

## I. Diadochus and Evagrius

Born around 400 and dying before 486, Diadochus was Bishop of Photice in northern Greece. He was a supporter of the Council of Chalcedon, but little more is known of his biography. In their Introductory Note to 'St Diadochos of Photiki' the editors of the English translation of *The Philokalia* make this observation with regard to the Diadochus-Evagrius relationship: 'St Diadochos borrows many of the Evagrian technical terms, but his work contains certain features not found in Evagrios: an emphasis, for instance upon the primacy of love (see especially chapters 90–92), upon the sacraments, and upon the heart as well as the intellect' (*nous*).[1]

This summary of the Diadochus-Evagrius relationship does not represent the majority opinion within modern scholarship. Those scholars who have ventured to offer insights into the *Capita centum* have been

1 Palmer, Sherrard and Ware, *Philokalia, Vol. I*, 251.

noticeably reticent in referring to any Evagrian dependency on the part of Diadochus. Either they have ignored the Evagrian linkage altogether, or else they have compared the Evagrian influence unfavourably with that of other authorities, notably Pseudo-Macarius.

### *1. Irénée Hausherr*

Hausherr, as we have seen in *Noms du Christ et voies d'oraison*, includes a description of Diadochus as a 'witness to an intermediate stage in the evolution towards a fixed formula of prayer to Jesus'.[2] In an account whose substance was to be later taken up by David Hester,[3] Hausherr explains that Diadochus spoke constantly about the memory of God, but only as a means to a higher goal of love (ἀγάπη). The original simplicity of the intellect (νοῦς), divided by the fall into two operations, needed to be recovered. The unity of the νοῦς implied the unity of the sense (αἴσθησις), that is, consciousness both relating to the intellect and to volitional acts. The αἴσθησις is an integral property of the νοῦς. The intellectual sense is distinct from the five bodily senses.

Disobedience withdrew the soul from the unifying influence of the νοῦς and made it a hotbed of psychic passions. Evil is seen as a habit actualized whenever free will accepts demonic suggestion, a schizophrenic condition. How is it healed? That is, how is the simplicity of the νοῦς recovered? Hausherr argues that Diadochus prescribes a reverse order to that which caused the sickness: free choice, memory, sense, intellect. The final goal of asceticism is to 'strip off the memory of evil and put on the love of God'.[4]

Freedom must be trained to move towards the good. The person must keep the commandments as well as thinking noble thoughts. The soul must

2 Hausherr, *Noms du Christ*, 210; Cummings, *Name of Jesus*, 229.

3 David Hester, 'Diadochos of Photiki: The Memory and its Purification', *SP* 23 (Leuven: Peeters Press, 1989), 49–52.

4 Hausherr, *Noms du Christ*, 205; Cummings, *Name of Jesus*, 223.

maintain what counterattacks the devil's purposes, that is, the μνήμη θεοῦ (memory of God), in the invocation of Jesus. Empowered by the Spirit, through the grace of baptism, the image and likeness of God are renewed. There is a need for asceticism for the re-integration of memory. Diadochus' spirituality, Hausherr insists, is based on μνήμη θεοῦ, in line with Basil of Caesarea and Mark the Ascetic. Nowhere in this account of the thinking behind the relevant passages in the *Capita centum* does Hausherr make any reference to Evagrian influence.

## *2. Édouard des Places*

Similarly, whilst being prepared to make some reference to Evagrius in the introduction to his edition of the *Capita centum*, Édouard des Places sees no linkage between the writings of the Pontic monk and Diadochus' understanding of the spiritual life, either with regard to the love of God, or to the invocations of the name of Jesus.[5]

## *3. Theodoritus Polyzogopoulos*

Theodoritus Polyzogopoulos, in a comprehensive article,[6] proffers only four references to Evagrius. In the first of these, he simply acknowledges that along with Evagrius, and others, Diadochus follows the Platonic tripartition of the human soul into the intelligent (λογιστικόν), the incensive (θυμικόν), and the appetitive (ἐπιθυμητικόν) aspects.[7] In the second, he briefly notes that Diadochus' conception of the soul is 'between the Origenistic theory

5 Édouard des Places, ed., *Oeuvres spirituelles, Diadoque de Photicé*, introduction, texte critique, traduction et notes, SC 5 (Paris: Éditions du Cerf, 1955), 48–52.

6 Theodoritus Polyzogopoulos, 'The Anthropology of Diadochus of Photice', in *Theologia: Hiera Synodos tēs Ekklēsias tēs Hellados* 55 (Athens: Brabeion Akadēmias Athēōn, 1984), 1072–101.

7 Ibid., 1083.

of the soul, which has been accepted by Evagrius, and the Stoic conception, which is found in the Messalians and Ps. Macarius'.[8]

In the third, he draws a distinction between the Evagrian and the Diadochian understanding of the heart as follows: 'Diadochus used the term <heart> in its biblical meaning, that is the centre of all man's psycho-physiological life, whereas in Origen, Gregory of Nyssa and Evagrius <heart> becomes a synonym of the Platonic terms mind or soul'.[9] And finally, he sees fit to differentiate between the Evagrian and Diadochian treatment of evil thoughts: 'Diadochus speaks about evil thoughts δαιμονικῶν λογισμῶν but he does not reproduce any specific Evagrian enumeration'.[10]

## *4. Marcus Plested*

More significantly, Marcus Plested has given a much more thorough consideration of he extent of Evagrian influence on Diadochus in *The Macarian Legacy: the place of Macarius-Symeon in the Eastern Christian tradition*.[11]

Unsurprisingly in a work bearing such a title, Plested consistently presses the case that Pseudo-Macarius played a greater role than Evagrius in the thinking of Diadochus. For example, he describes how Diadochus' understanding of αἴσθησις, particularly in relation to his use of the phrase αἴσθησις νοερά ('spiritual sense'), owes more to the Macarian tradition than to the Origenistic-Evagrian understanding.[12]

Nevertheless, he goes on to describe how Diadochus' approach to dreams and visions is to some extent dependent on Pseudo-Macarius, but how in his extreme caution on the subject the Bishop of Photice shows himself to be 'operating far more obviously in the tradition of Evagrius'.[13]

8 Ibid., 1086.

9 Ibid., 1090.

10 Ibid., 1096.

11 Marcus Plested, *The Macarian Legacy: the place of Macarius-Symeon in the Eastern Christian tradition* (Oxford and New York: Oxford University Press, 2004), 133–75.

12 Plested, *Macarian Legacy*, 134–40; see also Nicholas Madden, 'Αἴσθησις νοερά (Diadochus-Maximus)', SP 23 (Leuven: Peeters Press, 1989), 53–60.

13 Plested, *Macarian Legacy*, 150.

With regard to his teaching on the passions and ἀπάθεια (passionlessness or impassibility), Plested argues that Diadochus is both like and unlike Evagrius: 'Diadochus' teaching on the harnessing of the *thumos* recalls Evagrius' teaching on the role of the incensive power of the soul in the fight against the demons. Diadochus does not, however, make use of Evagrius' classification of the eight principal vices'.[14]

Similarly, he notes that Diadochus does not follow Evagrius in associating particular demons with particular vices, but that he does follow Evagrius, and Pseudo-Macarius, in his insistence that ἀπάθεια does not bring an end to the ascetic struggle.[15] He takes Diadochus' allusion to the 'confines of impassibility' in *Capita centum* 54 as a reference to Evagrius, but sees his concept of ἀπάθεια as the fruit of love as derivative from Pseudo-Macarius, in contrast to the Evagrian version, which has love as the offspring of ἀπάθεια.[16]

Most telling, for the purpose of the present chapter, is Plested's assertion that in his treatment of prayer and the language of mystical experience, Diadochus follows Pseudo-Macarius and diverges from Evagrius. Thus, he observes: 'Prayer, for Diadochus, is the activity of the intellect in and through the heart. It is the activity of the whole human person – precisely as in Macarius. One is not to turn from this prayer towards any imagination or fantasy (φαντασία) (ibid.). Diadochus does not say "free from images", nor does he speak of the "naked intellect"; his prayer is not the non-iconic prayer of Evagrius'.[17]

Again, Plested continues: 'Diadochus' focus on the repetition of the holy name would certainly seem to entail a constant meditation on the person of Christ: something that would not sit easily with Evagrian non-iconic prayer'.[18]

14 Ibid., 164.
15 Ibid., 165.
16 Ibid., 165–6.
17 Ibid., 169.
18 Ibid., 170.

## 5. *Andrew Louth*

Bucking the trend displayed by the scholars considered thus far is Andrew Louth. In *The Origins of the Christian Mystical Tradition*,[19] Louth argues that the apparently diverse traditions of Evagrianism and Messalianism converge in the thought of Diadochus. He claims that despite Diadochus' opposition to the fundamental doctrines of the Messalians, he is nonetheless prepared to use some of their language, and also some of that derived from Pseudo-Macarius, which is at variance with that of Evagrius. However, Louth insists that Diadochus' Evagrianism is 'no less marked', and he proceeds to catalogue the evidence for this statement.

Thus, Louth cites as belonging to both Evagrius and Diadochus:

> the same understanding of the progressive purification of the soul, beginning with the desiring part and advancing to the passionate part, the same doctrine that visions for one who has attained *apatheia* are the work of the demon of vainglory, the same understanding of the way in which the demons attack the soul (which doctrine he uses to explain why the Messalians mistakenly imagine that the demons still dwell in the souls of the baptized), and much else.[20]

He goes on to argue that Diadochus' understanding of the spiritual nature of prayer is his most important similarity to Evagrius, eschewing the materialism of the Messalians, but neither adopting an entirely intellectualist approach. And, he says, in his spiritual theology, the Bishop of Photice seeks to combine what is good in both Evagrianism and Messalianism by making use of the idea of the soul's *αἴσθησις νοερά*, a word which 'indicates his bold conjunction of feeling and the mind, the heart and the intellect, Macarius and Evagrius'.[21]

Again, in the context of Diadochus' refutation of the Messalian view of sin dwelling in the human heart even after baptism, Louth describes how he employs the Evagrian explanation of the demonic mode of attack upon the soul. In this understanding, which Diadochus endorses, the demons

19 Andrew Louth, *The Origins of the Christian Mystical Tradition*, Second Edition (Oxford and New York: Oxford University Press, 2007), 122–7.

20 Ibid., 123.

21 Ibid., 124.

unleash λογισμοί upon the soul which the soul can convert into sin by rendering to them its consent, but which have no power of themselves to inflict harm upon the soul without that consent.[22]

### *6. Summary*

In summary, most of the scholars considered above, who have wrestled with the theology of Diadochus, have seen fit to place some distance between the expression of the thought of the Bishop of Photice and that of the Pontic monk. Nor, according to these scholars who have focused their attention on the Diadochian passages relating to the invocation of Jesus, is there any suggestion of Evagrian influence therein.

Nevertheless, it should also be noted that, even within this majority, Evagrius is not without relevance to the Diadochian development. And furthermore, the contention of Andrew Louth that the work of Diadochus represents a convergence of Evagrianism and Messalianism, and a uniting of the Evagrian and Macarian traditions has real substance to it. From what has been written, therefore, it is certainly possible to concur with the view of the editors of the English translation of the *Philokalia*, and to put forward the thesis that, while he was prepared to borrow from Evagrius, Diadochus also displayed a consummate freedom to remould the material and to apply it in ways which would not necessarily have been conducive to the former's thinking.

## II. Evagrian psalmody: Luke Dysinger

Whilst, as we have seen, no Evagrian connection with the invocatory passages of the *Capita centum* has been established by the aforementioned authors, a more fruitful search emerges as a result of turning towards a

22 Ibid., 124–5.

consideration of Evagrius' approach to psalmody. Here we return to our discussion in Chapter 3 of Dysinger's *Psalmody and Prayer in the Writings of Evagrius of Pontus*, in which the author describes a threefold role for the hearing and the chanting of the psalms in Evagrius' understanding of monastic spirituality.

Firstly, we saw how, according to Dysinger, Evagrius teaches that the Psalter functions as a spiritual remedy. Much of this is bound up with the capacity of psalmody to subdue θυμός and the other passions. Secondly, Dysinger says that for Evagrius the Psalter is a spiritual weapon. Psalmody is part of the spiritual warrior's arsenal. Thirdly, Dysinger describes the Psalter as contemplative vision in the Evagrian structure, whereby it can serve as a school for prayer for the Christian contemplative. Here the person aspiring to knowledge of the divine, learns to perceive the Λόγος in the salvation events narrated in the psalms. Let us now consider those texts in the *Capita centum*, in which Diadochus highlights the value and the significance of the constant invocation of the name of Jesus.

## III. The invocation of Jesus in the *Capita centum*

References to the invocation of the name of Jesus may be found in eight of Diadochus' *Capita centum de perfectione spirituali*. These are Chapters 31, 32, 33, 59, 61, 85, 88 and 97. One of the most striking features of these chapters is the ease with which they correlate to the three classifications of Evagrian psalmody as identified by Dysinger.[23] Thus in Chapters 61, 88 and 97 we see Diadochus promoting the invocation of Jesus as a spiritual remedy. In Chapters 31, 32, 33 and 85 we find him advocating the repetition of the divine name as a spiritual weapon. And in Chapter 59 we observe

23 See James F. Wellington, 'From Cantor to Contemplative: Evagrian Psalmody and the Invocation of Jesus in the *Capita centum de perfectione spirituali* of Diadochus of Photice', in *SP* 72 (Leuven: Peeters Press, 2014).

him heralding the divine invocation as contemplative vision. Let us examine each in turn.

## *1. Chapter 61*[24]

Diadochus makes reference to τὸ κύριε Ἰησοῦ without further explanation, suggesting that here we are dealing with a well-known, short invocatory prayer, to which he has already made reference in Chapter 33 (see below). This prayer is a weapon in the struggle to prevent the soul from forgetting God. Here Diadochus emphasizes the importance of the habitual recitation of the name of Jesus (Ἔχει γὰρ αὐτὴν τὴν χάριν τότε καὶ συμμελετῶσαν αὐτῇ ἡ ψυχὴ καὶ συγκράζουσαν τὸ κύριε Ἰησοῦ), which is strongly linked with the repression of evil thoughts through the entrenchment of the memory of God, according to Hausherr and Hester.

In this way the constant repetition of the holy name is of a much higher order in terms of significance than might be indicated in the simple phrase 'calling on Jesus'. Its aim is not merely a request for divine assistance but is also a means by which the soul can move towards an ever-closer intimacy with God. For Diadochus, this repetition is a key component in the healing process, which puts the effects of the fall into reverse, and restores the wholeness of the human person.

With the assistance of the Holy Spirit, Diadochus goes on to say, this constant repetition makes it possible for the soul to 'aspire to the remembrance of the love of our God and Father' (πρὸς τὴν τοῦ θεοῦ καὶ πατρὸς ἡμῶν κινηθῶμεν μνήμην τε καὶ ἀγάπην), and to be led more and more deeply into union with God in continual prayer. Thus the invocation of Jesus is a crucial movement along the pathway of restoration, reintegration and reunion of human beings with themselves and with God.

24 Des Places, SC 5, 120–1; Palmer, Sherrard and Ware, *Philokalia, Vol. I*, 271–2.

## 2. *Chapter 88*[25]

The Diadochian doctrine of the human person, as identified by Hausherr and Hester, is spelt out most vividly in this chapter. A form of schizophrenia has reigned in the human intellect since the fall. The intellect has become fragmented and divided into two separate compartments, the memory of the good and the memory of the bad. The fire of divine grace, which is kindled by the keeping of the commandments and by the constant invocation of the name of Jesus (οἵτινες ἄπαυστον ἔχουσιν ἐν τῇ καρδίᾳ τὴν μνήμην τοῦ κυρίου Ἰησοῦ), can bring about its reintegration and restoration to wholeness. The intellect's ability to supplant worldly thoughts with spiritual thoughts is made possible through this practice. And whilst the fire metaphor can be seen to carry with it a martial as well as a therapeutic meaning, it is clear that the latter is predominant in this passage.

## 3. *Chapter 97*[26]

Again in this chapter, Diadochus resorts to the ambiguous metaphor of fire to describe divine grace, and the effects of the ceaseless invocation of Jesus, asserting the intense importance of such a practice. The person desiring cleanliness and wholeness of heart must make this practice 'his only study and his ceaseless task'. Here Diadochus places the emphasis fairly and squarely on the continual aspect of this invocation, which he equates with the μνήμη θεοῦ. The remembrance of God, he says, is ineffective if it is practised only occasionally.

The fruit of such perseverance, he says, is the gradual incineration of the evil within the human heart (ἵν' οὕτω κατ' ὀλίγον τοῦ κακοῦ ὑπὸ τοῦ πυρὸς τῆς τοῦ ἀγαθοῦ μνήμης δαπανωμένου). In addition, the soul is

25 Des Places, SC 5, 147–8; Palmer, Sherrard and Ware, *Philokalia, Vol. I*, 287.

26 Des Places, SC 5, 159–160; Palmer, Sherrard and Ware, *Philokalia, Vol. I*, 293–4.

restored to a state which even surpasses its original radiance. Again, within the double metaphor, the medical meaning appears to trump the military inference.

## *4. Chapter 31*[27]

Here and in the following two chapters we find Diadochus addressing the challenge posed by the illusion of grace. He calls upon those who wish to learn from him to cleave 'fervently to the remembrance of the glorious and holy name of the Lord Jesus' ('Εάν οὖν εὑρεθῇ ἐν θερμῇ λίαν μνήμη κρατῶν ὁ νοῦς τὸ ὄνομα τὸ ἅγιον τοῦ κυρίου Ἰησοῦ...). In this appeal the word κρατῶν carries with it the inference of grasping closely and gaining mastery over this form of prayer, as one might grasp and master a tool or weapon. This invocatory prayer is to be used as a weapon against the wiles of the devil.

## *5. Chapter 32*[28]

Here we see Diadochus using the phrase μνήμη του θεοῦ as a virtual synonym for the act of remembering the Lord Jesus. Again he is responding to the threat posed by the illusion of grace to the inner life, and is articulating the necessity of combating it. Reciting the name of Jesus attentively (προσεχῶς) is the right strategy for the practitioner in this struggle, he says, and the purpose of such recitation or remembrance is to foil the enemy's battle-plan and the illusion which he seeks to instil, and to fight him with the confidence granted by the grace of God.

27 Des Places, SC 5, 101; Palmer, Sherrard and Ware, *Philokalia, Vol. I*, 261–2.

28 Des Places, SC 5, 102; Palmer, Sherrard and Ware, *Philokalia, Vol. I*, 262.

### *6. Chapter 33*[29]

Diadochus' reference in this chapter to calling upon the 'holy name' (εἰ καὶ τῷ ἁγίῳ κέχρηται ὀνόματι) must be understood to refer to the invocation of the Lord Jesus. This invocation is made 'not now simply out of love for God, but in order to repel the evil one'. It enables the soul to identify the illusion of grace for what it is, as something which is being offered to it by the demons. Again, as in the previous two chapters, Diadochus salutes and promotes the invocation of the name of Jesus as a weapon (τῇ μνήμῃ τοῦ θεοῦ κατ' αὐτῶν ὁπλίζηται), as a means by which the soul may equip itself in the ongoing warfare against the temptations, enticements and wiles of the evil one.

It is clear from this passage that Diadochus' reference to the 'Lord Jesus!' (τὸ κύριε 'Ιησοῦ), using the vocative form, is identifying a form of invocatory prayer well known to those reading his treatise. His usage of the definite article τὸ, which is translated in the English by inverted commas, points to a prayer which consists of more words than just κύριε 'Ιησοῦ, in the same way that 'the Our Father' is a prayer which is made up of more than two words. However, it is impossible to reconstruct the precise text of the prayer to which Diadochus was referring. It may or may not be the Κύριε 'Ιησοῦ Χριστέ, υἱὲ τοῦ Θεοῦ, ἐλέησόν με of the *Peri tou Abba Philēmon*.

### *7. Chapter 85*[30]

Diadochus begins this chapter with a side swipe at the Messalians, and also indeed Pseudo-Macarius, in rejecting the claim that both Satan and the Holy Spirit can co-exist within the human soul. He insists that it is the grace of God which permits the devil to wound the soul, but only for the sake of its own progress. This progress can be achieved by keeping the commandments and by the ceaseless invocation of Jesus (ἐπικαλοῖτο τὸν κύριον 'Ιησοῦν).

29 Des Places, SC 5, 102–4; Palmer, Sherrard and Ware, *Philokalia, Vol. I*, 263–4.
30 Des Places, SC 5, 144–5; Palmer, Sherrard and Ware, *Philokalia, Vol. I*, 285–6.

He goes on to say that this invocation is effective in enabling the fire of grace to incinerate the weeds within the earth of the soul (τὰ ζιζάνια τῆς ἀνθρωπείας γῆς πληροφορητικῶς καταφλέγουσα) and to put a stop to the demonic attacks. Here, once again, we find Diadochus resorting to the fire metaphor in both a therapeutic and a martial sense. In this passage, however, the emphasis is clearly on the military imagery. It is apparent from the context that, whether as medical remedy or tool of war, the fire of divine grace is enkindled by the constant calling upon the name of Jesus. Diadochus is also at pains to affirm the primacy of grace within this whole operation. Unaided human effort is insufficient.

## *8. Chapter 59*[31]

Diadochus asserts without qualification the prominence which should be given to the invocation of Jesus in the form of 'Lord Jesus!' (τὸ κύριε Ἰησοῦ). Here again, in this passage, he makes use of the *double-entendre* character of the fire metaphor. On the one hand, it is therapeutic in so far as it incinerates and destroys what is dangerous to the soul (πάντα τὸν ἐπιπολάζοντα ῥύπον ἐν τῇ ψυχῇ ἐν αἰσθήσει ἱκανῇ καταφλέγει). On the other hand, though implicit rather than explicit in this text, it carries with it a combative inference in that it obliterates the attacks of the evil one.

However, the task of leading the intellect into a vision of light, within its own inner shrine (οὗτοι καὶ τὸ φῶς αὐτῶν τοῦ νοῦ δύνανται ὁρᾶν ποτε), undistracted by mental images, is the most important thrust of this chapter. This is where Diadochus sounds more like Evagrius than in any other section of the work. Here we see the role of the invocation of Jesus in parallel with the third Evagrian category of psalmody, relating to contemplative vision. The intellect is open to the glory of divine love by which it may be impregnated, resulting in a joy beyond words, if only it can be unencumbered by unnecessary baggage.

31 Des Places, SC 5, 119; Palmer, Sherrard and Ware, *Philokalia, Vol. I*, 270–1.

## IV. Summary

The analysis of these texts in the *Capita centum* has produced material of great relevance to the question as to whether there is any linkage between such passages and the role of psalmody in the works of Evagrius, as identified by Dysinger. From the evidence which has been discussed, it may be said with some confidence that in the eight chapters under investigation Diadochus replicates in his understanding of the role of the invocation of Jesus the threefold Evagrian categorization of the role of psalmody, as spiritual weapon, spiritual remedy and contemplative vision.

In Chapters 31, 32 and 33 Diadochus portrays the fervent remembrance of the Lord Jesus as an essential weapon in the battle against the deceptions of Satan, and particularly in the struggle to withstand the illusion of grace with which the demonic power seeks to seduce the soul. The acquisition of the mastery of this tool of the spiritual arsenal also brings advancement in discernment and in the art of discrimination, and welds the soul to the love of God.

Diadochus' call to say the prayer attentively recalls Evagrius' insistence that, in order for it to produce the right spiritual fruits, psalmody must be chanted with understanding and with good rhythm. Like Evagrius, in his teaching on psalmody and prayer, Diadochus is also happy to use erotic imagery to convey the unitive character of contemplation. However, unlike Evagrius he uses the imagery to warn against diabolical seduction rather than to make allusion to the joys of nuptial bliss with the divine.

Again, whilst encouraging his readers to use the invocation of Jesus in an antirrhetic way to destroy the demonic enemies and to thwart their regular attacks, Diadochus makes no attempt, unlike Evagrius, to identify the nature of such attacks with reference to particular λογισμοί. His chief concern is with the broad issue of the illusion of grace, and he satisfies himself with promoting the use of the 'Lord Jesus!' as a form of defence and counterattack in place of the psalm-texts so beloved by Evagrius, and also without the latter's more detailed classification.

In Chapters 61, 88 and 97 Diadochus is extremely well served by the metaphorical fire of divine grace, a metaphor also employed by Evagrius in his exposition of the Psalter,[32] which, while carrying with it something of a martial connotation, is used principally to portray the invocation of Jesus as a spiritual remedy. The constant, as opposed to occasional, repetition of the name of Jesus is understood by Diadochus, in this context, to be what to-day we would see as a type of radio-therapy, consuming and burning up the cancer of evil within the human heart and intellect.

This cancer takes the form of the memory of evil which, through the invocation of Jesus, has to be destroyed and replaced by the memory of the good, that is the remembrance of God, in order that the human person, torn apart internally as a result of Adam's disobedience, may be reintegrated and made whole. It is a form of treatment which needs to be continual in order to produce the desired healing for the fragmented soul.

Again, we see similarity and dissimilarity with the teaching of Evagrius. The Evagrian emphasis, with regard to psalmody as a spiritual remedy, is placed firmly on the role of θυμός. The purpose of psalmody here is to cool down the passion, to redirect it, and to prevent it from distracting the intellect from pure prayer, from conversation with God. Diadochus, on the other hand, places the emphasis more firmly upon the memory, and upon its need for healing and reordering. Rather than cooling things down, his language is all about hotting things up. The employment of the fire metaphor introduces a dynamism into the healing role of the invocation of Jesus, which contrasts with the more static model offered by Evagrius in relation to the therapy provided by psalmody.

Such dynamism is particularly evident in what Diadochus writes in Chapter 85. Here Diadochus moves well beyond the therapeutic understanding of the fire metaphor, and couches his language much more directly in terms of spiritual conflict. His choice of the parable of the wheat and the tares is instructive, in so far as the tares are described by Jesus as the 'children of the evil one',[33] the demonic offspring of the enemy.

Finally, in Chapter 59, Diadochus presents his readers with his concept of the invocation of Jesus as a means towards contemplative vision.

32 See for example *Scholion* 18 on Psalm 36.20 (3), PG 12, 1317D.

33 Matthew 13.38.

He holds out to them the possibility that the constant repetition of the prayer τὸ κύριε 'Ιησοῦ will set them free from the distractions of mental images, a clear allusion to Evagrius, and will transport them through an inner intensity into the radiance of divine love. The Evagrian influence of this passage is further underlined by Diadochus' claim that those meditating unceasingly upon the name of Jesus 'can sometimes see the light of their own intellect'. Evagrius' belief that prayer is a vehicle of light-visions is, according to Konstantinovsky,[34] based upon his own experience. What Diadochus appears to be doing in this passage is to take this Evagrian experience at face value, and to reapply it to serve his case for the practice of the invocation of Jesus, a practice which was most certainly not part of Evagrius' own teaching. Once again we find an example of how Diadochus adopts an Evagrian term or concept and reworks and develops it according to the needs of his own theological and ascetical concerns.

This examination certainly points us in the direction of the hypothesis that Diadochus was fully prepared to borrow not only technical terms from Evagrius, but also components of his structural thinking, that is, his threefold categorization of the role of psalmody in the ascetic's progress, and to develop them in a new way. For the latter, the remedial, antirrhetic and visionary elements in the recitation of the Psalter helped to propel the monk towards a true γνῶσις. For the former, the same elements in the recitation of the holy name helped to lead him towards a spiritual contemplation (πνευματική θεωρία).

What all of this tells us is that within a couple of generations of the death of the Pontic monk the roles which Evagrius has assigned to psalmody are now being fulfilled by a new form of contemplative prayer, consisting of the habitual and continual recitation of the invocation, κύριε 'Ιησοῦ. Furthermore, the possibility that Diadochus developed his thinking on the short, Christocentric, invocatory prayer in the light of the Evagrian teaching on the threefold role of psalmody is fully consistent with what we have discovered in Chapter 3 about the Pontic monk's understanding of the relationship between psalmody and prayer. It could be argued that

34 Konstantinovsky, *Making of a Gnostic*, 78–9.

such a development would have been a natural product of the *symbiōsis* and the mutualism of these two expressions of monastic discipline, which ensured a recurring interchange of their respective characteristics, and which informed and influenced the understanding of subsequent contemplatives. This would suggest that Diadochus' input into the story of the evolution of the Jesus Prayer is rather more pronounced than that allowed by Hausherr.

PART THREE

# The Invocation of Christ

CHAPTER SIX

# Other Commentaries

Whilst Evagrius's role in the development of Eastern monastic spirituality in the late fourth and early fifth centuries cannot be overstated, the individuals and communities which dedicated themselves to anchoritic, semi-anchoritic and cenobitic forms of Christian discipleship during this period had at their disposal other resources for the purpose of guiding them towards a deeper life with God. With regard to their understanding of the psalms, it is clear that they had recourse to a number of commentaries ascribed to Eastern authors whose availability would have assisted them to fulfil the Evagrian injunction to 'sing psalms with understanding' (ψάλλε συνετῶς).

The purpose of this third part of the study is to examine a selection of these commentaries in order to explore how the recitation of the Psalter was understood to involve the invocation of the person of Christ, in ways other than those manifested in Evagrius' *Scholia ad psalmos*. To this end, the present chapter will provide a brief summary of the critical background to a series of documents which reveal a pattern of such invocation which is consistently expressed in four key ways. In so doing, this exercise is largely dependent on the most comprehensive study of the material produced to date, in Rondeau's first volume of *Les Commentaires Patristiques du Psautier*.

In an introductory note to the work, Rondeau informs us that the literature in question 'has come to us in an often deplorable state'.[1] She acknowledges the difficulties surrounding the dating and authorship of the documents, and observes that their more recent critical study has undermined the confidence placed in some of them by earlier scholarship. She cites the work of Georg Karo and Johannes Lietzmann, Giovanni Mercati,

1 Rondeau, *Commentaires Patristiques du Psautier, Vol. I*, 25.

Robert Devreesse and Marcel Richard, who have assisted the quest to 'recover, in whole or in part, the psalmic exegesis of the authors concerned', but warns of the limits of their outcomes.[2]

Armed with this very strong *caveat*, with regard to the reliability of the material in question, Rondeau then proposes to present 'author by author, in an approximate chronological order, the state of our documentation'.[3] There follows a chapter relating to the psalm-commentaries attributed to a number of Greek Fathers from Hippolytus to Hesychius of Jerusalem. Of these, Origen's *Selecta in psalmos*, Eusebius of Caesarea's *Commentarii in psalmos*, Athanasius's *Expositio in psalmos*, Didymus the Blind's *Expositio in psalmos* and Theodoret of Cyrrhus' *Commentarius in psalmos* are those which are of concern to our investigation. Let us summarize her account of these.

Rondeau's comprehensive review of the critical study of psalm-commentaries accredited to these patristic authorities results in a picture which is not altogether satisfactory with regard to arriving at a greater understanding of the background of the documents in question. Indeed her introductory comment that much of the material 'has come to us in an often deplorable state' is a disappointingly accurate description of the subject matter.

This description is particularly poignant with regard to the commentaries assembled under the names of Origen, Athanasius and Cyril, where issues of lost material, pseudonymity, and fragmentation vie with one another to deprive the enquirer of any accurate picture of the original exegeses of the psalms on the part of those authors. And furthermore, even in relation to the commentaries ascribed to Eusebius, Didymus and Theodoret, where the material in question is capable of delivering a more fruitful outcome, the end product is far from ideal.

Despite the noble efforts of a succession of scholars, the failure to produce modern critical editions of most of the commentaries under investigation inevitably throws the enquirer back on the mercy of the various

2 Ibid.
3 Ibid.

collections assembled in Jacques-Paul Migne's *Patrologiae cursus completus* series. The unsatisfactory nature of this situation is regularly highlighted by Rondeau in her review. As a consequence of this, it is essential, at this point, to focus clearly on the nature of the exercise which is being undertaken in this third part of the study.

Our task here is, most emphatically, not to attempt to recreate anything resembling the original forms of the psalm-commentaries attributed to the patristic authors in question. Such a task would constitute a major study in its own right, and would serve only as a distraction from the goal of this investigation. On the contrary, what is being attempted here is to uncover the insights, the themes and the thrusts of those documents which were in circulation in the East during the late fourth and early fifth centuries, and which would have assisted in informing and shaping the understanding of the psalmody which was being read, chanted or listened to by early Eastern monastics.

To this end, therefore, questions as to the authorship, or for that matter the integrity, of these various works are not deemed to be of essence to this study, except in so far as they impinge upon the dating of the commentaries. The subject under consideration does not involve a comparison of the respective theologies of the different exegetes, but rather the acquisition of a total picture of the Christological interpretation given to the psalms by this body of early Christian literature.

This being the case, the use throughout the following chapters of the names of the scholars will therefore not prejudge any critical enquiry into the authorship of the works in question. It will merely be employed as a form of short hand, a convenient way of avoiding the pedantry of either placing the name of the relevant Father in italics or quotation marks, or of qualifying each and every reference with the phrase 'as attributed to'.

Neither will the study engage with the debate surrounding the respective merits of the relevant sources. Despite its many acknowledged flaws, and in the absence of modern critical alternatives, it will focus its attention chiefly on Migne's *Patrologiae*. Notwithstanding Rondeau's constant criticism of the quality of those manuscripts, they are nonetheless the sources to which she continually appeals in the second volume of *Les Commentaires Patristiques du Psautier*. Thus the editions collected by Migne will be used as sources for all bar two of the commentaries, which are both attributed to Didymus. The sources used for these will be the edition compiled by Ekkehard Mühlenberg from the chains, or collections of texts, known the *catenae*, and that assembled by Michael Gronewald from papyri discovered at Tura in Egypt. Despite their faults, the editions used here provide us with significant evidence of insights, themes and thrusts appertaining to the patristic understanding of the meaning of the Psalter in the fourth and fifth centuries.

In the course of the next four chapters we will consider some significant ways in which each of these documents present psalmody as an invocation of Christ. Firstly, we will explore those psalm-texts in which Christ is identified as the divine name (ὄνομα). Secondly, we will examine those verses in which he is defined as the face or countenance (πρόσωπον) of God. Thirdly, we will analyse those passages where Christ is recognized as the addressor of prayers for divine assistance. Fourthly, we will investigate those *scholia* where he is invoked as the addressee of such petitions.

Before we proceed, it has to be acknowledged that in the course of this exploration some liberty is being taken with the use of the word 'invocation'. Many of the relevant texts are framed in the third person, making statements about Christ, or in the second person, making statements to Christ, rather than being in the form of a direct appeal to Christ, as the normal usage of the word would require. However, 'invocation' is being employed in this study in the lighter sense of making reference to Christ. The purpose of this is to avoid the inadequacy of a more passive term, such as 'encounter', and to convey to the reader the degree to which those who would chant, read or listen to the psalms were being encouraged by the commentators to understand the recitation of the Psalter as an active engagement in dialogue with the Son of God.

CHAPTER SEVEN

# The Invocation of Christ as *Onoma*

'While now people rage against the kingdom of the Saviour, there will come a time when they will confess his great name'.[1] Eusebius of Caesarea's gloss on the text of Psalm 98.3 specifically identifies the 'your great name' of the psalmist with that of Christ. This is but one of many texts in the psalm-commentaries attributed to Origen Eusebius, Athanasius, Didymus, Cyril and Theodoret where the exegete associates the divine ὄνομα of the Psalms of the Septuagint with the Second Person of the Trinity.

The purpose of this chapter is to examine the extent to which and the manner in which the aforesaid works invite the reader or the singer to accept a Christological understanding of those psalm-verses which refer to the 'name of the Lord'. From these psalm-commentaries it will draw on seventy-one texts, which, taken together, provide a considerable body of material for the investigation.

Of the thirty-five psalms in which the relevant texts appear, Psalm 88 is the most well-endowed with seven texts, while Psalms 98 and 117 account for four each. Three such texts are to be found in each of Psalms 44, 47, 71, 79, 104 and 112, while Psalms 19, 43, 53, 65, 67, 73, 74, 82, 90, 95, 101 and 105 each provide two. A single text is to be located in each of Psalms 5, 7, 17, 22, 28, 60, 75, 85, 91, 114, 121, 137, 142 and 149.

Before examining the patristic texts themselves, we will make a short excursion into the *milieu* of Rabbinic Judaism, which will provide a useful background to an exploration of the question of how psalm-texts relating to the divine name were understood in a setting contemporaneous with, though theologically distinct from, the environment which produced the commentaries which feature in this study. For the sake of convenience,

1 PG 23, 1236C.

psalm-references are based on the notation of the Septuagint rather than on that of the Hebrew Bible.

A perusal of the Targum Psalms which relate to those psalm-texts in which the Fathers have equated the divine name with that of Christ reveals some interesting insights. There is a substantial number of variations from the Hebrew text in the Aramaic, and these throw some light on how the invocation of the divine name was understood in Rabbinic Judaism. Throughout this study the Aramaic variations from the Hebrew text will be placed in italics. The following merit attention.

In three psalm-texts the word 'God' in the Hebrew has been substituted by the word *Lord*. Thus Psalm 47.10–11 reads: 'We have considered, O *Lord*, your goodness in the midst of your temple. As is your name, O *Lord*, so is your praise to the ends of the earth'.[2] Similarly, Psalm 43.9 reads: '...and in your name, O *Lord*, we will give thanks for ever'.[3] And again, in Psalm 74.2 we find: 'We give thanks to you, O *Lord*, we give thanks, for *the Shekinah of* your name is near; they recount your wonderful deeds'.[4]

In these texts the substitution of *Lord* for 'God' provides the pray-er of the psalm with a more reverential approach to their act of worship. The divine name is thus endowed with a greater air of sanctity. The insertion of *Shekinah* in the text further enhances this tendency, and is a matter to which we will return.

The concern to magnify, and indeed to intensify, the sacral nature of the act of prayer is also manifested in the repeated practice of using additional words or phrases to describe the dwelling-place of the divine, whether on earth or in heaven. For example, the 'house' of the Lord is converted into *the house of the sanctuary* of the Lord in Psalms 19.2–3, 76.2–3, 98.5, 117.26, and 134.1–2.[5] Similarly, *his holy dwelling-place of heaven* finds its way into the text of Psalm 19.7–8.

2 David M. Stec, trans., *Targum Psalms* (London: T. & T. Clark, 2004), 101.

3 Ibid., 94.

4 Ibid., 147.

5 Ibid., 55, 148, 182, 210 and 228–9.

By the same token, however, the holiness of the divine name is safeguarded by the Aramaic reading of Psalm 73.7: 'They have set on fire *the house of* your sanctuary: to the ground they have desecrated the dwelling-place *in which your name is invoked*.'[6] The insertion of *the house of* is clearly designed to place some distance between the enemy's ability to damage the temple building and his capacity to harm the divinity. And again, by substituting 'of your name' by *in which your name is invoked*, the text reinforces the transcendence of the divine name.

By far the most significant interpolations in the Targum Psalms in question are those regarding the use of the word *Memra*, and to a far lesser extent *Shekinah*. As David Stec indicates in a footnote to his introduction, '*Memra* is used almost exclusively where God and humans relate to one another, as a device for keeping a proper distance between them'.[7] Furthermore, Robert Hayward makes this observation, linking *Memra* and *Shekinah*: 'Like the Shekhina of the Lord, the *Memra* of the Lord is used as the subject of verbs of divine action, and the Lord is described as being present, revealed, redeeming, creating in or by means of His *Memra*'.[8]

The *Jewish Encyclopedia* describes the *Memra* as the manifestation of divine power, or as a divine messenger, representing God himself, and performing a mediatorial role.[9] It goes on to outline the influence of *Memra* on Philo's doctrine of the *Logos*, and, for our purposes, to note how in the *Apostolic Constitutions* (chapters xxvi–xxxviii) Early Church liturgy, adopted from the Synagogue, changed the word *Logos*, in the sense of 'the Word by which God made the world, or made His Law or Himself known to man', into *Christ*.[10]

6 Ibid., 145.

7 Ibid., 12.

8 C. T. Robert Hayward, 'Memra and Shekhina: A Short Note', in *Journal of Jewish Studies* 31 (Oxford: Oxford Centre for Postgraduate Hebrew Studies, 1980), 210–13.

9 *Jewish Encyclopedia, Vol. VIII* (New York and London: Funk and Wagnalls, 1904), 465.

10 Ibid. See also Alexander Roberts and James Donaldson, ed., *Ante-Nicene Christian Library, Vol. XVII* (Edinburgh: T. & T. Clark, 1870), 187–199; see also David A. Fiensy, *Prayers Alleged to be Jewish: An Examination of the Constitutiones Apostolorum*, Brown Judaic Studies 65 (Chico, California: Scholars Press, 1985).

In the psalm-texts in question, where the psalmist is addressing God, *your Memra* is used instead of *you*, as a way of underlining the gap between creature and Creator in Psalms 5.11 and 43.6.[11] The *Memra of the Lord* is preferred to 'the Lord' in Psalms 9.10, 33.3–4, and 39.4–5, and to 'God' in Psalm 43.9,[12] while *his Memra* finds its way into the text of Psalm 32.21.[13] On the other hand, where God is addressing the psalmist, in Psalm 90.14, 'because he delights in me' becomes 'because he delights in *my Memra*'.[14]

In five texts variations the phrase *the name of the Memra* is employed in order to add an even greater emphasis to the dividing line between mortality and immortality. Thus in Psalm 62.5 *in the name of your Memra* replaces 'in your name'.[15] In Psalm 88.25 God says '*in the name of my Memra* his glory shall be exalted', instead of 'in my name…'.[16] And in Psalms 117.10 and 26, and 123.8 'in the name of *the Memra of the Lord*' is substituted for 'in the name of the Lord'.[17]

Finally, in the psalm-texts under investigation the *Shekinah* of the Lord makes two intrusions. Firstly, in Psalm 74.2, as we have seen, the psalmist does not give thanks that the divine name is near, but because '*the Shekinah of* your name is near'.[18]

Again, in Psalm 121.4 the tribes of the Lord go up to the holy city, not simply to give thanks to the name of the Lord, but also *testifying to Israel that his Shekinah dwells among them, when they go*.[19] However, this is designed less to emphasize the differentiation of finite and infinite, and rather more to stress the indwelling presence of the God of Israel with his people.

11 Stec, *Targum Psalms*, 34 and 93.
12 Ibid., 38–9, 74, 85 and 94.
13 Ibid., 74.
14 Ibid., 175.
15 Ibid., 123.
16 Ibid., 169.
17 Ibid., 209, 210 and 222.
18 Ibid., 147.
19 Ibid., 220.

# I. Themes

We now move on to a closer scrutiny of the seventy-one psalm-texts which form the basis of this study. For the sake of convenience, rather than strict accuracy, we will catalogue the texts under the headings of the themes of δόξα, παρουσία, ὁμοούσιος, σωτηρία, ἐκκλησία and πόλεμος, whilst recognizing that a significant number of the texts could be located, with justification, in one of more of the groupings.

## *1. Doxa*

It should come as no surprise that a large number of psalm-texts appertaining to the divine name should be categorized under a heading which speaks of the glory or δόξα of God. Again and again in the Psalter, the psalmist calls upon his fellow worshippers to give glory to the name of the Lord, and in the texts which follow we will see how the exegete understands that the name to be glorified is the name of Christ.

Inevitably, music plays a crucial role in this call to worship, and in a host of these texts the musicians are called upon to honour the name of the Son. Thus, commenting on the text of Psalm 65.1–2, 'Make a joyful noise to God, all the earth; do make music to his name',[20] Athanasius associates the making of music to the divine name with the coming of Christ.

In his commentary on Psalm 65.4, 'Let all the earth worship you, and make music to you',[21] Theodoret gives the verse a definite Christological gloss, as he announces that Christ is named as Most High by everyone (καὶ ὁ Δεσπότης Χριστὸς ὕψιστος παρὰ πάντων καλεῖται).

With regard to the text of Psalm 7.18, 'I will give to the Lord the acknowledgement due to his righteousness, and make music to the name

20 Ἀλαλάξατε τῷ Θεῷ πᾶσα ἡ γῆ, ψάλατε δὴ τῷ ὀνόματί αὐτοῦ: PG 27, 288B.

21 Πᾶσα ἡ γῆ προσκυνησάτωσάν σοι, καὶ ψαλάτωσαν. Ψαλάτωσαν δὲ τῷ ὀνόματί σου, Ὕψιστε: PG 80, 1364B.

of the Lord, the Most High',[22] Cyril associates making music to the name of the Lord Most High with salvation from sin and death in Christ, and the recognition that the truth is the Son of God (καὶ ἐπιγνωσθέντος ἤδη τοῦ κατὰ ἀλήθειαν Υἱοῦ τοῦ Θεοῦ).[23] Again, the title the 'Most High' (του ὑψίστου) is interpreted Christologically, alluding to the one who is both exalted to heaven and lifted high upon the cross for our salvation. And, with regard to Psalm 67.5, 'Sing to God, make music to his name',[24] he understands this verse as an imperative to sing the praise of 'Christ who is the Saviour of us all' (δῆλον δὲ ὅτι τοῦ πάντων ἡμῶν Σωτῆρος Χριστοῦ).

Here the Targum text offers some interesting information. It reads, 'Sing *before* God, extol his *glorious* name; *praise him who sits upon the throne of glory in Arabah*; his name is the Lord, exult before him'.[25] The doxological character of the imperative is thus enhanced, the psalmist imploring the people to sing in the presence of God to a name which is 'glorious', and where the divine abode is to be located, figuratively, in the deserts. Whether or not the Fathers detected a Christological reference here, in terms of the story of the temptations in the wilderness, or an ecclesiological reference, in terms of the growth of monasticism in the sandy wastes, is open to speculation.

When he comes to Psalm 91.2, 'It is good to acknowledge the Lord, to make music to your name, O Most High',[26] Cyril understands the purpose behind singing praises to the name of the Lord in terms of what we owe to 'our Saviour Christ' (Ὀφείλομεν δὲ τῷ πάντων ἡμῶν Σωτῆρι Χριστῷ), while in Psalm 95.2, 'Sing to the Lord, bless his name; tell of his salvation from day to day',[27] he associates the call to bless the name of the Lord with the truth that the Son is called 'mercy and justice (Ἔλεος δὲ καὶ δικαιοσύνη ὀνομάζει τὸν Υἱόν).[28]

22 Ἐξομολογήσομαι τῷ Κυρίῳ κατὰ τὴν δικαιοσύνην αὐτοῦ, ψαλῶ τῷ ὀνόματι Κυρίου τοῦ ὑψίστου: PG 69, 756C.

23 PG 69, 756D.

24 Ἄισατε τῷ Θεῷ, κ.τ.λ: PG 69, 1144C.

25 Stec, *Targum Psalms*, 129.

26 Ἀγαθὸν τὸ ἐξομολογεῖσθαι τῷ Κυρίῳ: PG 69, 1225B.

27 Εὐαγγελίζεσθε ἡμέραν ἐξ ἡμέρας τὸ σωτήριον αὐτοῦ, κ.τ.λ: PG 69, 1244A.

28 PG 69, 1244B.

Paul's Philippian hymn provides the Fathers with an important key for unlocking the spiritual meaning of some of the psalm-verses which refer to the divine name; and doxological, Christological, and soteriological themes coalesce in the reflections prompted by this text. For the purposes of this study, two of these references have been categorized under the current heading, for the dominant, though not exclusive, interest appears to be in the future glorification of the name of Jesus.

As we have seen, Eusebius uses this hymn to interpret Psalm 98.3, 'Let them acknowledge your great name, for it is awesome and holy',[29] noting that 'While now people rage against the kingdom of our Saviour, there will be a time when they will confess his great name' (ἐν ᾧ καὶ αὐτοὶ ἐξομολογήσονται τῷ ὀνόματι αὐτοῦ τῷ μεγάλῳ), and proceeding to quote from Philippians 2.10–11.

Athanasius, similarly, specifically identifies the name of Jesus with the 'awesome and holy' name in the psalm-verse (Μέγα αὐτοῦ τὸ ὄνομα τὸ, Ἰησοῦς, καθὸ καὶ σωτηρία λαοῦ ἑρμηνεύεται), though the Philippian reference is implicit rather than explicit.[30]

Eusebius also uses the Philippian hymn to interpret Psalm 44.18, 'I will remember your name in every generation upon generation; therefore the people will acknowledge you forever even forever and ever'.[31] Here he makes a direct connection between the 'name' to be remembered in every generation in the psalm-verse and the name of Jesus in Philippians 2.10.

Athanasius, on the other hand, appears to understand this verse in an ecclesiological fashion.[32] He interprets 'In place of ancestors, your sons were born', in verse 17, to refer to the 'sons of the Church, appointed as rulers over all the earth by the Lord Jesus' (κατεστάθησαν δὲ ἄρχοντες ἐπὶ πᾶσαν τὴν γῆν παρὰ τοῦ Κυρίου Ἰησοῦ). However, having quoted verse 18, he then notes, 'in the sacred syllables the name of God is remembered', and concludes the commentary on the psalm by saying, 'Through the proclamation, the word

29 Ἐξομολογησάσθωσαν τῷ ὀνόματί σου τῷ μεγάλῳ, ὅτι φοβερὸν καὶ ἅγιόν ἐστι: PG 23, 1236C.

30 PG 27, 421B.

31 Διὰ τοῦτο λαοὶ ὑμνήσουσί σε εἰς αἰῶνα διηνεκῶς: PG 23, 405A.

32 μνησθήσονται τοῦ ὀνόματός σου ἐν πάσῃ γενεᾷ καὶ γενεᾷ: PG 27, 213B.

is as if [addressed] to Christ (ὡς πρὸς τὸν Χριστὸν δὲ ὁ λόγος)'. In contrast to the two above, Cyril is simply content to link the remembrance of the divine name directly with the remembrance of Christ.[33]

Three texts focus on the theme of rejoicing or 'boasting in the Lord'. Thus in Psalm 5.12–13, 'But let all who hope in you be glad; forever they will rejoice, and you will tent among them, and those who love your name will boast in you',[34] Eusebius interprets this verse in the light of Paul's teaching in Galatians 6.14 and 1 Corinthians 1.31, thus clearly identifying 'your name' and 'you' with Christ (Τοιοῦτοι περὶ ὧν ὁ λόγος, ἠγαπηκότων αὐτοῦ τὸ ὄνομα).[35]

Here we see a clear example of how the reading of the Targum Psalm, 'But let all who trust in your *Memra* rejoice',[36] coincides with a patristic reference to ὁ λόγος in the exegesis of the same verse. Where the Targum introduces the *Memra*, the patristic authority introduces the divine Word.

Eusebius reads Psalm 104.3, 'Be commended in his holy name; let the hearts of those who seek the Lord be glad',[37] in a similar light. His gloss on this verse is that Christians rejoice in the knowledge and consideration of the true God (ἐν τῇ τοῦ ἀληθινοῦ Θεοῦ γνώσει καὶ προμηθείᾳ καὶ τῷ καλεῖσθαι Χριστιανούς), and in being called Christians.

Theodoret, on the other hand, makes exactly the same point by linking the holy name in the psalm-verse directly with Paul's injunction in 2 Corinthians 10.17 to 'boast in the Lord'.[38] It may be worth noting *en passant* that here the Targum Psalm refers not to 'those who seek the Lord', but to 'those who seek *instruction from* the Lord', thus identifying a didactic element in the text, which is not followed by the Fathers.

33 PG 69, 1045D.

34 καὶ εὐφρανθήτωσαν ἐπὶ σοὶ πάντες οἱ ἐλπίζοντες ἐπὶ σέ· εἰς αἰῶνα ἀγαλλιάσονται, καὶ κατασκηνώσεις ἐν αὐτοῖς.

35 PG 23, 117D.

36 Stec, *Targum Psalms*, 34.

37 Ἐπαινεῖσθε ἐν τῷ ὀνόματι τῷ ἁγίῳ αὐτοῦ· εὐφρανθήτω καρδία ζητούντων τὸν Κύριον: PG 23, 1300A.

38 PG 80, 1709B.

Δόξα, as a general theme, lies behind several texts to which the exegete attributes an exposition which identifies the divine name in the psalm with that of Christ. The royal psalm, Psalm 71.17–19, is a source for such an exegesis on the part of Eusebius, Didymus and Cyril: 'Let his name be blessed through the ages, his name shall endure as long as the sun... And blessed be his glorious name forever even forever and ever'.[39]

Having set down the text of the verses 18 and 19,[40] Eusebius proceeds to equate 'his glorious name' (Ὄνομα δὲ δόξης αὐτοῦ) with the name given by Gabriel to Joseph, according to Matthew 1.21, that is, Jesus.

Didymus makes a direct connection between the glorious name in verse 17 and Jesus' glorification by his death, as in Hebrews 2.9 (καὶ τὸ Τὸν ἠλαττωμένον βλέπομεν Ἰησοῦν διὰ τὸ πάθημα τοῦ θανάτου δόξῃ καὶ τιμῇ ἐστεφανωμένον).[41] 'For where is Christ not?' (Ποῦ γὰρ οὐκ ἔστι Χριστὸς), Cyril rhetorically exclaims, in response to 'Let his name be blessed' (Ἔστω τὸ ὄνομα αὐτοῦ εὐλογημένον),[42] thus identifying the glorified name with that of the Son of God.

Cyril goes on to explain verse 19, 'Blessed be his glorious name' (Καὶ εὐλογητὸν τὸ ὄνομα τῆς δόξης αὐτοῦ)[43] with reference to John 17.1, making a direct connection between the divine name in the psalm-verse and the person of Christ: 'Therefore this name, he says, is surely the Son, indeed, Christ Jesus'.[44]

These passages should be read in the light of the Targum's gloss on verse 17, which is clearly eager to underline the pre-existent nature of the name in question: 'May his name be *remembered* for ever – *even before the*

39 ἔστω τὸ ὄνομα αὐτοῦ εὐλογημένον εἰς τοὺς αἰῶνας, πρὸ τοῦ ἡλίου διαμενεῖ τὸ ὄνομα αὐτοῦ ... καὶ εὐλογητὸν τὸ ὄνομα τῆς δόξης αὐτοῦ εἰς τὸν αἰῶνα καὶ εἰς τὸν αἰῶνα τοῦ αἰῶνος: see PG 23, 820A-C, Mühlenberg 2, 763, 104, and PG 69, 1184B-D.

40 Εὐλογητὸς Κύριος ὁ Θεὸς Ἰσραὴλ ὁ ποιῶν θαυμάσια μόνος. Καὶ εὐλογητὸν τὸ ὄνομα τῆς δόξης αὐτοῦ εἰς τὸν αἰῶνα: PG 23, 820BC.

41 *In Ps. caten.* 71.17–19, Mühlenberg 2, 763, 104.

42 PG 69, 1184B.

43 PG 69, 1184C.

44 Τοῦτο τοίνυν τὸ ὄνομα, φησὶν, τουτέστι τὸ Υἱὸς ἤτοι Χριστὸς Ἰησοῦς: PG 69, 1184D.

*sun existed his name was being prepared* – and may all the nations be blessed through *his merit, and say, "Blessed be he!"*'.[45]

Didymus focuses on the general theme of glory in Psalm 95.7–8, 'Bring to the Lord the glory due to his name; raise offerings, and enter into his courts'.[46] Here he interprets these words in the light of James 2.7, where the name of the Lord in the psalm-verse is connected directly to the name of Christ, which is invoked over his slaves, and by which they bear his glory.[47]

In Psalm 112.1, 'Praise the Lord, O servants; praise the name of the Lord',[48] Athanasius observes that the new people are taught as if 'our Lord has been taken up, and is at the right hand of the Father',[49] thus affirming the glory of Christ's ascension into heaven.

In *Psalm* 28.2, however, Theodoret shifts the δόξα emphasis in the direction of the Trinity: 'Bring to the Lord, O sons of God, bring to the Lord glory and honour. Bring to the Lord glory for his name; worship the Lord in his holy court'.[50] He links this psalm-verse with Christ's great commission to the apostles to baptize people everywhere in the name of the Father and of the Son and of the Holy Spirit, as in Matthew 28.19, and notes that the psalmist goes on to speak about holy waters.[51]

To conclude these doxological psalm-texts, we find Origen, Eusebius and Didymus all at one in linking the name in the same psalm-verse with the glory of Christ's transfiguration.

Origen explains the text of Psalm 88.13, 'The north and the seas you created; Tabor and Hermon will rejoice in your name'.[52] He identifies Tabor as the 'mountain of Galilee on which Christ was transfigured' (ἐφ'οὗ

45 Stec, *Targum Psalms*, 140.

46 ἐνέγκατε τῷ κυρίῳ δόξαν ὀνόματι αὐτοῦ, ἄρατε θυσίας καὶ εἰσπορεύεσθε εἰς τὰς αὐλὰς αὐτοῦ.

47 δόξαν ἐνέγκωμεν τῷ ἐφ'ἡμᾶς ὀνόματι τοῦ Χριστοῦ: *In Ps. caten.* 95.7–8, Mühlenberg 2, 933, 203.

48 Αἰνεῖτε, παῖδες, τὸν Κύριον, αἰνεῖτε τὸ ὄνομα τοῦ Κυρίοῦ: PG 27, 465D.

49 εἰ καὶ ἀνελήφθη ὁ Κύριος ἡμῶν, καὶ ἔστιν ἐν δεξιᾷ τοῦ Πατρὸς: PG 27, 465D–468A.

50 Ἐνέγκατε τῷ Κυρίῳ, υἱοὶ Θεοῦ, ἐνέγκατε τῷ Κυρίῳ υἱοὺς κριῶν. Ἐνέγκατε τῷ Κυρίῳ δόξαν καὶ τιμὴν· ἐνέγκατε τῷ Κυρίῳ δόξαν ὀνόματι αὐτοῦ· προσκυνήσατε τῷ Κυρίῳ ἐν αὐλῇ ἁγίᾳ αὐτοῦ: PG 80, 1064B.

51 καὶ ὁ ψαλμὸς γὰρ, μετὰ τὰ εἰρημένα, εὐθὺς τῶν ἱερῶν ὑδάτων ἀνέμνησε: PG 80, 1065A.

52 Θαβὼρ καὶ Ἑρμὼν ἐν τῷ ὀνόματί σου ἀγαλλιάσονται: PG 12, 1548D.

μετεμορφώθη Χριστὸς). Hermon is identified with the city of Nain, 'in which Christ raised the widow's son' (ἐν ᾗ ἤγειρε τὸν χήρας υἱὸν ὁ Χριστός). It follows that he associates the name in which the mountains rejoice with the name of Christ.

For Eusebius the text reads as, Θαβὼρ καὶ Ἑρμὼν ἐν τῷ ὀνόματί σου αἰνέσουσι.[53] Like Origen, he connects the reference to Mount Tabor's rejoicing in the divine name with the transfiguration of Christ.[54] And while he is not remotely as explicit as the other two, Didymus would appear to be making an allusion to the transfiguration in his commentary.[55]

## 2. *Parousia*

In broad terms, the collection of psalm-texts which may be codified, loosely, as Christological may be divided further into two sub-categories. The first of these include those texts where the reference to the divine name is understood in prophetic terms, regarding the coming of Christ (παρουσία). The second of these involve those passages where the exegete uses the divine name as a basis for reflection on the relationships within the Godhead (ὁμοούσιος).

Four passages in Eusebius's *Commentarii in psalmos*, where the divine name is given a Christological spin, are understood by the writer as prophecies of Christ's παρουσία. In Psalm 17.50, 'Therefore I will acknowledge you, O Lord, among the nations, and make music to your name',[56] he associates the singing of this verse by David ('the anointed') with the coming of 'our Saviour' (ὥσπερ ὁ Δαυῒδ μετὰ τὴντοῦ Σωτῆρος ἡμῶν παρουσίαν).

Similarly, with regard to Psalm 19.8, 'Some glory in chariots, and some in horses, but we will glory in the name of the Lord our God',[57] he

53 PG 23, 1092D.

54 καὶ οἶμαί γε ἐν τούτοις τοῖς ὄρεσι τὰς παραδόξους τοῦ Σωτῆρος ἡμῶν γεγονέναι μεταμορφώσεις: PG 23, 1092D.

55 ὡς ἐκτὸς μὲν τὸ Θαβώρ, φωτὸς δὲ μετεωρισμὸς τὸ Ἑρμωνιείμ.: *In Ps. caten.* 88. 12–13, Mühlenberg 2, 886, 170.

56 Διὰ τοῦτο ἐξομολογήσομαι σοι ἐν ἔθνεσι, Κύριε, καὶ τῷ ὀνόματί σου ψαλῶ: PG 23, 185B.

57 Οὗτοι ἐν ἅρμασιν καὶ οὗτοι ἐν ἵπποις, ἡμεῖς δὲ ἐν ὀνόματι Κυρίου Θεοῦ ἡμῶν ἐπικαλεσόμεθα: PG 23, 197AB.

understands this verse as a prophecy relating to the 'time of the appearing of the salvation given' (κατὰ τὸν καιρὸν τῆς τοῦ ἀποδοθέντος σωτηρίου ἐπιφανείας). That this should be interpreted in a Christological context is borne out by a reference to Simeon's prophecy, which follows.

It is worth noting in passing that in the Targum the previous verse inserts an emphasis on the celestial abode of the divine name: 'Now I know that the Lord has delivered his anointed one; *he has accepted his prayer* from *his holy dwelling place in heaven*'.[58]

In his commentary on Psalm 85.9, 'All the nations you made shall come and bow down before you, O Lord, and shall glorify your name',[59] Eusebius understands this psalm-verse concerning the future glorification of God's name as a prophecy of the coming of Christ.[60]

And again, in Psalm 105.47, 'Save us, O Lord our God, and gather us together from among the nations, that we may acknowledge your holy name and boast in your praise',[61] he sees the present experience of the Saviour shining on men (ἤδη τοῦ Σωτῆρος ἡμῶν ἐπιλάμψαντος ἀνθρώποις) as a fulfilment of the psalmist's prayer for salvation, and his hope that he and his people may acknowledge the divine name.

Athanasius ponders the text for Psalm 104.1, 'O acknowledge the Lord and call on his name, announce his deeds among the nations'.[62] He associates the invocation of the divine name with the ruling of the Holy Spirit over the apostles, the manifestation of miraculous works to the people of the nations, and the coming of the Lord (ἐπὶ παρουσίας αὐτοῦ ὁ Κύριος).

He understands Psalm 121.4, 'For there the tribes went up, the tribes of the Lord, as was solemnly charged to Israel, to acknowledge the name of the Lord',[63] as prophecy that the kingdom of David, in which the tribes

58 Stec, *Targum Psalms*, 55.

59 Πάντα τὰ ἔθνη ὅσα ἐποίησας, ἥξουσι καὶ προσκυνήσουσιν ἐνώπιον σου, Κύριε, καὶ δοξάσουσι τὸ ὄνομα σου: PG 23, 1032D.

60 καὶ μέση τῶν περὶ τοῦ Χριστοῦ προφητειῶν παρεμβέβληται: PG 23, 1033A.

61 Σῶσον ἡμᾶς, Κύριε ὁ Θεὸς ἡμῶν, καὶ ἐπισυνάγαγε ἡμᾶς ἐκ τῶν ἐθνῶν, τοῦ ἐξομολογεῖσθαι τῷ ὀνόματί σου τῷ ἁγίῳ, τοῦ ἐγκαυχᾶσθαι ἐν τῇ αἰνέσει σου: PG 23, 1320A.

62 Ἐξομολογεῖσθε τῷ Κυρίῳ, καὶ ἐπικαλεῖσθε τὸ ὄνομα αὐτοῦ, ἀπαγγείλατε ἐν τοῖς ἔθνεσι τὰ ἔργα αὐτοῦ: PG 27, 441D.

63 Τοῦ ἐξομολογήσασθαι τῷ ὀνόματι Κυρίου: PG 27, 512D.

go up to acknowledge the name of the Lord, will be restored through the grace of Christ (δι'ὧν ἡ βασιλεία Δαυῒδ ἀνορθοῦται χάριτι τοῦ Χριστοῦ).

The Targum insertion is of particular interest here, where the verse reads: 'to which the tribes, the tribes of the Lord go up, *testifying to Israel that his Shekinah dwells among them, when they go* to give thanks to the name of the Lord'.[64] Here the *Shekinah* is directly associated with the divine name in the same psalm-verse which the patristic witness interprets Christologically.

Theodoret comments on Psalm 67.5, 'Sing to God, make music to his name; make a way for him who rides upon the sunset – his name is the Lord – be exultant before him'.[65] He understands this psalm-verse as a prophetic word to the apostles (Ἐνταῦθα ὁ προφητικὸς λόγος τοῖς ἱεροῖς ἀποστόλοις), with reference to Christ's command to them to baptize in the name of the Trinity, in Matthew 28.19 (as he does in relation to Psalm 28.2), and with the ministry of John the Baptist in Matthew 3.5.

Didymus reflects on Psalm 79.18–19, 'But let your hand be upon the man at your right hand, and upon the son of man whom you made strong for yourself. Then we will never turn away from you; you will revive us, and we will call upon your name'.[66] He reads this verse in the light of the prophecy of Zechariah 5.12–13,[67] where he identifies the 'man at your right hand' of the psalm and the 'Dawn' (Ἀνατολὴ) of the prophecy with God the Word (αὕτη δέ ἐστιν ὁ θεὸς λόγος), concluding the commentary on this verse with a quotation from Romans 10.13.[68]

He also comments on Psalm 142.11, 'For your name's sake, O Lord, you will quicken me',[69] observing that 'We were completely quickened at the

64 Stec, *Targum Psalms*, 220.

65 Ἄισατε γὰρ, φησὶ, τῷ Θεῷ· ψάλατε τῷ ὀνόματι αὐτοῦ· ὁδοποιήσατε τῷ ἐπιβεβηκότι ἐπὶ δυσμῶν. Κύριος ὄνομα αὐτῷ, καὶ ἀγαλλιάσθε ἐνώπιον αὐτοῦ: PG 80, 1377A.

66 γενηθήτω ἡ χείρ σου ἐπ' ἄνδρα δεξιᾶς σου, καὶ ἐπὶ υἱὸν ἀνθρώπου ὃν ἐκραταίωσας σεαυτῷ· καὶ οὐ μὴ ἀποστῶμεν ἀπὸ σοῦ· ζωώσεις ἡμᾶς, καὶ τὸ ὄνομά σου ἐπικαλεσόμεθα.

67 Ἰδοὺ ἀνὴρ, Ἀνατολὴ ὄνομα αὐτῷ...: Brenton, *Septuagint with Apocrypha*, 1118.

68 *In Ps. caten.* 79.18–19, Mühlenberg 2, 829, 139.

69 ἕνεκα τοῦ ὀνόματός σου, Κύριε, ζήσεις με ἐν τῇ δικαιοσύνῃ σου, ἐξάξεις ἐκ θλίψεως τὴν ψυχήν μου.

time that Christ our life was made manifest' (ζησόμενοι τελείως τὸ τηνικαῦτα ὅταν φανερωθῇ Χριστὸς ἡ ζωὴ ἡμῶν)[70] in an allusion to Colossians 3.4.

In a text which may be accredited to Evagrius, Origen offers comment on Psalm 112.3, 'From the rising of the sun to its setting, praise the name of the Lord'.[71] He identifies the sun in the psalm-verse with the 'sun of righteousness' (τῆς δικαιοσύνης ἥλιος) and with the 'spiritual and celestial sun' (ὁ πνευματικὸς καὶ ἐπουράνιος ἥλιος), a clear reference to the person of Christ, thus associating τὸ ὄνομα Κυρίου with him.

Commenting on the same verse, Theodoret says, 'This psalm prophesied the knowledge of God provided to the nations after the incarnation of the Only-begotten',[72] thus linking the divine name in the psalm-verse with the coming of the Son.

The Philippian hymn provides him with food for thought in terms of his interpretation of Psalm 101.16, 'The nations will fear the name of the Lord, and all the kings of the earth your glory',[73] where he associates the psalm-verse with Philippians 2.10, and observes that fear of the Lord's name came after the incarnation of the Saviour.[74]

### 3. *Homoousios*

Eight texts, in all, reflect the exegetes' interest in associating the divine name in the psalms with the unity of relationships within the Godhead. Didymus places his interpretation of Psalm 82.19, 'Let them know that your name is the Lord; you alone are most high over all the earth',[75] within a Trinitarian

70 *In Ps. caten.* 142.11, Mühlenberg 2, 1244, 342.

71 Ἀπὸ ἀνατολῶν ἡλίου μέχρι δυσμῶν αἰνετὸν τὸ ὄνομα Κυρίου, κ.τ.έ.: PG 12, 1572B.

72 Τὴν μετὰ τὴν ἐνανθρώπησιν τοῦ Μονογενοῦς τοῖς ἔθνεσι παρασχεθεῖσαν θεογνωσίαν ὁ ψαλμὸς προεθέσπισε: PG 80, 1785A.

73 Καὶ φοβηθήσονται τὰ ἔθνη τὸ ὄνομά Κυρίου, καὶ πάντες οἱ βασιλεῖς τῆς γῆς τὴν δόξαν σου: PG 80, 1680C.

74 Τοῦτο δὲ κυρίως καὶ ἀληθῶς μετά τὴν τοῦ Θεοῦ καὶ Σωτῆρος ἡμῶν ἐνανθρώπησιν γέγονε: ibid.

75 Καὶ γνώτωσαν ὅτι ὄνομά σοι Κύριος· σὺ μόνος Ὕψιστος ἐπὶ πᾶσαν τὴν γήν.

context, focusing on the words 'most high', which is applicable to Father, Son and Holy Spirit (ὁ γὰρ τὸν πατέρα ὕψιστον εἰπὼν καὶ τὸν υἱὸν καὶ τὸ πνεῦμα τὸ ἅγιον δηλοῖ).[76] Thus for him, the divine name in the psalm is equally applicable to the Son, and indeed to the Spirit, as it is to the Father.

In his assessment of the same verse, Theodoret indicates very clearly that the divine name in the psalm-verse is that of Christ (ὡς αὐτός ἐστι μόνος καὶ Θεὸς καὶ Δεσπότης), the God from God and only-begotten Son (ὁ ἐκ Θεοῦ Θεὸς, ὁ μονογενὴς Υἱός).[77]

The same commentary text for Psalm 88.25, 'My truth and steadfast love shall be with him; and in my name his horn shall be exalted', is to be found in the works of both Athanasius and Cyril.[78] They affirm the unity of Father and Son, and appear to indicate that, as with 'steadfast love' (ἔλεος), so 'name' can be said to refer to both.[79]

Once more the Targum's witness provides us with some relevant material: 'And my faithfulness and my goodness shall be with him; and in *the name of my Memra* his glory shall be exalted'.[80] Here again we find a Christological interpretation of the divine name in a psalm-text coinciding with the insertion of the *Memra motif* in the same text by Rabbinic Judaism. Where the Targum text introduces the *Memra*, so the patristic scholar introduces the divine Word.

Psalm 117.26, 'Blessed is the one who comes in the name of the Lord', provides us with similar material. Origen understands this verse, Εὐλογημένος ὁ ἐρχόμενος ἐν ὀνόματι Κυρίου, κ.τ.ἑ.,[81] as a prophecy of the coming of Christ.[82] But his constant use of Κύριος in the commentary implies an equation between the divine name in the psalm and the title of Christ.

76 *In Ps. caten.* 82.19b, Mühlenberg 2, 842, 146–7.

77 PG 80, 1537AB.

78 Καὶ ἐν τῷ ὀνόματί μου ὑψωθήσεται τὸ κέρας αὐτοῦ: PG 27, 389B; PG 69, 1213A.

79 Τοῖς γὰρ ὀνόμασιν, οἷς μάλιστα πρέπουσι τῷ Πατρί, καὶ αὐτὸς ὁ Υἱὸς δοξάζεται: PG 27, 389B; cf. PG 69, 1213A.

80 Stec, *Targum Psalms*, 169.

81 PG 12, 1584CD.

82 Καὶ ταύτην τὴν φωνὴν οἱ εὐαγγελισταὶ περὶ Χριστοῦ προφητείαν εἶναι ἐξειλήφασιν: ibid.

In interpreting the same verse, Theodoret is more explicit. He easily identifies Jesus as the one who comes in the name of the Lord, after Matthew 21.9, 14–16, and is eager to emphasize the identity of his title with that of the Father: 'Being Lord, he has come in the name of the Lord'.[83]

Again, the Targum offers a similar background to that regarding Psalm 88.25, where the verse reads: '"Blessed is the one who comes in the name of *the Memra of* the Lord," *said the architects*. "We bless you from the house of *the sanctuary of* the Lord", *said David*'.[84] Here in the context of an antiphonal chant, Rabbinic Judaism both introduces the *Memra* and also amplifies the sacral nature of the divine dwelling in the same psalm-text where the patristic authorities equate the divine name with that of the Word of God. In two further texts the Philippian hymn is introduced in order to associate the divine name in the psalm with the theme of the relationship of the Father and the Son. Cyril makes such an observation with regard to Psalm 98.3, 'Let them acknowledge your great name, for it is awesome and holy',[85] where he interprets the verse in the light of Philippians 2.11, and uses the text as an opportunity to affirm the consubstantiality of God the Word with the divine name.[86]

Didymus takes the same approach to Psalm 137.2, 'I will bow down towards your holy shrine and acknowledge your name for your steadfast love and your truth; for you magnified your oracle upon every name'.[87] He links the divine name in the verse directly to Jesus with a reference to Philippians 2.10, for 'he alone came in the name of the Father, so that the holy name of God might be magnified upon all'.[88]

83 Κύριος δὲ ὤν, ἐν ὀνόματι Κυρίοῦ ἐλήλυθεν: PG 80, 1817C; Robert C. Hill, trans., *Theodoret of Cyrrhus, Commentary on the Psalms, Psalms 73–150*, The Fathers of the Church102 (Washington D.C.: The Catholic University of America Press, 2001), 243.

84 Stec, *Targum Psalms*, 210.

85 Ἐξομολογησάσθωσαν τῷ ὀνόματί σου τῷ μεγάλῳ: PG 69, 1257AB.

86 πλὴν ὅτι μόνος ὁ ἐξ αὐτοῦ καὶ ἐν αὐτῷ καὶ ὁμοούσιος αὐτῷ Θεὸς Λόγος: ibid.

87 προσκυνήσω πρὸς ναὸν ἅγιον σου, καὶ ἐξομολογήσομαι τῷ ὀνόματί σου ἐπὶ τῷ ἐλέει σου καὶ τῃ ἀληθείᾳ σου, ὅτι ἐμεγάλυνας ἐπὶ πᾶν ὄνομα τὸ ἅγιόν σου.

88 μόνος γὰρ οὗτος ἐλήλυθεν ἐν ὀνόματι τοῦ πατρὸς, ἵνα μεγαλυνθῇ ἐπὶ πάντας τὸ ὄνομα τὸ ἅγιον τοῦ θεοῦ: *In Ps. caten.* 137.2d, Mühlenberg 2, 1204, 322.

A relatively insignificant variant in the Targum version of this psalm-verse has the psalmist bowing down *before* rather than 'toward' the holy temple, and the divinity exalting '*the words of your praise* above all your name'.[89]

Finally, there are, within this section, two texts which stand apart from either of these two sub-categories. Firstly, in his exegesis of Psalm 47.11, 'Your name, O God, just like your praise, is to the ends of the earth; your right hand is full of justice',[90] Cyril gives a Christological interpretation to the second part of the verse, following the reference to the divine 'right hand'.[91]

Here once more, the evidence from the Targum comes into play, where the relevant verse reads: 'As is your name, O *Lord*, so is your praise to the ends of the earth....'[92] The replacement of 'God' with *Lord* thus takes place in the same text which the patristic exegete associates with the 'only-begotten Word of God'.

To complete this section, Origen tackles the text of Psalm 75.2, 'In Judah God is known; his name is great in Israel',[93] and interprets this verse in the light of the incarnation. God is known in Judah, the place where he has revealed himself in Christ, on whose account, therefore, his name is great in Israel.

## 4. *Sōtēria*

We now move on to those passages where the interpretation has been guided by salvation or σωτηρία. Athanasius comments on the text of Psalm 53.3, 'Save me, O God, in your name, and you will judge me in your power'.[94] He explicitly identifies the power of God with the person of Christ (Καὶ

89 *Targum Psalms*, 232.

90 Κατὰ τὸ ὄνομά σου, ὁ Θεὸς, οὕτως καὶ ἡ αἴνεσίς σου ἐπὶ τὰ πέρατα τῆς γῆς ... Δικαιοσύνης πλήρης ἡ δεξιά σου: PG 69, 1064A.

91 πλὴν ὅτι κατὰ ἀλήθειαν ὁ ἐξ αὐτοῦ πεφηνὼς μονογενὴς Θεοῦ Λόγος: PG 69, 1064B.

92 Stec, *Targum Psalms*, 101.

93 Γνωστὸς ἐν τη Ἰουδαίᾳ, ἐν τῷ Ἰσραὴλ μέγα τὸ ὄνομα αὐτοῦ: PG 12, 1536B.

94 Ὁ Θεὸς, ἐν τῷ ὀνόματί σου σῶσόν με: PG 27, 249BC.

ἐν δυναστείᾳ σου, τουτέστι τῷ Υἱῷ σου), thus indicating that it is in the Son's name that the psalmist pleads for salvation. In like manner, with regard to the same verse, Theodoret makes a specific link between the divine name in the psalm-verse and the name of Christ, this time with reference to the name invoked in Acts 3.16.[95]

Commenting on another plea for salvation, in Psalm 105.47, 'Save us, O Lord our God, and gather us together from among the nations, that we may acknowledge your holy name and boast in your praise',[96] Theodoret links the confession of the divine name with vocation, recognition of truth and faith in the Lord Christ.[97]

For Didymus, the words of Psalm 98.3, 'Let them acknowledge your great name, for it is awesome and holy!', prompt him to associate a cry for salvation with the name of Christ. After an allusion to Acts 4.12, he connects the 'great and awesome name' not only with Christ but also with Christians.[98]

The Lord's promise of deliverance in Psalm 90.14, 'Because in me he hoped I will deliver him; I will protect him because he knew my name', provides both Eusebius and Athanasius with the opportunity to interpret the divine name Christologically.

Eusebius sets out this psalm-verse thus: Ὅτι ἐπ' ἐμὲ ἤλπισε, καὶ ῥύσομαι αὐτόν·σκεπάσω αὐτὸν, ὅτι ἔγνω τὸ ὄνομά μου.[99] In his commentary he links the person who knows the divine name with the man who is made perfect in Christ (τοῦ ἐν Χριστῷ τετελειωμένου ἀνδρὸς), whereas Athanasius, while focusing on the second half of the verse, notes that Jesus Christ is our salvation (Εἴη δὲ τὸ σωτήριον ἡμῶν Ἰησοῦς Χριστὸς).[100]

95 Ἐν τῷ ὀνόματι γὰρ, φησὶν, Ἰησοῦ Χριστοῦ ἔγειραι, καὶ περιπάτει: PG 80, 1265A.

96 Σῶσον ἡμᾶς, Κύριε ὁ Θεὸς ἡμῶν, καὶ ἐπισυνάγαγε ἡμᾶς ἐκ τῶν ἐθνῶν· τοῦ ἐξομολογήσσθαι τῷ ὀνόματί σου τῷ ἁγίῳ, τοῦ ἐγκαυχᾶσθαι ἐν τῇ αἰνέσει σου: PG 80, 1733C.

97 ἀλλα κλῆσιν καὶ ἐπίγνωσιν ἀληθείας, καὶ πίστιν εἰς τὸν Δεσπότην Χριστὸν: PG 80, 1733D.

98 πάντας γοῦν τοὺς ἀπὸ πάντων τῶν ἐθνῶν σωζομένους Χριστιανοὺς ἀπὸ Χριστοῦ καλουμένους ἔστιν ἰδεῖν: *In Ps. caten.* 98.3–4a, Mühlenberg 2, 954, 214.

99 PG 23, 1164B.

100 PG27, 404B.

It is worth noting that in the Targum text of this verse the words are: 'Because he delights in *my Memra*, I will rescue him, I will set him on high because he knows my name'.[101] The replacement of 'me' by *my Memra* thus occurs within the same passage where the Fathers associate the person of Christ with the name of the Lord. Where the Targum introduces *Memra*, so the Father introduces the divine Word.

Origen, or more probably Evagrius, considers the prayer for deliverance in Psalm 114.4, 'Then I called on the name of the Lord, "Ah, Lord, rescue my soul"'.[102] He understands this psalm-verse in the light of Paul's Christological interpretation in Romans 10.9–13, following his explicit Pauline reference in his exegesis of the previous verse (ὡσ ὁ εἰπὼν Παῦλος). τὸ ὄνομα Κυρίου is therefore clearly identified with the name of Christ.

Both Origen and Cyril see justification for their Christianization of the divine name in the cry for help in Psalm 43.27, 'Rise up, O Lord, come to our help; redeem us for the sake of your name'.[103] Origen interprets this psalm-verse as a prayer addressed to Christ, as he lay in the heart of the earth 'at the time of his sufferings', to give help and deliverance 'for the sake of your name', i.e. the name of Christ. He 'who gave his life as a ransom for many does such things for the glory of his name' (ὑπὲρ τῆς δόξης τοῦ ὀνόματος αὐτοῦ).

Cyril interprets the phrase 'for the sake of your name' (ἕνεκεν τοῦ ὀνόματός σου) with reference to showing mercy to the unworthy, to 'those who out of the horn of their own ignorance sharpen their swords against Christ' (οἱ τῆς ἑαυτῶν ἀγνοίας τὸ κέρας ἀκονήσαντες τῷ Χριστῷ).

Two further passages from Origen, the first most likely Evagrian, link the divine name in the psalm with that of Christ within a soteriological context. Psalm 79.19b,'You will revive us, and we will call upon your name',[104] begins with a verb (Ζωώσεις) which carries with it a sense of the imperative. The name invoked here is clearly the name of Christ, for 'No

101 Stec, *Targum Psalms*, 175.

102 Καὶ τὸ ὄνομα Κυρίου ἐπεκαλεσάμην, κ.τ.ἑ.: PG 12, 1573D.

103 Ἀνάστα, Κύριε, βοήθησον ἡμῖν, καὶ λύτρωσαι ἡμᾶς ἕνεκεν τοῦ ὀνόματος σου, κ. τ. ἑ.: PG 12, 1428BC; PG 69, 1025B.

104 Ζωώσεις ἡμᾶς, καὶ τὸ ὄνομά σου ἐπικαλεσόμεθα, κ.τ.ἑ.: PG 12, 1544C.

one can give us life, except him who says, "I am the life"' (Οὐδεὶς δύναται ζωοποιῆσαι ἡμᾶς, εἰ μὴ ὁ εἰπών: Ἐγώ εἰμι ἡ Ζωή).

And in Psalm 19.2, 'The Lord hearken to you in the day of trouble; the name of the God of Jacob protect you',[105] Origen associates the help given by the name of the God of Jacob in the day trouble with the help given by Christ.[106]

The reading of the Targum equivalent of this verse and verse 3 reveals a couple of insertions into the Hebrew text: 'May the Lord *accept your prayer* in the day of trouble, the name of the God of Jacob lift you high. May he send your help from *the house of his* sanctuary, and may he aid you from Zion'.[107]

Finally in this section, we find Eusebius making a Christological-soteriological connection with regard to Psalm 22.3, 'He restored my soul; he led me into righteous paths for his name's sake',[108] where he associates the leading 'into righteous paths for his name's sake' with the granting of eternal life to him who believes in the Son of God.[109]

## 5. *Ekklēsia*

In eight passages within the works in question the Fathers place an ecclesiological emphasis in their exposition of the relevant psalm-text. Eusebius and Athanasius adopt such an approach to Psalm 47.11, 'Like your name, O God, your praise is to the ends of the earth. Your right hand is full of justice'.[110]

105 Ἐπακούσαι σου Κύριος ἐν ἡμέρᾳ θλίψεως, ὑπερασπίσαι σου τὸ ὄνομα τοῦ Θεοῦ Ἰακώβ: PG 12, 1245C.

106 ἀγγελικῆς ἤ τινος τοιαύτης ἐξαποστελλομένης ἡμῖν τῆς βοηθείας, ἢ βοηθείας τοῦ Χριστοῦ: *ibid.*

107 Stec, *Targum Psalms*, 55.

108 Ὡδήγησέ με ἐπὶ τρίβους δικαιοσύνης ἕνεκεν τοῦ ὀνόματος αὐτοῦ: PG 23, 217C.

109 ὡς ἄρα ὁ πιστεύων εἰς τὸν Υἱὸν τοῦ Θεοῦ: *ibid.*

110 Κατὰ τὸ ὄνομά σου, ὁ Θεὸς, οὕτως καὶ ἡ αἴνεσίς σου ἐπὶ τὰ πέρατα τῆς γῆς· δικαιοσύνης πλήρης ἡ δεξία σου: PG 23, 425AB; see also PG 27, 221AB.

Having associated the divine name with the rejoicing of Mount Sion (Εὐφρανθήτω ὄρος Σιών), and the foundation of the Church, Eusebius declares 'Therefore the rock and the mountain was Christ himself' (Ἡ πέτρα οὖν καὶ τὸ ὄρος αὐτὸς ἦν ὁ Χριστὸς), while Athanasius makes a direct link between the universality of the divine name in the psalm-verse and Paul's dictum on the inclusivity of believers in the Body of Christ in Galatians 3.28.

Both Origen and Didymus identify the divine name in Psalm 74.2, 'We will acknowledge you, O God; we will acknowledge and call upon your name',[111] with that of Christ within the context of an ecclesiological *motif*. Origen observes that the psalmist states in two verses that the Church is in Christ (Ἡ ἐν Χριστῷ Ἐκκλησία). Hence it is the name of Christ which is invoked here. Didymus, on the other hand, appears to link the invocation of the divine name with the grace enjoyed by those who love the Lord Jesus Christ with an undying love, as in Ephesians 6.24.[112]

The Targum psalm-text reads as follows: 'We give thanks to you, O *Lord*, we give thanks, for *the Shekinah of* your name is near; they recount your wonderful deeds'.[113] Here we see both the substitution of *Lord* for 'God', and the use of *Shekinah* to establish a greater element of transcendence for the divine name, in a text where the patristic commentators see references to him who is both Lord and the presence of God.

Cyril and Eusebius, similarly, find common cause in their respective exegeses of 'and they will rejoice in your name' in Psalm 88.17.[114] For Cyril the name in the text is none other than the 'beautiful name of Christ' (Ἀεὶ γὰρ ἡμᾶς στεφανοῖ τὸ καλὸν ὄνομα τοῦ Χριστοῦ τὸ ἐπικληθὲν εἰς ἡμᾶς), through whom 'we are called Christians'. For his part, in a lengthy exposition of these verses, Eusebius observes that the Christian is not only

111 Ἐξομολογησόμεθά σοι, ὁ Θεὸς, ἐξομολογησόμεθα, καὶ ἐπικαλεσόμεθα τὸ ὄνομά σου, κ.τ.ἑ.: PG 12, 1533B.

112 Ἡ χάρις γάρ φησι μετὰ τῶν ἀγαπώντων τὸν κύριον ἡμῶν Ἰησοῦν Χριστὸν ἐν ἀφθαρσίᾳ.: *In Ps. caten.* 74.1–2, Mühlenberg 2, 778a, 111.

113 Stec, *Targum Psalms*, 147.

114 Ἐν τῷ ὀνόματί σου ἀγαλλιάσονται (PG 69, 1212C; see also PG 23, 1093C).

enlightened but also exalted in the name of Christ (ἔτι καὶ τῷ ὀνόματι αὐτοῦ σεμνυνόμενος).[115]

Eusebius also takes the ecclesiological route in his explanation of the nature of the divine name in Psalm 79.18–19,[116] where he associates the name in the psalm with the name of Christ: 'But from your name of Christ, we are called Christians' (ἀπὸ δὲ τοῦ σοῦ ὀνόματος τοῦ Χριστοῦ Χριστιανοὶ χρηματίσομεν).

Finally, Theodoret follows a similar path in identifying the name of Christ in the text of Psalm 60.6, 'For you, O God, listened to my vows; you gave a heritage to those who fear your name'.[117] He interprets this verse in the light of Matthew 25.34, in which parable the lambs receive a heritage on account of their service of Christ in the needy.[118]

## 6. *Polemos*

We now, finally, turn our attention to those passages in which the exposition reflects that of conflict or πόλεμος, where Christ is invoked as the Divine Warrior, the God of Battles.

Two texts from Origen bear witness to this tendency. In relation to Psalm 149.3, 'Let them praise his name with a dance; let them make music to him with drum and harp',[119] Origen associates the praise of God's name in a dance with 'crucifying the principalities and powers with Christ' (τῷ Χριστῷ συσταυροῦσθαι τὰς ἀρχὰς καὶ τὰς ἐξουσίας). With regard to Psalm 117.10, 'All nations surrounded me, and in the name of the Lord I fended them off',[120] he interprets this verse in the light of the opposition to Christ

115 PG 23, 1096B.

116 Ζωώσεις ἡμᾶς, καὶ τῷ ὀνόματί σου κληθησόμεθα: PG 23, 968B.

117 Ὅτι σὺ, ὁ Θεὸς, εἰσήκουσας τῶν εὐχῶν μου· ἔδωκα κληρονομίαν τοῖς φοβουμένοις τὸ ὄνομά σου: PG 80, 1325C.

118 Ταύτην τὴν κληρονομίαν τοῖς φοβουμένοις αὐτὸν δώσειν ὁ Δεσπότης ὑπέσχετο: ibid.

119 Αἰνεσάτωσαν τὸ ὄνομα ἐν χορῷ, κ.τ.ἑ...Ἐν τυμπάνῳ καί ψαλτηρίῳ ψαλάτωσαν αὐτῷ, κ.τ.ἑ.: PG 12, 1680C.

120 Πάντα τὰ ἔθνη ἐκύκλωσάν με, καὶ τῷ ὀνόματί Κυρίου ἠμυνάμην αὐτοὺς: PG 12, 1580D.

by 'all the nations'. By implication it is in his name, 'by the wisdom of God' (τῇ σοφίᾳ τοῦ Θεοῦ), that the holy man rejects many kinds of teachings.

Here we find another incidence where the Targum replaces the phrase 'the name of the Lord' with 'the name of *the Memra of* the Lord', for its version of the texts reads: 'All the peoples have surrounded me; in the name of *the Memra of* the Lord *I trust that* I shall uproot them'.[121] Here again, where the Targum introduces the *Memra* the patristic exegete introduces the divine Word.

Theodoret follows Origen's lead in his exposition of Psalm 117.12,[122] where he makes it clear, with recourse to his Christological title 'Master' (Δεσπότης), that it is in the name of Christ that the psalmist emerges victorious over the foes.[123] In two passages Eusebius sets his Christianizing of the divine name against the background of spiritual warfare. He comments on the text of Psalm 101.16, 'The nations will fear the name of the Lord, and all the kings of the earth your glory'.[124] Reflecting on the verse in the light of present-day opposition to the Church, Eusebius laments, 'Neither the nation, nor the kingdom does obeisance to the glory of Christ (ἡ μὴ προσκυνοῦσα τὴν δόξαν Χριστοῦ), in whole or in part', thus identifying Christ as the addressee of the text, and, consequently, the name of Christ with τὸ ὄνομά σου.

He makes a similar identification with regard to Psalm 73.10–11: 'How long, O Lord, will the enemy rebuke, the opponent utterly provoke your name? Why do you turn away your hand, and your right hand from within your bosom completely?'[125]

In a consideration of the divine response to enemy attacks, Eusebius moves easily from references to the divine name, and to the right hand,

121 Stec, *Targum Psalms*, 209; see also verses 11 and 12.

122 Καὶ τῷ ὀνόματι Κυρίου ἠμυνάμην αὐτούς: PG 80, 1813A.

123 τὸν γὰρ ἐμὸν Δεσπότην πᾶσιν ἐκείνοις ἀντέταξα, καὶ δι' αὐτοῦ τὴν νίκην ἐκομισάμην: ibid.

124 Καὶ φοβηθήσονται τὰ ἔθνη τὸ ὄνομά σου, Κύριε, καὶ πάντες οἱ βασιλεῖς τὴν δόξαν σου: PG 23, 1260A.

125 Ἕως πότε, ὁ Θεὸς, ὀνειδίζει ὁ ἐχθρὸς. παροξύνει ὑπεναντίος τὸ ὄνομά σου εἰς τέλος...: PG 23, 860B.

and the bosom of God to a Christological reflection on John 1.18, noting in passing that the bosom of God is full of good things (ὁ κόλπος τοῦ Θεοῦ ἀγαθῶν ἐστι πλήρης), that is, the Only-begotten Son.[126]

It is of some interest to note, *en passant*, that the Targum version of Psalm 73.7 reads: 'They have set on fire *the house of* your sanctuary; to the ground they have desecrated the dwelling place *in which your name is invoked*',[127] a text which appears to attempt to put some distance between the act of sacrilege and the transcendence of divinity. It may be that the Christological interpretation of this passage is a patristic attempt to step into that particular void.

Finally, Didymus also understands that the divine name in Psalm 73 refers to that of Christ, this time with regard to verses 18–21: 'Remember this your creation, the enemy reproached the Lord, and a foolish people provoked your name... Let him not be turned away humbled and in shame; the poor and needy will praise your name'.[128]

He makes a direct link between the provocation of the divine name in the psalm-verse, and the provocation of Christ's name by Caiaphas and the Jewish people as they demanded his crucifixion.[129]

## II. Summary

The study of the works in question has revealed a readiness on the part of the patristic authors to link the divine ὄνομα of the Septuagint Psalter with that of Christ, either by direct equation or by strong association. In the

126 PG 23, 860C.

127 Stec, *Targum Psalms*, 145.

128 μνήσθητι ταύτης τῆς κτίσεώς σου. ἐχθρὸς ὠνείδισεν τὸν κύριον, καὶ λαὸς ἄφρων παρώξυνεν τὸ ὄνομα αὐτοῦ ... μὴ ἀποστραφήτω τεταπεινωμένος καὶ κατῃσχυμμένος· πτωχὸς καὶ πένης αἰνέσουσιν τὸ ὄνομά σου.

129 παρώξυνε δὲ τὸ ὄνομα αὐτοῦ λαὸς ἄφρων ὁ τῶν Ἰουδαίων.: *In Ps. caten.* 73. 18–21, Mühlenberg 2, 777a, 111.

course of this extensive linkage a significant number of New Testament texts have been employed by the Fathers to identify the person of Christ with the divine ὄνομα. Of these, by far the most prominent has been Philippians 2.9–11, a passage in which the above themes have coalesced, and a text which almost on its own has given the patristic authors both the permission and the authority to equate so easily the 'name of the Lord' in the Psalter with the name of the Son of God.

It is worth noting that while the Pauline text itself would appear to identify the divine ὄνομα with Κύριος, the working assumption of the patristic authorities, and indeed of later hymn-writers, appears to interpret the Philippian passage as referring to Ἰησοῦς or Χριστός. Either way, the readiness with which the Fathers associated the divine ὄνομα of the Psalter with the Second Person of the Trinity is clearly derived from Pauline theology.

At the same time, the background of Rabbinic Judaism has thrown up some very interesting information with regard to the Targum's propensity to enhance the element of divine transcendence within those same texts in which the patristic scholars detect the presence of the Word of God.

From what we have seen, it would appear that, with regard to the Targum psalms, there is in play a dialectic concerning God's presence among his people, a drive to establish both divine distance and divine presence at the same time. For Rabbinic Judaism, God is present in a transcendent sense, in a way in which he cannot be captured or circumscribed. This is a willed presence, as his *Shekinah* is seen to depart from his people when they choose to abandon his laws.

Where the Targum attempts to create space between the transcendent divinity and his fallible creatures, there the Fathers, over and over again, resolve to place Christ, the incarnate Word. The Fathers are clearly intent on holding onto the transcendent element within the divine ὄνομα, in so far as they consistently point to Jesus Christ as the name which is glorified and honoured in the psalmody, and, as we have seen, δόξα is a powerful theme in those name-texts which they choose to interpret Christologically.

However, their preference for interpreting the ὄνομα of Philippians 2.9–11 as Ἰησοῦς or Χριστός, rather than as Κύριος, suggests a different kind of motivation and interest from that of the Targum. It is surely no coincidence that their favoured New Testament passage for linking the divine ὄνομα of the Septuagint Psalter with the person of Christ begins not with a statement of divine transcendence and apartness but with the affirmation of divine humility and humiliation, of divine condescension, and incarnation.

To this extent it could be argued that, in sharp contrast to contemporary Rabbinic Judaism, the Fathers give a greater priority to the soteriological motivation and interest than to the doxological. The main thrust of the various patristic exegeses is to proclaim the saving work of the divine ὄνομα, that is, Christ, who is 'born in human likeness', rather than to safeguard the sanctity of God. In contrast to contemporary Judaism, the effect of their approach to the divine name in the Psalter is consistently to prioritize the nearness of God, placing the Word made flesh into the gap between divinity and humanity. This opens up the possibility that the Fathers are deliberately attempting to make a radical distinction between the Christian and Jewish understandings of God in these passages.

Moving on from the witness of Rabbinic Judaism, another important matter which has been raised in this study concerns the relationship of the divine name to the persons within the Godhead. Hilarion Alfeyev makes this comment with regard to the psalm-commentary of John Chrysostom:

> The text (Com Col 9.2) shows that Chrysostom thinks that the name of the Son is equal in power to the name of the Father, and the invocation of the name of all the persons of the Trinity is equal to one of them. This is provided that, and this is important, the name of God 'is pronounced with faith'. Elsewhere, explaining that the Trinity is glorified in Christ, Chrysostom makes this clear: 'To that the prophet has added in agreement, "Bless his name", which you say of the Father, of the Son, or of the Spirit, the name of the Trinity is God' (Com Ps 95.1, PG 55, 772).[130]

There is surely some linkage here with those texts which were explored under the rather loose description of 'Christological'. Again, it is worth asking the question as to whether Cyril's use of ὁμοούσιος to explain the

130 Hilarion Alfeyev, *Le Nom grand et glorieux. La vénération du Nom de Dieu et la prière de Jésus dans la tradition orthodoxe*. Traduction du russe par Claire Jounievy, Hieromoine Alexandre [Siniakov] et Dom André Louf (Paris: Les Éditions du Cerf, 2007), 86.

meaning of Psalm 98.3, his and Athanasius's focus on the unity of Father and Son in their commentary on Psalm 88.25, Origen and Theodoret's apparent equation of the title of those same persons in their exposition of Psalm 117.26, Didymus's resort to the Trinity in his exegesis of Psalm 82.19 and his identification of Jesus as the bearer of the divine name in his understanding of Psalm 137.2 are suggesting, with Chrysostom, that within the Godhead there is a unity of name (ὄνομα) which corresponds to a unity of substance (οὐσία).

Whatever the answer to questions such as this, the chapter certainly shines a useful light on how the early Eastern monastics were being led by contemporary patristic authorities to understand the meaning of the psalm-verses which they were chanting. Again and again, those authorities were encouraging the cantors to believe that, in their constant eulogizing of the name of the Lord, they were in fact singing the praises of Jesus Christ himself.

CHAPTER EIGHT

# The Invocation of Christ as *Prosōpon*

In response to Psalm 79.8, 'Bring us back, O God of hosts, show your face, and we shall be saved',[1] Origen comments, quoting Colossians 1.15: 'Here he has called Christ "face" (Πρόσωπον ἐνταῦθα τὸν Χριστὸν ὠνόμασεν), "For he is the image of the invisible God, the first-born of all creation"'. The purpose of this chapter is to explore texts such as this, to be found in the psalm-commentaries featured in this study, where the word πρόσωπον, as it appears with relation to God in the psalm-verses of the Septuagint, is interpreted Christologically.

In all, there are sixty-eight psalm-verses in the Septuagint Psalter in which the word πρόσωπον is used in relation to God. Within the commentaries under consideration, fifty-four texts have been located in which the exegete clearly identifies the πρόσωπον of God with the person of Jesus Christ, and these are to be found in twenty-five different psalms. Of these, Psalm 118 is the most prolific for this purpose, in accounting for five texts, while Psalm 79 accounts for seven and Psalm 67 for four. Three texts are provided by each of Psalms 16, 23 and 30, while Psalms 17, 20, 41, 43, 44, 94, 96 and 104 each supply two. Finally, a single text is contributed by each of Psalms 9, 15, 33, 45, 67, 88, 89, 138, 139 and 142.

Before proceeding to an investigation of the relevant texts, it is necessary to acknowledge the invaluable contribution which has been made to this subject by Rondeau in her second volume of *Les Commentaires Patristiques du Psautier*. Whilst the primary focus of that work is firmly on the prosopological exegesis employed by the various writers, Rondeau, nevertheless, has some useful things to say about how the particular authors understood the word πρόσωπον itself, in relation to the person of Christ.

1 Καὶ ἐπίφανον τὸ πρόσωπον σου, καὶ σωθησόμεθα: PG 12, 1544B.

In general, Rondeau is at pains to protect the fourth-century exegetes from the reprimand of a fifth-century Chalcedonian orthodoxy, insisting that they were using the word in a far less clearly defined way than that which prevailed by the year 451.

For Origen, she says, the word πρόσωπον has only modest instrumental value.[2] She continues: 'In contrast to what happens in Trinitarian theology, where the word *persona* serves to distinguish three persons in God, the word *prosopon/persona* serves here to mark the relationship which exists between God and Man'.[3] And she concludes, 'The word has no precise theological affectation'.[4]

She acknowledges that in Eusebius the use of the word πρόσωπον may appear to be in contravention to the Christology of Chalcedon. However, she notes that Eusebius uses it to distinguish characters in a scene, and that each character does not necessarily possess a 'personal consistency'.[5] Overall, she claims that πρόσωπον appears to have a fluid sense in Eusebian exegesis, sometimes commanding a strong sense, and sometimes a much weaker one.[6] With regard to Athanasius, her main interest in πρόσωπον seems to be to show that the writer uses it both in relation to Christ as a person of the Trinity, and also in relation to Christ as at one with all humanity, speaking for us.[7]

Finally, she finds herself questioning Adolphe Gesché's conclusion, following his analysis of Didymus' exegesis of Psalms 30.17, 30.21, 33.1 and 39.2 in the Tura commentary.[8] Here Gesché argues that Didymus' use of πρόσωπον in a Christological context is at variance with Chalcedon, in so far as, for Didymus, πρόσωπον refers to a manifestation or appearance of Christ rather than to the interiority of his being. Against this, Rondeau

2 Rondeau, *Commentaires Patristiques du Psautier, Vol. II*, 126.

3 Ibid., 132.

4 Ibid., 135.

5 Ibid., 173.

6 Ibid., 172–6.

7 Ibid., 199–206.

8 Adolphe Gesché, *La christologie du Commentaire sur les Psaumes découvert à Toura* (Gembloux: Éditions J. Duculot, 1962), 314–18.

insists that the intensive use of the prosopological formula by Didymus suggests a stronger, more substantial conception of the word on his part.[9]

We now turn our attention to the themes underlying those usages in the exegeses in question. These can be conveniently grouped under five headings, consisting of light (φῶς), salvation (σωτηρία), righteousness (δικαιοσύνη), joy (χαρά) and seeking or longing (ζητέω), though, again, there will be some inevitable overlapping of the categories.

## I. Themes

### *1. Phōs*

In eleven of the fifty-four psalm-texts it is the light generated by the πρόσωπον which leads the exegete, directly or indirectly, to identify the face, the countenance, the manifestation or the presence of God with the person of Christ. In Psalm 4.7, 'Many are saying, "Who will show us good things? The light of your face was made to shine upon us, O Lord!"', Athanasius, Didymus and Cyril all interpret the verse Christologically.

Athanasius sees in τὸ φῶς τοῦ προσώπου σου a reference to Christ, for 'Christ is the light of the world'.[10] Didymus, who provides us with the lion's share of these psalm-texts, identifies the light of the face of God with Christ through allusions to Hebrews 1.3 and Colossians 1.15,[11] where he states explicitly, 'And this is the only-begotten Son of God'.[12] Meanwhile, Cyril associates the face of God with the Son and the light of the face with the Spirit.[13]

9 Rondeau, *Commentaires Patristiques du Psautier, Vol. II*, 230.

10 Τὸ φῶς τοῦ κόσμου ὁ Χριστός ἐστι: PG 27, 73A.

11 Δυνατὸν Φῶς τοῦ θεοῦ τὸν χαρακτῆρα τῆς ὑποστάσεως καὶ εἰκόνα αὐτοῦ τοῦ ἀοράτου θεοῦ εἰπεῖν: *In Ps. caten.* 4.7b, Mühlenberg 1, 21, 129.

12 οὗτος δὲ ὁ μονογενής ἐστι τοῦ θεοῦ υἱός: ibid.

13 πρόσωπον μὲν τοῦ Θεοῦ καὶ Πατρὸς ὁ Υἱὸς, φῶς δὲ τὸ ἐξ αὐτοῦ πεμπόμενον Πνεῦμα εἰς ἡμᾶς: PG 69, 740B.

To Origen, Didymus, Cyril and Theodoret, 'May God have compassion on us and bless us, and display his face to us' (ἐπιφάναι τὸ πρόσωπον αὐτοῦ ἐφ' ἡμᾶς) in Psalm 66.2 speaks of the light of Jesus.

To Origen, this prayer to God to be merciful to us and to bless us is seen in the context of a divine hymn (Θείος ... ὁ ὕμνος) where the Saviour manifests his acts and great contemplation (καὶ θεωρίαν αὐτῶν μεγίστην). The psalm prophesies the Epiphany of the Word of God (Προκηρύττει τοῦ Θεοῦ Λόγου την ἐπιφάνειαν...) and the salvation of all nations.[14]

Didymus, here and in several other passages, uses an allusion to Hebrews 1.3 to identify τὸ πρόσωπον αὐτοῦ with the person of Christ.[15] For Cyril, commenting on this prayer to God to have compassion upon us and for his face to shine upon us, this face is the Son.[16] And Theodoret introduces a Marian element, asserting that the prayer for God's compassion and blessing is made to 'God the Word in person, immutably born of the Virgin': '...the psalmist says, *may his face shine upon us*. We saw him face to face, of course (Εἴδομεν γὰρ αὐτὸν πρόσωπον πρὸς πρόσωπον), but once made man; we saw him presenting no other form but God the Word in person immutably born of the Virgin' (αὐτὸν Θεὸν Λόγον ἀτρέπτως ἐκ Παρθένου γενόμενον εἴδομεν).[17]

For Eusebius, it is Christ who does the lighting up in the text of Psalm 89.8, 'You set our lawless deeds before you; our lifetime became lit up by your countenance'.[18] Commenting on this verse, he makes a link between the divine countenance of the psalm-verse and the coming of the Saviour, by way of Isaiah 59.5: 'These things the prophet declared, sending forth the word upon the constitution of the people after the coming of our Saviour'.[19]

14 PG 12, 1504B.

15 ἐπιφαίνεται δὲ τὸ πρόσωπον τοῦ πάντων δημιουργοῦ, ὅταν ἐπιδημήσῃ ὁ χαρακτὴρ τῆς ὑποστάσεως αὐτοῦ ἄνθρωπος...: *In Ps. caten.* 66.2, Mühlenberg 2, 676a, 61.

16 τουτέστι τὸν Υἱόν: PG 69, 1140C.

17 PG 80, 1372C; Hill, Fathers of the Church 101, 377.

18 Ἔθου τὰς ἀνομίας ἡμῶν ἐναντίον σου· ὁ αἰὼν ἡμῶν εἰς φωτισμὸν τοῦ προσώπου σου: PG 23, 1136C.

19 ...μετὰ τὴν παρουσίαν τοῦ Σωτῆρος ἡμῶν: PG 23, 1137A.

Again, the same author, in the company of Athanasius and Didymus, sees the face of Christ in the text of Psalm 118.135, 'Make your face shine upon your slave'.[20] This Eusebius does with reference to the Second Coming of the Saviour (Τὴν δευτέραν τοῦ Σωτῆρος), and with help from John 14.9. For his part, Athanasius comments on this verse: 'He eagerly desires to see the coming of the Lord',[21] thus appearing to identify Τὸ πρόσωπόν σου with the person of Christ. And Didymus, like Eusebius, makes use of John 14.9 in order to link the divine face with the person of Christ.[22]

## 2. *Sōtēria*

Closely associated with the theme of light, salvation and other expressions of divine assistance account for some sixteen of the psalm-texts. In six of these the light *motif* is especially evident.

Thus Didymus sees Christ as the πρόσωπον of God in Psalm 30.17, 'Let your face shine upon your slave; save me in your steadfast love'.[23] In his commentary, with the help of Hebrews 1.3, Colossians 1.15 and Philippians 2.7, he attributes the following paraphrase of this verse to Christ:

> I am your face, the imprint of your substance (ὁ χαρακτὴρ τῆς ὑποστάσεως σου), your image of you, the invisible God (ἡ εἰκών σου τοῦ θεοῦ τοῦ ἀοράτου). Since I have taken the form of a servant, make your face look upon your servant. Show that your servant has this form, that the face has lived in this servant, so that 'deliver me' may be said according to the perspective of the servant (κατ'ἐπίνοιαν τοῦ δοῦλου), and the word 'face' according to the perspective of the truth (κατ'ἐπίνοιαν τῆς ἀληθείας) of the imprint of the divine substance (τοῦ χαρακτῆρος τῆς θεικῆς ὑποστάσεως).[24]

20 Τὸ πρόσωπόν σου ἐπίφανον ἐπὶ τὸν δοῦλοόν σου: PG 23, 1388C.

21 Τὴν παρουσίαν ἐπιποθεῖ τοῦ Κυρίου Θεσάσθαι: PG 27, 501D.

22 Τὸ πρόσωπον σου ἐπίφανον, ὅπερ ἰδών τις σὲ ὁρᾷ. αὐτὸς γὰρ περὶ ἑαυτοῦ λέγει Ὁ ἑωρακὼς ἐμὲ ἑώρακε τὸν πατέρα: *In Ps. caten.* 118.135, Mühlenberg 2, 1131, 292.

23 ἐπίφανον τὸ πρόσωπόν σου ἐπὶ τὸν δοῦλόν σου, σῶσόν με ἐν τῷ ἐλέει σου: *In Ps. Tura* 30.17, T 149, 14, Gronewald 3, 102.

24 *In Ps. Tura* 30.17, T 149, 15–18, Gronewald 3, 102; based on the translation of Rondeau, *Commentaires Patristiques du Psautier, Vol. II*, 236.

Here Christ, as the speaker of the psalm-verse identifies himself as the 'face of God', though as one who addresses God from two different perspectives. Incidentally, in her consideration of Didymus's treatment of this and the following verse, Rondeau rejects Gesché's claim that Christ speaks from two different *personae*.[25]

In Psalm 43.4, both Didymus and Cyril read the 'illumination of your countenance' (ὁ φωτισμὸς τοῦ προσώπου σου), as a reference to Jesus. Didymus associates τοῦ προσώπου σου with the 'only-begotten Son'.[26] He also explicitly identifies 'your right hand, your arm, and the light of your countenance' with the Saviour.[27] Cyril, on the other hand names the Son of the Father as the πρόσωπον τοῦ Θεοῦ, on the basis that he is the 'unchangeable image' of God.[28]

With regard to Psalm 79.4 and verse 8, Origen, Cyril and Theodoret all see an opportunity for Christological reflection. In verse 8 with regard to 'Bring us back, O God of Hosts, show us your face and we shall be saved',[29] Origen comments, quoting Colossians 1.15, 'Here he has called the face Christ, "For he is the image of the invisible God, the first-born of all creation"'.[30] Theodoret interprets the psalm's plea to the Lord to let his face shine upon his people in the light of the 'coming in the flesh', thus identifying τὸ πρόσωπόν σου with the incarnate Christ.[31] With regard to the exegesis of the similar text in verse 4, Cyril insists that this is a prayer for the epiphany of the Son, for they call Christ the face of our God and Father.[32]

In two texts the soteriological theme arises specifically against the background of a conflict with enemies. Thus is Psalm 9.4, Cyril interprets

25 Rondeau, *Commentaires Patristiques du Psautier, Vol. II*, 237; Gesché, *Christologie du Commentaire*, 270–274, 314–16.

26 τουτέστι τοῦ μονογενοῦς υἱοῦ: *In Ps. caten.* 43.3b-4, Mühlenberg 1, 439, 331.

27 καὶ ὁ βραχίων αὐτοῦ καΐ ἡ δεξιὰ καὶ ὁ φωτισμὸς τοῦ προσώπου αὐτοῦ ὁ σωτήρ ἐστιν: *In Ps. Tura* 43.4, T 310, 23, Gronewald 5, 116.

28 Πρόσωπον μὲν γὰρ τοῦ Θεοῦ καὶ Πατρός ἐστιν ὁ Υἱὸς, εἰκὼν ἀπαράλλακτος ὑπάρχων αὐτοῦ: PG 69, 1020A.

29 Καὶ ἐπίφανον τὸ πρόσωπόν σου, καὶ σωθησόμεθα: PG 12, 1544B.

30 Ibid.

31 ἐπιφάνειαν λέγων τὴν ἔνσαρκον παρουσίαν: PG 80, 1513B.

32 Πρόσωπον τοῦ Θεοῦ καί Πατρὸς ὀνομάζουσιν τὸν Υἱόν: PG 69, 1197C.

'When my enemy turns back, they shall grow weak and perish before you'[33] to mean that they will come to nothing in the presence of Christ. Again he claims that the Son is the πρόσωπον of the Father on the basis that he is the 'unchangeable image' of the Father.[34]

And Psalm 67.2, 'Let God arise and let his enemies be scattered; let those who hate him flee before him',[35] is taken by Theodoret to point to the rising of the Son of God. The inference is therefore that ἀπὸ προσώπου αὐτοῦ also refers to Christ.[36]

Elsewhere, in Psalm 30.23,[37] Didymus understands the words which prompt God's saving activity, 'I have been cast from your sight' as a reference to Christ. In his comment on this verse, Didymus implies an identification of Christ with the divine presence through an ecclesiological observation. He says, in the context of 1 Corinthians 12.27: 'As all those who come in faith are the body of Christ (σῶμα Χριστοῦ) and individually members of it, so the body of God is the full measure of the divine powers and rational beings'.[38]

For Didymus it would appear that the issue is the possibility of separation from the body of Christ, which he understands by the phrase 'from your sight' (ἀπὸ προσώπου τῶν ὀφθαλμῶν σου). The same author, in Psalm 45.6, also identifies the Saviour as the countenance of God in 'God shall help her with his countenance'.[39]

'I implored your face with all my heart' (Ἐδεήθην τοῦ προσώπου σου) of Psalm 118.58 is taken as a reference to Christ by Origen and Didymus. For Origen, the prayer is to God to have mercy on the psalmist, who has

33 Ἀσθενήσουσι καὶ ἀπολοῦνται ἀπὸ προσώπου σου: PG 69, 764B.

34 πρόσωπον τοῦ Θεοῦ καὶ Πατρὸς ὁ Υἱὸς, ὅς ἐστιν εἰκὼν αὐτοῦ ἀπαράλλακτος: ibid.

35 Ἀναστήτω ὁ Θεὸς, καὶ διασκορπισθήτωσαν οἱ ἐχθροὶ αὐτοῦ· καὶ φυγέτωσαν ἀπὸ προσώπου αὐτοῦ οἱ μισοῦντες αὐτόν: PG 80, 1376A.

36 ἀλλὰ καὶ τὸ ἀναστῆναι τὸν Σωτῆρα τοῦ κόσμου διὰ τριῶν ἡμερῶν: PG 80, 1376B.

37 ἐγὼ δὲ εἶπα ἐν τῇ ἐκστάσει μου Ἀπέριμμαι ἀπὸ προσώπου τῶν ὀφθαλμῶν σου: *In Ps. Tura* 30.23, T 154, 21, Gronewald 3, 128.

38 *In Ps. Tura* 30.23, T 154, 31–2, Gronewald 3, 130.

39 βοηθήσει αὐτῇ ὁ θεὸς τῷ προσώπῳ: Brenton, *Septuagint with Apocrypha*, 725; *In Ps. caten.* 45.6b, Mühlenberg 1, 477, 346.

sought his face with his whole heart. This is linked to Matthew 5.8 and contains a loose association between Christ and the face and mercy of God.[40] Didymus immediately associates *τοῦ προσώπου σου* in the psalm-verse, inevitably, with Hebrews 1.3,[41] and concludes the passage with Jesus' words from the same Matthean text.[42]

And finally, with regard to Psalm 142.7, 'Listen to me quickly, O Lord; my spirit failed; do not turn your face from me, or I shall be like those who go down to the pit',[43] Eusebius associates this prayer with David's prayer to Christ, thus identifying the face of God with Christ.[44]

### *3. Dikaiosynē*

In nine of the texts the psalm-verse which gives rise to an identification of the πρόσωπον of God with Christ focuses on the *motif* of righteousness. In these texts the πρόσωπον is presented as the location of such divine characteristics as righteousness, or justice, and the power and authority to render judgment.

Thus in Psalm 16.2, 'From you may my vindication come; let my eyes see the right',[45] Athanasius identifies Christ, the Only-begotten, as the one who vindicates, in his commentary on the psalm-verse.[46]

Similarly, in Psalm 16.15, Didymus and Theodoret understand the face, referred to in 'I shall appear before your face in righteousness',[47] as the Son. On the words 'in righteousness I shall appear in your sight', Theodoret

40 PG 12, 1600B.

41 Πρόσωπον θεοῦ ὁ χαρακτὴρ τῆς ὑποστάσεως αὐτοῦ: *In Ps. caten.* 118.58, Mühlenberg 2, 1101, 282.

42 *In Ps. caten.* 118.58, Mühlenberg 2, 1101, 283.

43 Ταχὺ εἰσάκουσόν μου, κ.τ.λ. Μὴ ἀποστρέψῃς τὸ πρόσωπόν σου ἀπ'ἐμοῦ: PG 24, 49B.

44 προσήκει ὁμοίως τῷ Δαυῒδ λέγειν εὐχομένους τὰ Χριστοῦ, Εἰσάκουσόν μου: Κύριε, PG 24, 49C.

45 Ἐκ προσώπου σου τὸ κρῖμά μου ἐξέλθοι: PG 27, 105D.

46 Σαφῶς εὔχεται τὸν Μονογενῆ κριτὴν ἑαυτῷ καταστῆναι: ibid.

47 Ἐγὼ δὲ ἐν δικαιοσύνῃ ὀφθήσομαι τῷ προσώπῳ σου.

comments, 'that is, to your Son'.[48] Didymus understands this verse with reference to the 'face to face' (Πρόσωπον πρὸς πρόσωπον) of 1 Corinthians 13.12, and he links the 'glory of God' with the 'only–begotten Son'.[49]

For both Athanasius and Cyril the 'fire flamed before him' (πῦρ ἀπο προσώπου αὐτοῦ) in Psalm 17.9 is interpreted in the context of the judgment given by the Son of God. Athanasius understands πῦρ ἀπο προσώπου αὐτοῦ in the light of the Son of God's battle against his enemies.[50] Cyril identifies the source of the fire in the psalm-verse with the person of Christ.[51]

Eusebius reads 'at the rebuke of your countenance they will perish' (ἀπὸ ἐπιτιμήσεως τοῦ προσώπου σου ἀπολοῦνται) in Psalm 79.17 in the light of the coming judgment of the Saviour. Here he makes an apparent link between the 'divine manifestation of the Saviour' (τὴν τοῦ Σωτῆρος θεοφάνειαν) and 'they will perish at the rebuke of your countenance' (ἀπὸ ἐπιτιμήσεως τοῦ προσώπου σου ἀπολοῦνται).[52]

For Didymus Psalm 88.15, 'Righteousness and judgment are the foundation of your throne, steadfast love and truth will go before your face',[53] lead him to connect the addressee of the psalm-verse with the Son. With another allusion to Hebrews 1.3, Didymus interprets 'mercy and truth shall go before your face' as a reference to Christ.[54]

And finally, the judgment of Christ is for Eusebius and Cyril the key to understanding the meaning of πρόσωπον in Psalm 96.5: 'The mountains melted like wax before the Lord (ἀπὸ προσώπου Κυρίου), before the

48 τῷ Παιδί σου: PG 80, 972B.

49 δυνατὸν ὀφθησομένην θεοῦ δόξαν ἐκλαβεῖν τὸν μονογενῆ υἱὸν περὶ οὗ γέγραπται, *In Ps. caten.* 16.15, Mühlenberg 1, 109, 187.

50 Ταῦτα γὰρ Ὁ τοῦ Θεοῦ Υἱὸς ἐνεργεῖ ἀφανῶς κατὰ τῶν ἀντικειμένων δυνάμεων τὸ πῦρ αὐτῶν σβεννὺς ἑτέρῳ πυρὶ κρείττονι καὶ δυνατωτέρῳ: PG 27, 109D.

51 ἠκολούθησε δὲ καὶ πῦρ, ἡ παντελὴς πάντως τοῦ πολεμίου φθορὰ γενομένη ἀπὸ προσώπου τοῦ Θεοῦ, τουτέστιν ἀπὸ Χριστοῦ: PG 69, 821B.

52 PG 23, 965B.

53 δικαιοσύνη καὶ κρίμα ἑτοιμασία τοῦ θρόνου σου. ἔλεος καὶ ἀλήθεια προπορεύσεται πρὸ προσώπου σου.

54 Εἰ δὲ πρόσωπον τοῦ πατρὸς ὁ υἱὸς λέγοιτο τῷ χαρακτὴρ εἶναι τῆς ἑαυτοῦ ὑποστάσεως, προπορευθῆναι τούτου τοῦ προσώπου δεῖ ἐν τοῖς διὰ καθαρότητα τῆς καρδίας... *In Ps. caten.* 88.14–15, Mühlenberg 2, 887, 171.

Lord of all the earth'.[55] Eusebius links this psalm-verse with the eschatological upheavals accompanying the Second Coming of Christ,[56] while Cyril interprets the mountains melting like wax in the presence of God Christologically.[57]

## 4. *Chara*

Predictably, the spirit of worship in the psalmody leads the Fathers to offer Christological reflection on some of the psalm-verses which convey a mood of joy and gladness, and in six of their passages relating to this mood the word πρόσωπον is identified with the Saviour.

Psalm 15.11, 'You made known to me the ways of life; you will fill me with gladness along with your presence (μετὰ τοῦ προσώπου σου); in your right hand are delights, completely',[58] presents Didymus with the opportunity of referring to the image and imprint of God. He identifies μετὰ τοῦ προσώπου σου with Christ, through an allusion, once more, to Hebrews 1.3: 'The face of God, it is he who is his image, and the imprint of his substance'.[59]

Both Athanasius and Didymus link μετὰ τοῦ προσώπου σου in Psalm 20.7, 'You will give him blessing forever and ever; you will make him glad with the joy of your presence',[60] with the Son of the Father. Athanasius interprets μετὰ τοῦ προσώπου σου Christologically: 'The Son is the Πρόσωπον of the Father'.[61]

55 Τὰ ὄρη ὡσει κηρὸς ἐτάκησαν ἀπὸ προσώπου Κυρίου, ἀπὸ προσώπου Κυρίου πάσης τῆς γῆς: PG 23, 1228C; also PG69, 1249B.

56 διὰ τοῦ πυρὸς καὶ τῆς διατούσης ἀστραπῆς ἐν τῇ δευτέρᾳ Χριστοῦ παρουσίᾳ: PG 23, 1228D.

57 Ἄς κατέτηξεν ὁ Σωτὴρ ὡσεὶ κηρὸν: PG 69, 1249C.

58 ἐγνώρισάς μοι ὁδοὺς ζωῆς· πληρώσεις με εὐφροσύνης μετὰ τοῦ προσώπου σου· τερπνότητες ἐν τῇ δεξιᾷ σου εἰς τέλος.

59 θεοῦ δὲ πρόσωπον ἡ εἰκὼν αὐτοῦ καὶ ὁ χαρακτὴρ τῆς ὑποστάσεως αὐτοῦ: *In Ps. caten.* 15.11, Mühlenberg 1, 98, 181; see also *In Ps. Tura* 20.7, T 18, 14–26, Gronewald, 1, 70.

60 εὐφρανεῖς αὐτὸν ἐν χαρᾷ μετὰ τοῦ προσώπου σου.

61 Πρόσωπον τοῦ Πατρὸς ὁ Υἱός, PG 27, 129A.

Didymus picks up the ambiguity of this verse as noted by Origen in *Contra Celsum* 1.46, where the πρόσωπον of God is he who is rejoiced in and he who rejoices, and also presents the double function of the Word incarnate as the face of God and the face of man.[62] He goes on to identify μετὰ τοῦ προσώπου σου with Christ through a customary allusion to Colossians 1.15 and Hebrews 1.3: 'The face here, is the face of the Lord of whom the texts speaks: it is the Son, his image, the imprint of his substance'.[63]

In Psalm 94.2, both Eusebius and Athanasius make a direct connection between 'Let us anticipate his presence (τὸ πρόσωπον αὐτοῦ) with acknowledgement, and let us make a joyful noise to him with psalms',[64] and the Word or Son of God. Eusebius immediately makes a direct connection between the 'presence' (τὸ πρόσωπον) of God in the psalm-verse and the coming of the Word of God.[65] And Athanasius makes a direct connection between τὸ πρόσωπον αὐτοῦ and the Son of God.[66]

Finally, in Psalm 139.14, 'But the righteous shall acknowledge your name, and the upright shall live in your presence',[67] is construed by Didymus as a reference to Christ. Before concluding the exegesis of this verse with a quotation from 2 Corinthians 5.17, Didymus identifies the presence in which the upright shall live with Christ through yet another allusion to Hebrews 1.3.[68]

62 Rondeau, *Commentaires Patristiques du Psautier, Vol. II*, 233–4.

63 ἐστὶν δὲ ὁ υἱὸς ἡ εἰκὼν αὐτοῦ, ὁ χαρακτὴρ τῆς ὑποστάσεως αὐτοῦ: *In Ps. Tura* 20.7, T 18, 27–8, Gronewald 1, 70; see also *In Ps. caten.* 20.6–8a, Mühlenberg 1, 167, 219.

64 Προφθάσωμεν τὸ πρόσωπον αὐτοῦ ἐν ἐξομολογήει, καὶ ἐν ψαλμοῖς ἀλαλάξωμεν αὐτῷ: PG 23, 1209B.

65 Ἐπὶ μὲν τῆς πρώτης αὐτοῦ παρουσίας τὸ πρόσωπον αὐτοῦ το ἔνθεον ἀποκρύψας ὁ τοῦ Θεοῦ Λόγος: ibid.

66 τὸ πρόσωπον αὐτοῦ, ἔστι δὲ ὁ υἱὸς: PG 27, 413B.

67 πλὴν δίκαιοι ἐξομολογήσονται τῷ ὀνόματί σου, καὶ κατοικήσουσιν εὐθεῖς ἐν τῷ προσώπῳ σου.

68 πρόσωπον δὲ θεοῦ ἀποδέδεικται ὁ χαρακτὴρ τῆς ὑποστάσεως, αὐτοῦ κατοικοῦντος ἐν τούτῳ τῷ προσώπῳ παντὸς περὶ οὗ λέγεται Εἴ τις ἐν Χριστῷ, καινὴ κτίσις: *In Ps. caten.* 139.13–14, Mühlenberg 2, 1227, 334.

*5. Zēteō*

In nine texts the divine πρόσωπον appears as an object of seeking or longing, analogous to the erotic sense of the human yearning to behold the face of a loved one. Three of these feature as commentaries on Psalm 23.6, 'This is the company of people who seek him, who seek the face of the God of Jacob'.[69] Here 'the face of the God of Jacob' (τὸ πρόσωπον τοῦ Θεοῦ Ἰακώβ) is identified with the Saviour by Eusebius, Theodoret and Didymus.

With reference to τὸ πρόσωπον τοῦ Θεοῦ Ἰακώβ, Eusebius writes: 'Perhaps through question and answer they teach all men about the kingdom of our Lord Jesus Christ'.[70] Theodoret understands this verse as a prophecy fulfilled through the incarnation, when 'all land and sea' abandoned their ancestral gods and sought the face of the God of Jacob, that is, in Jesus Christ.[71]

Throughout his exegesis of this verse Didymus identifies τὸ πρόσωπον τοῦ Θεοῦ Ἰακώβ with the person of Christ. He refers to the 'resurrection of the Saviour'.[72] He identifies the 'King of glory' (ὁ βασιλεὺς τῆς δόξης) with the Saviour.[73] And he concludes the passage with a quotation from Acts 1.3.[74]

In Psalm 41.3, 'My soul thirsted for the living God; when shall I come and appear before the face of God?',[75] the face (τῷ προσώπῳ τοῦ Θεοῦ)

69 Αὕτη ἡ γενεὰ ζητούντων αὐτὸν, ζητούντων τὸ πρόσωπον τοῦ Θεοῦ Ἰακώβ: PG23, 221C; cf. PG 80, 1032B.

70 Ἴσως δὲ διὰ τῆς πεύσεως καὶ ἀποκρίσεως διδάσκουσι πάντας ἀνθρώπους τὴν δεσποτείαν τοῦ Κυρίου ἡμῶν Ἰησοῦ Χριστοῦ: PG 23, 221D.

71 Μετὰ γὰρ τὴν ἐνανθρώπησιν τοῦ Θεοῦ καὶ Σωτῆρος ἡμῶν, πᾶσα ἡ γῆ καὶ θάλασσα τῷ θείῳ πεισθεῖσα κηρύγματι, κατέλιπε μὲν τούς πατρῴους θεοὺς, τοῦ δὲ Ἰακὼβ ἐπιζητεῖ: PG 80, 1032C.

72 ἐλέγομεν δὲ τὴν ἀνάστασιν τοῦ σωτῆρος: *In Ps. Tura* 23.6, T 70, 25–6, Gronewald, 2, 60.

73 *In Ps. Tura* 23.6, T 71, 11, Gronewald, 2, 62.

74 θεώρει ὅτι καὶ διὰ τοῦ συναλίζεσθαι ζῶντα ἑαυτὸν μετὰ τὸ παθεῖν παρέστησεν: *In Ps. Tura* 23.6, T 72, 2–4, Gronewald, 2, 64.

75 Πότε ἥξω, καὶ ὀφθήσομαι τῷ προσώπῳ τοῦ Θεοῦ: PG 27, 201A.

before which the psalmist longs to appear is the Word of God, according to Athanasius. His immediate comment on this psalm-verse is, 'The Word is the face of God'.[76] Having made reference to the Πρόσωπον πρὸς πρόσωπον of 1 Corinthians 13.12, Didymus goes on to identify τῷ προσώπῳ τοῦ Θεοῦ with Christ, using his recurring allusion to Colossians 1.15.[77]

The text of Psalm 44.13, 'The daughters of Tyre will worship him with gifts, the rich of the people will entreat your face',[78] invites both Athanasius and Theodoret to equate the face to be entreated by the 'rich people' with Christ. Athanasius appears to associate Τὸ πρόσωπόν σου in this psalm-verse with the person of Christ when he adds the commentary, 'Worship the Church, that is its Lord'.[79] Theodoret resorts to Ephesians 1.22 to explain that as the head of the body, the Lord is the face of the Church, and thus identifies Τὸ πρόσωπόν σου with the person of Christ.[80]

And finally, with regard to Psalm 104.4, 'Seek the Lord and be strengthened; seek his presence continually',[81] both Eusebius and Didymus affirm that the presence of the Lord (τὸ πρόσωπον αὐτοῦ) which the psalmist exhorts his readers to seek continually is the Son of God. Eusebius is explicit that the divine presence (πρόσωπον) which the addressee is being exhorted to seek is that of the Son.[82] Didymus, for his part, once again makes use of the texts of Hebrews 1.3 and Colossians 1.15 to identify τὸ πρόσωπον αὐτοῦ with the person of Christ.[83]

76 Πρόσωπον τοῦ Θεοῦ ὁ Λόγος: ibid.

77 ὅπως τελείως ὀφθῇ τῷ προσώπῳ τοῦ θεοῦ οὐχ ἑτέρου τυγχάνοντος τῆς εἰκόνος τοῦ θεοῦ τοῦ ἀοράτου: *In Ps. caten.* 41.3, Mühlenberg 1, 424, 325.

78 Τὸ πρόσωπόν σου λιτανεύσουσιν οἱ πλούσιοι τοῦ λαοῦ: PG 27, 212D.

79 Προσκύνησον τὴν Ἐκκλησίαν, ἤτοι τὸν ἑαυτῆς Κύριον: ibid.

80 Πρόσωπον δὲ τῆς Ἐκκλησίας κυρίως μὲν αὐτὸς ὁ Δεσπότης: PG 80, 1196B.

81 Ζητήσατε τὸν Κύριον καὶ κραταιώθητε· ζητήσατε τὸ πρόσωπον αὐτοῦ διαπαντός: PG 23, 1301A.

82 Τὸ γὰρ τῆς οὐσίας πρόσωπον οὐδεὶς ὄψεται καὶ ζήσεται. Πρόσωπον δὲ αὐτοῦ καὶ ὁ Υἱός, PG 23, 1301C.

83 πρόσωπον δὲ θεοῦ ὁ χαρακτὴρ τῆς ὑποστάσεως ἐστι, τυγχάνων εἰκὼν τοῦ θεοῦ τοῦ ἀοράτοῦ: *In Ps. caten.* 104.4b, Mühlenberg 2, 1002, 241.

## *6. Miscellanea*

Three further texts complete this summary. To Didymus, the hiddenness of the divine πρόσωπον, which features in the text of Psalm 30.21, 'In the secret place of your face you will hide them from human disturbance; you will shelter them in a tent from contentious tongues',[84] speaks of the person of Jesus. Having noted that God has an apparent face in the creation and a hidden face in the Son, Didymus goes on to say, with reference to 2 Corinthians 5.16:

> Jesus has had two *prosopa*, of man and of God (δύο πρόσωπα εἶχεν Ἰησοῦς, ἀνθρώπου καὶ θεοῦ). All those who know him according to the flesh grasp him in the manifestation of the *prosopon* (ἐν τῇ φανερώσει τοῦ προσώπου). But all those who are being deterred from knowing him according to the flesh have arrived at knowing him as God the Word. On the other hand, since I said that the exterior representation of the world is the face (of God), the Word, through whom all things have been made, healed and are managed and governed, is the secret of the face of God.[85]

Here Didymus is able to speak freely about two faces or manifestations in Christ, the one human, the other divine. Again, there is some debate between Rondeau and Gesché as to the precise sense of πρόσωπον.[86] As with verse 17, it is remarkable that even when he designates Christ as the speaker of the psalm-verse, Didymus can nevertheless allow Christ to appropriate for himself the title of the face of God.

The same author is more interested in the theme of change in relation to the πρόσωπον of Christ, by which he understands David's change of face or appearance (ἠλλοίωσεν τὸ πρόσωπον αὐτοῦ) in Psalm 33.1, 'Pertaining to David, when he changed his face/appearance before Abimelech, and he let

84 κατακρύψεις αὐτοὺς ἐν ἀποκρύφῳ τοῦ προσώπου σου: *In Ps. Tura* 30.21, T 151, 9, Gronewald 3, 112.

85 *In Ps. Tura* 30.21, T 151, 23–7, Gronewald 3, 112–114; based on the translation of Rondeau, *Commentaires Patristiques du Psautier, Vol. II*, 230.

86 Rondeau, *Commentaires Patristiques du Psautier, Vol. II*, 230; Gesché, *Christologie*, 314–18.

him go, and he went away'.[87] With reference to John 1.14 and Philippians 2.7, Didymus interprets the alteration in David's face/appearance before the King of Gath in terms of the Christ's assumption of the form of a slave at his incarnation. He observes: 'When the Word becomes flesh and takes the form of a slave, he is altered as to his πρόσωπον, not according to a change (οὐ κατὰ μεταβολήν) … but according to an assumption' (ἀλλὰ κατὰ πρόσληψιν).[88] While the text clearly refers to the face/appearance of David, Didymus prefers to use it as an opportunity to describe Christ as the πρόσωπον of God.

Finally, again, it is Didymus who focuses on the theme of omnipresence when he refers to the divine face from which it to be impossible to flee (καὶ ἀπὸ τοῦ προσώπου σου ποῦ φύγω) in the text of Psalm 138.7, 'Where should I go from your spirit, or where should I flee from your face?'.[89] He identifies this face with the person of Christ, through a predictable allusion to Hebrews 1.3 and Colossians 1.15.[90]

## II. Summary

In terms of the themes covered by the relevant Septuagint psalm-texts, those of an epiphanic or salvific nature have been shown to constitute roughly half of the total, thus highlighting the predominance of revelatory or soteriological interests on the part of the chosen range of exegetes. As well as Didymus' recourse, almost *ad nauseam*, to Hebrews 1.3 and Colossians 1.15, two other texts lie behind much of the Christological reflection on the divine πρόσωπον in these texts.

87 Τῷ Δαυίδ, ὁπότε ἠλλοίωσεν τὸ πρόσωπον αὐτοῦ ἐναντίον Ἀβιμέλεχ, καὶ ἀπέλυσεν αὐτόν, καὶ ἀπῆλθεν: *In Ps. Tura* 33.1, T 184, 3, Gronewald 3, 198.

88 *In Ps. Tura* 33.1, T 185, 12–13, Gronewald 3, 204.

89 Ποῦ πορευθῶ ἀπὸ τοῦ πνεύματός σου; καὶ ἀπὸ τοῦ προσώπου σου ποῦ φύγω.

90 ὁ μονογενὴς αὐτοῦ υἱὸς εἰκὼν τυγχάνων αὐτοῦ ὄντος θεοῦ ἀοράτου, ἀλλὰ καὶ χαρακτὴρ τῆς ὑποστάσεως αὐτοῦ τοῦ θεοῦ εἰρημένος: *In Ps. caten.* 138.7–8, Mühlenberg 2, 1213, 325.

The words of Paul in 2 Corinthians 4.6, 'For it is the God who said, "Let light shine out of darkness", who has shone in our hearts to give the light of the knowledge of the glory of God in the face of Jesus Christ', and those of Jesus in John 14.9, 'Whoever has seen me has seen the Father', underpin much of the drive to identify the divine face of the psalm-verses with the Only-begotten Son of God.

It is clear, from all that has been said above, that these authors were encouraging their readers to read, pray or chant the relevant psalms on the understanding that in so doing they were consistently engaging with and invoking the presence of the Son of God. In one-sixth of the Psalter, the users of these commentaries were being taught that the recitation of words or phrases relating to the face, outward appearance, countenance or presence of God represented a living encounter with the Lord Jesus Christ, the Son of God, the Word of God, the Only-begotten.

For the monks of the Eastern monastic communities of the late fourth and early fifth centuries this daily recitation therefore led to the constant invocation of Christ, the πρόσωπον of God. Monastic psalmody at this time, given the weight of the authority which filled its intellectual tanks, provided its participants with a continual engagement with him whom both the Scriptures and the Greek Fathers were pleased to describe as the 'image of the invisible God' and the 'imprint of his very being'.

CHAPTER NINE

# The Invocation of Christ as Partner

In his paper, 'Inspiration of the Scriptures', Andrew Louth writes:

> Take, for example, the psalms: how are we to read them? As works by inspired, largely unknown poets, living at various moments in the history of Israel? As a collection of songs, composed (largely) by King David? As a hymn book of the Second Temple? As a psalter of the Christian Church? A doctrine of inspiration forces one to decide, generally to decide on the earliest moment of composition. But I would rather say: all of these, in this way making our use of the psalms something through which we join our prayer with Christ, or use these as ways of praying to Christ (the two predominant Christian ways of understanding the psalms), but also doing this in solidarity with the whole chosen people of God down the ages, all of whom have, in the Spirit, taken these hymns or poems on their lips.[1]

The purpose of this chapter is to examine how the Greek Fathers of the fourth and fifth centuries approached the first of these 'two predominant Christian ways of understanding the psalms'. Through a careful study of the relevant psalm-commentaries we will consider the exegeses which reveal both the extent to which and the manner in which the Fathers understood certain psalm-verses to be the *vox Christi* and therefore, in effect, to be invitations to the Christian individuals and communities to join their prayer to that of Christ in their recitation of the Psalter.

In this understanding of the relevant psalm-verses Christ is effectively invoked as a partner in prayer. The individuals or communities, in reciting these texts, make his words their own. They are encouraged by the Fathers to see themselves in partnership with Christ in his prayers for

1 Andrew Louth, 'Inspiration of the Scriptures'. A paper given at the first colloquy of the Orthodox Theological Research Forum at Cuddesdon in August, 2003, and published in *Sobornost* 31:1 (Oxford: Fellowship of St Alban and St Sergius, 2009), 42.

salvation, mercy, deliverance, rescue, help, vindication and so on, and thus to acknowledge their solidarity with him and his solidarity with them in these supplications. The particular prayers under investigation are those which may be described as short invocatory prayers for divine assistance, and which include such phrases as ῥῦσαί με, ἐλέησόν με, σῶσόν με, βοήθησόν μοι and their equivalents, such as Θαυμάστωσον τὰ ἐλέη σου and εἰς τὴν βοήθειάν μου πρόσχες. There are indeed over one hundred of these prayers to be found in the Septuagint Psalter, some of which are understood to be invocations offered to the Father by Christ himself, and others of which are deemed to be addressed by the psalmist to the person of Christ. The present chapter will focus on the former group.

The analysis provided by this chapter relies heavily on the second volume of Rondeau's work on the patristic psalm-commentaries. In this work Rondeau identifies a number of commentaries as those in which the regular recurrence of the phrase ἐκ προσώπου Χριστοῦ (from the person of Christ), and its equivalents, reveals a readiness on the part of the exegete to regard Christ as the sole or main speaker of the psalm or part of the psalm. These commentaries, again, consist of those referred to in Chapter 6. They also include Diadore of Tarsus' *Interpretationes in psalmos* and Theodore of Mopsuestia's *Commentarius in psalmos*.

An initial survey of the commentaries of Diadore of Tarsus and Theodore of Mopsuestia, both of which feature significantly in the second volume of *Les Commentaires Patristiques du Psautier*, failed to uncover any short invocatory prayers attributed to Christ by the respective Fathers, and therefore have no part to play in this particular study. However, there is some relevant material in the jumble of texts attributed to Cyril of Alexandria under the title of *Expositio in psalmos* in Volume LXIX, 717–1274, of Migne's *Patrologiae*, which has been included in the present analysis, though excluded from Rondeau's catalogue. Let us now give summarize the data on which this chapter is based.

The practice of New Testament writers to attribute certain psalm-verses to the person of Christ provides the Fathers with a core of psalms which they interpret as having been spoken by the psalmist *ex persona Christi*. To this core they are accustomed to add others in which they claim to discern Christ's voice.

Thus for Origen, the psalms which are explicitly or implicitly imputed to Christ in the New Testament are Psalms 2.7–8, 15, 21, 68, 87 and 108. This scholar, as a result of his own exegesis of the Psalter, however, chooses to expand this list to include Psalms 3, 4, 17, 26 and 29.[2] Furthermore, as may be seen from the core list above, sometimes the author interprets the whole psalm as having been spoken ἐκ προσώπου Χριστοῦ, while at other times he is content to attribute merely a part of the psalm, or even just one psalm-verse, to Christ.

Where the psalm is considered to be μονοπροσώπος, that is, where Christ is deemed to be the one who pronounces the whole psalm, it follows that any short invocatory prayers in the psalm are, by definition, understood by the exegete to be offered by the Son of God. However, where the exegete chooses not to comment on those particular psalm-verses they have not been numbered, as a general rule, among the list of texts in this study.

For example, Eusebius does not comment on Psalm 40.5 and 11 specifically, but he understands the psalm to be spoken by Christ through the mouthpiece of David.[3] Therefore for him both these prayers are invocations by Christ, but they form no part of the current inventory.

Again, some psalms are interpreted to be μονοπροσώπος but contain no short introductory prayer for divine assistance. With regard to Origen's core list, both Psalms 15 and 87 fall within this category. This being the case, although Christ is identified as the sole addressor of the psalm, neither one of them features in this study.

In the psalm-commentaries in question some fifty-eight texts, commented on by the exegetes, may accurately be described to be interpreting the relevant psalm-verse as a prayer for help made by Christ to the Father. While it is true that in at least four of these texts there is some pronounced ambiguity, deliberate or otherwise, concerning the identification of the speaker as Christ, in the remaining texts the *ex persona Christi* nature of the exegeses is beyond reasonable doubt. This total serves to emphasize the significance attached by the Greek Fathers of the fourth and fifth centuries

2 Rondeau, *Commentaires Patristiques du Psautier, Vol. II*, 101–2.

3 See PG 23, 361A, and especially the reference to John 13.16.

to the Christological character of the short invocatory prayers to be found in the Septuagint Psalter.

Altogether there are twenty psalms which furnish us with the data for this investigation into these fifty-eight texts. Nine texts are drawn from Psalms 108 and 68, together contributing almost one-third of the total, while seven come from each one of Psalms 40 and 21. Three texts each are taken from Psalms 17, 69 and 70, while Psalms 16, 24, 34 and 55, each supply us with two. Finally, Psalms 3, 4, 9, 15, 30, 42, 56, 58 and 85 contribute just one text each to the present investigation.

It will come as no surprise to learn that every single one of the twenty psalms in question, in its title in the Septuagint, is attributed to David. It is this King of Israel who is seen to act consistently as the mouthpiece of the Son in the psalm-prayers which elicit the aid of the God of Israel.

An interesting variety of imperatives or their equivalents are interpreted by the scholars as the words and phrases used by the Son of God in the fifty-eight psalm-texts to advance his petitions to his Father. Of these, ῥῦσαι is the most popular, and is to be found in nineteen, or about one-third, of the psalm-texts. The two other most frequently used are ἐλέησον, which features in seventeen psalm-prayers, and σῶσον, which occurs in thirteen. λύτρωσαι is present in five texts, while four references to βοήθησον appear in the list. φύλαξον is the imperative in three of the texts, while ἴασται, δίκασον, ἐξελοῦ and κρῖνον account for two each. Finally, οἰκτείρησον, ἀνάστησον and πολέμησον each make just a single appearance. We will now examine the theological emphases which emerge from them.

## I. Themes

All but one of the fifty-eight psalm-prayers in question are linked by the exegetes to the passion of Christ. The suffering Son of God pleads to his Father for help, as he confronts his enemies, as he endures his humiliation, as he expires on the cross, and as he descends into Hades. Over and over again, as the New Testament writers before them, the scholars hear the *vox Christi* uttering its cry of distress in the words of the psalms in its foreshadowing of Calvary.

However, within this overall theme it is possible to discern a number of distinct, though overlapping theological emphases, in which the particular Christological, soteriological and ecclesiological interests of the Fathers compete with one another for the reader's attention. Of necessity, the delineation of these interests is, at best, an approximate science. Nevertheless, armed with this *caveat*, we will now interrogate the texts with a view to uncovering the different aspects of the person and work of Christ which come into play in the course of these exegeses.

## *1. Christ as human*

The overwhelming theological emphasis of these psalm-texts is that of the humanity of Christ. No doubt, in the light of the Christological controversies of the era, the scholars are constantly at pains in their exposition of Scripture to give prominence to the assertion that the Son of God was truly human. They underline this assertion in a number of ways.

Athanasius reflects upon the text of Psalm 17.44: 'You will deliver me from disputes with people; you will make me head of the nations; a people whom I did not know, served me'.[4] He goes on to emphasize the Davidic ancestry of the speaker: 'For, I say, the Lord Christ is one who is born of David according to the flesh (ἐκ Δαυὶδ κατὰ σάρκα τεχθεὶς) and who is named David himself according to the divine Ezekiel, who ruled over all the nations'.[5]

Theodoret, in a passage which is a duplicate of that of Athanasius, also identifies Christ as the speaker through the mouthpiece of his ancestor, offering a prayer for deliverance, which is linked to the Jews' frenzy against the Saviour.[6] He goes on to say of the following verse, 'He makes

4 Ῥύσαί με ἐξ ἀντιλογών λαού: PG 27, 121A.

5 Ὁ γὰρ ἐκ Δαυῒδ κατὰ σάρκα τεχθεὶς, Δαυῒδ καὶ αὐτὸς ὀνομάζόμενος κατὰ τὸν θεῖον Ἰεζεχιὴλ, ὁ Δεσπότης, λέγω, Χριστός, πάντων ἐβασίλευσε τῶν ἐθνῶν: PG 27, 121AB.

6 PG 80, 985CD.

this prediction in the person of Christ the Lord',[7] but it is as one born of the human line of David.

Eusebius affirms the humanity of Christ by way of placing the accent on his freedom, in his commentary on the text of Psalm 34.24: 'Vindicate me, O Lord my God, according to your righteousness, and may they not be happy over me'.[8] For Eusebius, Christ expresses himself in a human fashion (Ἀνθρωπίνως δὲ ἱκετεύει λέγων πρὸς τὸν ἑαυτοῦ Πατέρα). In verses 23–6 he points out that Christ's humiliation is a voluntary act, whereby Christ freely makes himself weak in order to suffer on the cross for us.[9]

This voluntary self-emptying (κένωσις) on the part of Christ is also seen by Cyril in terms of underlining Christ's humanity. He does so in his observations on the text of Psalm 68.2: 'Save me, O God, for the waters threatened my life'.[10] Cyril understands this to be a prayer of Christ against the background of Philippians 2.7–8: 'It is fitting that these events should be spoken about on the part of the Lord (ἐκ προσώπου τοῦ Κυρίου), since having been born as man he humbled himself to the point of death...' (ἐταπείνωσεν ἑαυτὸν μέχρι θανάτου).[11]

This prayer to God for salvation from the water is then linked to Jonah (Jonah 2.6), who is a 'type of Christ' (ὁ τύπος δὲ Χριστοῦ), and to Job (Job 38.16), where there is an allusion to Christ walking on the water (Ἦλθες ἐπὶ πηγὴν θαλάσσης).[12] The association of Christ with these two characters further stresses the significance of his humanity.

Again, Eusebius regards this verse in a similar light. For him, Christ is the exclusive speaker of the whole psalm. This prayer signifies Christ's incarnation (καὶ τοῦ Σωτῆρος ἡμῶν τὴν ἐνανθρώπησιν σημαίνει).[13] The Saviour addresses the Father, expressing himself in a human way. His cry

7 Ἐκ προσώπου ταῦτα προαγορεύει τοῦ Δεσπότου Χριστοῦ: PG 80, 988A; Hill, Fathers of the Church 101, 130.

8 κρῖνόν με, Κύριε, κατὰ τὴν δικαιοσύνην σου, Κύριε ὁ θεός μου, καὶ μὴ ἐπιχαρείησαν μοι.

9 PG 23, 313AB.

10 Σῶσόν με, ὁ Θεός, ὅτι εἰσήλθοσαν ὕδατα ἕως ψυχῆς μου: PG 69, 1161B.

11 PG 69, 1161B.

12 PG 69, 1161BC.

13 PG 23, 724D.

of distress proves that the Word of God appropriates to himself the sufferings of the humanity which he has assumed.[14]

For Athanasius, Psalm 21.20 is a prayer of Christ which provides an example for other human beings to follow: 'But you, O Lord, do not put your help far away! Attend to my support!'[15] Athanasius uses these words of Christ as a moral lesson, whereby the true human sets the pattern for all other humans: 'He is an example for us (Ὑποτύπωσις ἡμῖν γενόμενος), in needing to call upon God when tempted, and not to give in to carelessness, nor be enfeebled by tribulations'.[16]

Psalm 40.11[17] provides an opportunity for both Didymus and Theodoret to highlight Christ's human nature. Didymus offers this reflection on the prayer, once again emphasizing that Jesus prays as a man: 'These things are said more humanly, about the man Jesus'.[18]

Theodoret comments on this verse, placing the emphasis firmly on Christ speaking as a member of the human race, here with a recognition of his human vulnerability: 'All this was said on the part of the nature assumed (Καὶ ταῦτα πάντα ὡς ἀπὸ τῆς ληφθείσης εἴρηται φύσεως), which was involved also in the passion. Likewise in the sacred Gospels we hear Christ the Lord praying, "Father, save me from this hour", and again, "Father, if it is possible let this cup pass from me"'.[19]

Both Athanasius and Theodoret find in Psalm 108 an Aladdin's cave of treasures bearing witness to the humanity of Christ. In verse 21,[20] Athanasius highlights the expression of the true humanity of Christ in this psalm-verse: 'And the Lord Christ says these things humanly (ἀνθρωπίνως). For he has fulfilled all things human (Πάντα γὰρ τὰ ἀνθρώπινα) apart from sin'.[21]

14 PG 23, 724B-D.

15 Σὺ δέ, Κύριε, μὴ μακρὺνης τὴν βοήθειάν σου ἀπ' ἐμοῦ: PG 27, 136A.

16 Ibid.

17 σύ δέ, Κύριε, ἐλέησόν με καὶ ἀνάστησόν με, καί ἀνταποδώσω αὐτοίς.

18 ταῦτα πάλιν ἀνθρωπικώτερον λέγεται περὶ τοῦ κατὰ τὸν ἄνθρωπον Ἰησοῦν: *In Ps. Tura* 40.11, T 295, 2, Gronewald 5, 28.

19 PG 80, 1168AB; Hill, Fathers of the Church 101, 246.

20 Καὶ σὺ, Κύριε, Κύριε, ποίησον μετ' ἐμοῦ ἕνεκεν τοῦ ὀνόματός σου: PG 27, 460B.

21 Ibid.

For Theodoret also the psalm is a psalm of the passion: 'This psalm prophesies the saving passion, the Jews' madness, and the betrayal of Judas'.[22] On verse 21 Theodoret reflects, emphasizing Christ's human nature:

> Christ the Lord spoke this in human fashion (Καὶ ταῦτα ἀνθρωπίνως εἴρηκεν ὁ Δεσπότης Χριστός) after all, he discharged all human functions except sin, being born according to the law of nature: [to be born] of a woman belongs to human nature, but [to be born] of a virgin is beyond it. He accepted swaddling clothes, circumcision and nourishment from milk. He offered sacrifices, fasted, went hungry and thirsty, and felt weariness. He is likewise also constantly recorded in the sacred Gospels as praying. Consequently, at this point, too, in human fashion he invokes divine help (Καὶ ἐνταῦθα τοίνυν ἀνθρωπίνως τὴν θείαν ἐπικαλεῖται βοήθειαν).[23]

Athanasius comments on verse 22: 'Deliver me, for I am poor and lowly!'[24] He links this prayer of Christ to his statement in John 12.27, just prior to his passion, that his soul is troubled: 'This also we find said by him in the sacred Gospels. As he was about to approach the passion he said, "Now my soul is troubled. And what do I say? Father, save me from this hour? But it is because of this that I have come to this hour"'.[25]

The Christ whose soul is troubled at the prospect of his approaching doom is the same human Saviour who can pray, 'Deliver me, for I am poor and needy'. Theodoret duplicates Athanasius, with reference to John 12.27 and the prayer in Gethsemane.[26] Again, just as the Christ prays for deliverance in the psalm, so the man Jesus wrestles with the prospect of death.

Finally, Theodoret comments on verse 26: 'Help me, O Lord my God, and save me according to your steadfast love!',[27] again alluding to Gethsemane, and, as Eusebius in his exegesis of Psalm 34.24, placing the accent on the freedom with which Christ chose to suffer: 'Let them learn,

22 Τὸ σωτήριον πάθος ... οὗτος ὁ ψαλμὸς προθεσπίζει: PG 80, 1753C; Hill, Fathers of the Church 102, 200.

23 PG 80, 1761C; Hill, Fathers of the Church 102, 204–5.

24 Ῥῦσαί με, ὅτι πτωχὸς καὶ πένης εἰμι ἐγώ: PG 27, 460C.

25 Ibid.

26 PG 80, 1761D.

27 Βοήθησόν μοι, Κύριε ὁ Θεός μου, καὶ σῶσόν με κατά τὸ ἔλεός σου: PG 80, 1764B.

he is saying, that it was not against my will that they gave me over to the cross, but it was a work of your disposition: through my passion you wanted to grant human beings impassibility'.[28]

## 2. *Christ as intercessor*

Matching these texts which, in a general way, affirm the significance of Christ's humanity is a similar number of other texts which focus on one particular aspect of the humanness of Jesus, brought out in these psalm-prayers. In these the dynamic shifts towards a more overtly soteriological and ecclesiological emphasis.

In these texts, Christ is deemed to offer prayer to the Father not simply for himself, but also on behalf of the rest of the human race. The petitions in these passages are therefore interpreted as those issuing from a representative of corporate humanity, pleading to God for its salvation, deliverance, rescue, forgiveness, etc. The assumption underpinning this image is that Christ is well placed to act in this role as a 'man among men'.

Athanasius displays an especially acute understanding of this intercessory role of Christ. He observes in his introduction to Psalm 15 that the words are 'as if from the person of Christ' (ὡς ἐκ προσώπου τοῦ Χριστοῦ), and then makes an observation on verse 1, 'Protect me, O Lord, for in you did I hope'. Here he claims that Christ prays to God the Father 'in the name of humanity' (ὥσπερ πρόσωπον τῆς ἀνθρωπότητος), addressing God as Father and describing himself as a slave.[29] This representative role of Christ is key to the Christology of this commentary.

He comments on the text of Psalm 40.11,[30] a prayer which is offered 'humanly' (Ἀνθρωπίνως) to the Father as a result of his divine self-emptying (διὰ τὴν κένωσιν), and is linked to the resurrection. As his comment on the

28 Διὰ γὰρ τοῦ ἐμοῦ πάθους ἐβουλήθης τοῖς ἀνθρώποις τήν ἀπάθειαν δωρήσασθαι: PG 80, 1764C; Hill, Fathers of the Church 102, 205–6.

29 PG 27, 100CD.

30 Σύ δέ, Κύριε, ἐλέησόν με, καί ἀνάστησόν με, καί ἀνταποδώσω αὐτοίς: PG 27, 200A.

following verse makes clear, this kenotic prayer to the Lord to have mercy and to 'raise me up' is that of the Christ who speaks on behalf of humanity (ἐκ προσώπου τῆς ἀνθρωπότητος), and who is the mercy of God the Father and the resurrection and the life.[31] This, as has already been noted, is a major characteristic of Athanasius's Christological exposition of the Psalter. For him Christ lives, prays, suffers, dies, and rises again 'for humankind', ἐκ προσώπου τῆς ἀνθρωπότητος, a phrase encapsulating the Christological, soteriological and ecclesiological thrusts of his understanding of the texts.

In this, Athanasius follows the lead of Origen who gives a similar dynamic to this verse: 'He asks for mercy and for resurrection not for himself, but for us. On the one hand it is "Raise me up", in human fashion (ἀνθρωποπρεπῶς); on the other hand it is "I will rejoice over them", manifestly with regard to the enemies, in divine fashion (θεοπρεπῶς)... So we are strengthened in Christ, and so are made face to face with the Father (τοῦτο ἐνώπιον τοῦ Πατρὸς) in eternity'.[32]

We meet the same phrase again in Athanasius's commentary on the text of Psalm 56.2: 'Have mercy on me, O God, have mercy on me' ('Ελέησόν με, ό Θεὸς, ἐλέησόν με). The introduction to the psalm ('Υπόθεσις) associates David's flight from Saul with Christ's 'sufferings in the flesh' for us. Indeed, the psalm is said to refer to 'what Christ has accomplished for us'.[33] It is followed by a prayer for mercy from God in verse 2. The prayer is made 'on behalf of humanity' ('Εκ προσώπου τῆς ἀνθρωπότητος) by Christ, whose lament over Jerusalem in Matthew 23.37 is alluded to in the commentary on the verse, thus removing any doubt that Athanasius identifies the Saviour as the addressor of this plea which he makes on behalf of the human race.[34]

That treasure trove of psalm-prayers offered *ex persona Christi*, Psalm 68, also provides Athanasius with an occasion to affirm this representative-intercessory role of Christ. In the introduction Athanasius is explicit that

31 PG 27, 200A.

32 PG 12, 1413D–1416A.

33 Ἀναφέρεται δὲ καὶ εἰς τὰ πεπραγμένα ὑπὲρ ἡμῶν τῷ Χριστῷ: PG 27, 257C.

34 PG 27, 257CD.

Christ is the speaker of this psalm, which, again, is offered 'on behalf of humanity'.[35] He goes on to link the prayer in verse 2, 'Save me, O God, for the waters threatened my life',[36] with Isaiah 53.4, 'He bore our sins, and is pained for us'.[37] Thus he identifies it as the prayer of Christ, the Suffering Servant. It is both by his words and by his endurance that Christ intercedes on behalf of the rest of the human creation.

Didymus is also keen to emphasize the *pro nobis* nature of this psalm-prayer in his exegesis of verses 2 and 3. He explains how this 'psalm is said by Jesus on behalf of us, as he bears our weaknesses, and suffers for us'.[38] He goes on to raise the question of Jesus making a confession of sin. He says with regard to such an act of penitence: 'If therefore it is not for his own faults that he makes a confession, it is clear that it is for us that he makes it. In fact, those who beseech the king on behalf of the guilty, who have been exiled because of their crimes, appropriate to their own person the faults of those for whom they make this supplication'.[39]

In the same passage he also points out that Jesus descends into Hades freely, of his own accord, and quotes John 10.18, before reinforcing the point with the allusion to Philippians 2.8.[40] Thus Didymus both faces and resolves the dilemma of how a sinless Christ can offer a penitential prayer to the Father. Christ confesses not his own failings but the failings of those on whose behalf he intercedes. This serves to underline further the scholars' conviction that Christ, in these psalms, speaks not only, or sometimes not at all, from a personal point of view, but rather from a collective perspective.

35 ἐκ προσώπου τῆς ἀνθρωπότητος: PG 27, 305B.

36 Σῶσόν με, ὁ Θεός, ὅτι εἰσήλθοσαν ὕδατα ἕως ψυχῆς μου: PG 27, 305C.

37 Ἐπειδὴ τὰς ἁμαρτίας ἡμῶν ἀνέλαβε, περὶ ἡμῶν ὀδυνᾶται: ibid.

38 ἐκ προσώπου ἡμετέρου ὑπὸ Ἰησοῦ λέγεται τὰς ἀσθενείας ἡμῶν φέροντος καὶ ὑπὲρ ἡμῶν ὀδυνωμένου: *In Ps. caten.* 68.2–3, Mühlenberg, 2, 707, 75.

39 εἰς ἴδιον πρόσωπον τὰ ἁμαρτήματα τῶν ὑπὲρ ὧν δέονται ἀναφέροντες: *In Ps, caten.* 68.2–3, Mühlenberg, 2, 707, 76; based on the translation by Rondeau, *Commentaires Patristiques du Psautier, Vol. II*, 260.

40 εἰ καὶ μὴ ἀκουσίως ὑπεμείνε τοῦτο ὑπήκοος τῷ πατρὶ μέχρι θανάτου γενόμενος: *In Ps. caten.* 68.2–3, Mühlenberg, 2, 707, 76.

The same exegete seeks to broaden the concept of intercessor by use of the image of ambassador in his commentary on verses 17–19. Here he refers explicitly to the incarnation. The prayer in verse 19, 'Pay attention to me and redeem me; rescue me because of my enemies',[41] is understood against the background of Christ's self-description as an 'ambassador for all', and it is in this capacity that he makes the prayer:

> Since your mercy, which I invoke upon those for whom I pray, will be, from the fact of your abundant goodness, full of sweetness – in fact you will remit their faults – rescue me. In the same way you will cast your eyes upon me who am an ambassador for all (πρεσβευόμενον ὑπὲρ πάντων), it is according to the abundance of your mercies, not according to one or two, that they will be saved and that they will have an abundant profit.[42]

Didymus continues his exegesis of the passage, with a strong anti-Apollinarian thrust, reaffirming the reality of the human soul of Jesus:

> One can say also with truth that the soul of him who is ambassador is every soul which is intimately united with him (οἰκειωθεῖσαν αὐτοῦ). In the same way, someone like Moses and Elijah is said to be a 'man of God', likewise also it could be said 'his soul' which has united (κολληθεῖσα) with him and which has become one spirit with him (1 Corinthians 6.17). In fact, every soul of this kind he is united with in giving it the soul which he has assumed. Likewise, in fact, the body of Jesus is given for the body of men, in this way his soul is given for their souls so that a whole man may be given for all by the one who has assumed him.[43]

So here we see both a robust defence of Christ's true and full humanity, against Apollinarius, and also a clear affirmation of the corporate and representational nature of his intercession, arising from Didymus's holistic approach to soteriology.

41 πρόσχες τῇ ψυχῇ μου καὶ λύτρωσαι αὐτήν, ἕνεκα τῶν ἐχθρῶν μου ῥῦσαί με.

42 *In Ps. caten.* 68.17–19, Mühlenberg, 2, 716a, 80; based on the translation by Rondeau, *Commentaires Patristiques du Psautier, Vol. II*, 261–2.

43 ...οὕτως ἡ ψυχὴ αὐτοῦ ὑπὲρ τῶν ψυχῶν αὐτῶν, ἵν' ὅλος ἄνθρωπος ὑπὲρ πάντων δοθῇ πρὸς τοῦ αὐτὸν ἀνειληφότος: *In Ps. caten.* 68.17–19, Mühlenberg, 2, 716a, 81; based on the translation of Rondeau, *Les Commentaires Patristiques du Psautier, Vol. II*, 280.

Again, it is Athanasius who underlines this perspective in his commentary on the same verse, which he understands as a prayer by Christ to the Father on behalf of humanity: 'From the injuries which we have suffered from our noetic enemies (παρὰ τῶν νοητῶν ἐχθρῶν), to the mercy of our Father he raises us' (ἐπὶ τὸν ἔλεον τὸν ἡμέτερον διεγείρει τὸν Πατέρα).[44]

Eusebius interprets this psalm-text in much the same way. In the prayer he sees Christ praying to the Father for us.[45] Cyril also follows Athanasius's treatment of this verse, in so far as he draws attention to the spiritual warfare underlying the intercession. He links this prayer for deliverance to justification and faith in Christ ('Η ἐν Χριστῷ δικαίωσις, ἡ διὰ πίστεως σωτηρία), and to the Saviour's power to deliver from noetic enemies (Καὶ ὁ Σωτὴρ δὲ ἐξ ἧς πεπόνθαμεν ἀδικίας παρὰ τῶν νοητῶν ἐχθρῶν). For he is one who does not flee from temptations (οὐκ ἐξέφυγε τούς πειρασμοὺς).[46]

This overall collective perspective is very much to the fore in the commentary of Cyril on the text of Psalm 40.5, 'As for me, I said, "O Lord, have mercy on me; heal me, for I have sinned against you"'.[47] In a similar vein to that pursued by Didymus, Cyril, with a little help from Paul *via* Galatians 3.13, claims that this prayer for mercy and healing is made by Christ who, making our sins his own, died for us and was made a curse for us: 'The Saviour may say such things, having made our sins his own, as nature's first-fruits (τὰς ἁμαρτίας ἡμῶν οἰκειούμενος, ὡς ἀπαρχὴ τῆς φύσεως). For Christ died for us, having become a curse for us'.[48]

Following this trend, in his commentary on the same text, Theodoret focuses on Christ as the Lamb of God. He understands this psalm in the light of John 13.17–19, as a word of Christ.[49] He says of this prayer: 'Now I am the one who is poor, he is saying, who embraced voluntary poverty,

44 PG 27, 309D.

45 Ἐπὶ τούτοις οὖν καὶ παρακάλει τὸν Πατέρα ἐμβλέψαι καὶ θεάσασθαι τοὺς ἄθλους οὓς ὑπὲρ ἡμῶν ὑπέμεινε: PG 23, 748A.

46 PG 69, 1169AB.

47 Κύριε, ἐλέησόν με, ἴασαι τήν ψυχήν μου, ὅτι ἥμαρτόν σοι: PG 69, 993B.

48 PG 69, 993BC.

49 PG 80, 1161B.

the Lamb of God who takes away the sin of the world, who makes my own the sufferings of human beings, who though having committed no sin offers the prayer for human nature as nature's first-fruits'.[50] Christ freely embraces and asks forgiveness for humanity's sins as the Lamb of God, who intercedes for all both by his words and by his suffering.

With regard to Psalm 108.21–3, Didymus comments on this passage, reaffirming his view of Christ as the Johannine intercessor, and also introducing an element of ecclesiology. Rondeau notes that for Didymus, the Son as Son addresses the 'Father', but as the incarnate one, he calls him 'God' or 'Lord'.[51] Didymus writes:

> He who is clothed in the form of a slave (Philippians 2.7) speaks to his father as Lord. He tells the Lord how to act mercifully towards him: in doing good to those who believe, who are his body (ὄντας αὐτοῦ σῶμα). In fact, he attributes to himself what comes to his body (τὰ γὰρ εἰς τὸ σῶμα αὐτοῦ γινόμενα ἑαυτῷ λογίζεται). It is why he says, 'Act with me because of your name, because it is in this name that I have come to those to whom you have sent me' (cf. John 5.43).[52]

Finally, Cyril observes the Christological intercessory character of Psalm 69. Without making specific reference to the short invocatory prayer in verse 2, 'O God, attend to helping me', he offers in his commentary on the previous verse a significant reflection as to the meaning of this verse, which became for Cassian an introit for continual prayer. He claims that it is possible that Christ says this psalm on behalf of humanity (Δύναται δὲ καὶ ἀπὸ Χριστοῦ προσάγεσθαι ὑπὲρ ἀνθρωπότητος).[53] While sounding ambiguous, Cyril displays a willingness to contemplate the prospect of the Saviour offering this psalm-prayer as a representative of humankind.

50 ὑπὲρ τῆς ἀνθρωπείας φύσεως, ὡς ἀπαρχὴ τῆς φύσεως: PG 80, 1164C; Hill, Fathers of the Church 101, 244.

51 Rondeau, *Commentaires Patristiques du Psautier, Vol. II*, 266, note 751.

52 *In Ps caten.* 108.21, Mühlenberg, 2, 1036, 252; based on the translation of Rondeau, *Commentaires Patristiques du Psautier, Vol. II*, 266.

53 PG 69, 1177B.

### *3. Christ as one who suffers*

As well as the texts already cited, there are some in which the exegete is content simply, as it were, to leave the fact of Christ's suffering on the table, while making little or no explicit reference to his intercessory role.

Thus in his commentary on the text of Psalm 21.21, 'Deliver my soul from the sword, my only life from the power of the dog',[54] Origen associates the sword in the psalm-verse with the sword of Simeon's prophecy in Luke 2.35 (ῥομφαία νοητὴ), thus associating Christ with the speaker in the verse, as one who prays to be delivered from noetic attack.

Again, he offers his reflection on Psalm 68.15, 'Save me from the mud, so that I shall not get stuck; may I be rescued from those who hate me, and from the deep waters'.[55] Origen, or possibly Evagrius, interprets this verse as an allegory of what happened during Christ's descent into Hades, and therefore as a prayer of the Saviour from out of the depths: 'The point is not ordinary that this is written as an allegory of what happened to our Saviour (Σκοπὸς οὐχ ὁ τυχὼν ἀλληγορῆσαι τὰ γεγραμμένα ἐπὶ τοῦ Σωτῆρος ἡμῶν γεγονότα). I think all these things were accepted by him in his descent into Hades'.[56]

Eusebius reflects on the text of Psalm 69.5, 'Help me, O God, you are my helper and rescuer! O Lord, do not delay!'[57] He sees that David's prayer for help is linked to Christ becoming poor for us, according to 2 Corinthians 8.9.[58] This entire psalm is, for Eusebius, a prayer of Christ (ἀναπέμπει πρὸς τὸν Πατέρα λέγων· Ὁ Θεὸς, εἰς τὴν βοήθειαν μου πρόσχες..., καὶ τὰ τούτοις ἀκόλουθα).[59] He addresses himself to the Father in human fashion as one who suffers.

54 Ῥῦσαι ἀπὸ ῥομφαίας τὴν ψυχήν μου κ.τ.έ.: PG 12, 1257C.

55 Σῶσόν με ἀπὸ πηλοῦ, ἵνα μὴ ἐμπαγῶ' ῥυσθείην ἐκ τῶν μισούντων με, καὶ ἐκ τοῦ βάθους τῶν ὑδάτων, κ.τ.ὲ.: PG 12, 1513D.

56 PG 12, 1513D.

57 Ὁ Θεός, βοήθησόν μοι· βοηθός μου καί ῥύστης μου εἰ σύ, Κύριε, μὴ χρονίσῃς: PG 23, 772B.

58 Ibid.

59 PG 23, 772C.

Again, in Psalm 70.2 he hears the *vox Christi* crying out from dire distress. He lays out the text: 'In your righteousness, rescue me and deliver me; incline your ear to me and save me'.[60] He establishes that the prophecy of this psalm is spoken *ex persona Christi*.[61] He goes on to place a series of cries for help in the mouth of Christ.[62]

Finally, in his observation on the text of Psalm 55.2, 'Have mercy on me, O Lord, for people trampled on me; all day long fighters afflicted me',[63] Didymus appears to identify Christ as the speaker of this psalm-verse. Having linked it with the words of Jesus, 'They throw it away' ("Ἔξω βάλλουσιν αὐτό), in Luke 14.35, he goes on to say with regard to the prayer, whereby Christ speaks of his own suffering: '"Being trampled by men" also applies to the one who disparages Christ'.[64]

### *4. Christ as warrior*

For the Fathers in general, and, as we have seen, for Evagrius in particular, psalmody was acknowledged to be part of the armoury with which the follower of Christ engaged in spiritual warfare. In these exegeses Christ is invoked as a fellow warrior, a comrade-in-arms, who has fought against and prevailed over the same powers of evil which threaten the monastic.

Whereas, as we have seen above, Origen interprets the sword in Psalm 21.21 in terms of the warning given by Simeon to Mary of her Son's future suffering, Athanasius prefers to understand it more in the light of classic spiritual warfare. Having set out the text of Psalm 21.21–2,[65] he interprets this prayer of Christ as a plea to be saved from the sword which may also

60 ἐν τη δικαιοσύνῃ σου ῥῦσαί με, καὶ ἐχέλου με: PG 23, 772D.

61 ὁ δὲ προφητεία ἔοικεν ἐκ προσώπου τοῦ Σωτῆρος προενηνεγμένη, PG 23, 772D.

62 PG 23, 776A.

63 Ἐλέησόν με, Κύριε, ὅτι κατεπάτησὲν με ἄνθρωπος, ὅλην τὴν ἡμέραν πολεμῶν ἔθλιψέν με.

64 καταπατεϊσθαι ὑπὸ τῶν ἀνθρώπων καὶ περὶ τοῦ τὸν Χριστὸν ἐξευτελίζοντος γέγραπται: *In Ps caten*. 55.2, Mühlenberg, 2, 584, 17.

65 PG 27, 136BC.

be the devil (Ῥομφαία δὲ εἴ ἂν καὶ ὁ διάβολος). Incidentally, he also picks up the reference to 'my only life' (μονογενῆ) as an affirmation of the unity of Christ, as perfect God and perfect man: 'For Christ is one, out of two opposites (Εἷς γάρ ἐστιν ὁ Χριστὸς ἐκ δύο τῶν ἐναντίων), perfect God and perfect man.'[66]

Origen himself places the accent on the spiritual or noetic warfare in three texts. Firstly, he comments on Psalm 34.1, 'Render judgment, O Lord, on those who do me injustice; fight against those who fight against me.'[67] Here he appears to imply that this verse is spoken by Christ with respect to his enemies, as he clearly identifies the 'me' in the psalm-verse with the person of Christ: 'For all wrongdoers do harm to Christ (ἀδικοῦσι Χριστὸν) who is righteousness; and those who do not have peace in themselves have conflicts, and fight against Christ (πολεμοῦσι Χριστὸν), who is our peace.'[68]

Secondly, in his exegesis of Psalm 58.2, 'Deliver me from my enemies, O God; redeem me from those who rise up against me,'[69] Origen identifies Christ as the speaker, whose words, he claims, take the form of a dire warning to the world. Here he exchanges the image of the suffering intercessor for that of a judge who comes to combat the enemies of justice: 'The Saviour says this psalm (ὁ Σωτὴρ λέγει τὸν ψαλμόν). And on account of this, "Attend to the visitation (Πρόσχες τοῦ ἐπισχέψασθαι), all the nations"'.

Thirdly, in a text accredited to the Evagrian *Scholia ad psalmos*, he seeks to unpack the text of Psalm 70.4, 'Rescue me, O my God, from a sinner's hand, from the hand of a person who transgresses the law and practices injustice,'[70] where Origen establishes that the psalm is said by Christ.[71] In this prayer he identifies the 'sinner' and the one who 'transgresses the law and practices injustice' as Satan, the great adversary of both God and man.

66 PG 27, 136C.

67 Δίκασον, Κύριε, τοὺς ἀδικοῦντάς με, πολέμησον τοὺς πολεμοῦντάς με, κ.τ.ἑ.: PG 12, 1309BC.

68 PG 12, 1309C.

69 Ἐξελοῦ με ἐκ τῶν ἐχθρῶν μου, ὁ Θεὸς μου, κ.τ.ἑ.: PG 12, 1477A.

70 Ὁ Θεός μου, ῥυσαί με ἐκ χειρὸς ἁμαρτωλοῦ, ἐκ χειρὸς παρανομοῦντος καὶ ἀδικοῦντος, κ.τ.ἑ.: PG 12, 1520B.

71 PG 12, 1517D.

Eusebius also focuses on the conflict aspect of this text, though without identifying Satan in the prayer. According to him, Christ asks to be delivered from the hand of the sinner, 'lest by the practices he might become like the sinner or transgressor'.[72] Such an observation reinforces his interpretation that Christ prays in 'human fashion'. Christ recognizes his vulnerability as a human being in respect of his enemies, and therefore prays to be spared from the contamination which they might bring to him.

Further texts from Didymus, Cyril and Theodoret follow the same practice of laying emphasis upon their assertion that it is the background of spiritual battle which gives rise to the particular invocation. Didymus gives his verdict on Psalm 42.1, 'Vindicate me, O God, and defend my cause against a nation not devout; from a person who is unjust and deceitful deliver me'.[73] Here he identifies Christ as the addressor of this prayer, in the light of the passion story, and the Jewish nation and Judas as his enemies: 'But the person of the Saviour brought this word before the Father (τὸ πρόσωπον τοῦ σωτῆρος παρεισήγαγεν λέγον πρὸς τὸν πατέρα) in the psalm, and surely naming the Jews as the nation, and Judas as the one who is unjust and deceitful'.[74]

As we have already observed, Cyril comments on the text of Psalm 68.19, 'Pay attention to me and redeem me; rescue me because of my enemies',[75] linking together the roles of Christ as both intercessor and divine warrior.[76]

Finally, Theodoret understands the invocations in Psalm 21.21–22 in terms of Christ's victory over the devil.[77] For him the names of lion and dog and unicorn refer to the 'one with the power of death' (Hebrews 2.14) that is the

72 ἵνα μὴ ταῖς πράξεσιν ὅμοιος γένηται τῳ ἁμαρτωλῷ, μήδε τῷ παρανομοῦντι: PG 23, 776B.

73 Κρῖνόν με, ὁ θεός, καὶ δίκασον τὴν δίκην μου ἐξ ἔθνους οὐχ ὁσίου, ἀπὸ ἀνθρώπου ἀδίκου καὶ δολίου ῥῦσαί με.

74 *In Ps caten*. 42.1, Mühlenberg, 1, 434a, 329.

75 Πρόσχες τῇ ψυχῇ μου, καὶ λύτρωσαί αὐτήν…Ἕνεκα τῶν ἐχθρῶν μου ῥῦσαί με.

76 PG 69, 1169AB.

77 Σὺ δέ, Κύριε, μὴ μακρὺνης τὴν βοήθειάν σου ἀπ' ἐμοῦ…Ῥῦσαι ἀπὸ ῥομφαίας τὴν ψυχήν μου, καὶ ἐκ χειρὸς κυνὸς τὴν μονογενῆ μου. Σῶσόν με ἐκ στόματος λέοντος, καὶ ἀπὸ κεράτων των μονοκερώτων τὴν ταπείνωσίν μου: PG 80, 1017BC.

devil (τουτέστι τον διάβολον). And he links this plea of Christ to the Saviour's words in John 12.31, relating to the driving out of the ruler of this world, and in John 14.30, where the ruler of this world 'will find nothing in me'.[78]

## *5. Christ as God*

As is evident from all that has been said thus far, the overwhelming thrust of the exegetical emphasis with regard to these short invocatory psalm-prayers, which are attributed to Christ by the Fathers, revolves around the humanity of the Son of God. Christ as man, in these prayers, intercedes for us, suffers for us, and engages in conflict on with the noetic foes, as one of our race, and on our behalf.

Against this tidal wave, however, two psalm-texts provide us with a minor counter-current in which the exegete interprets the invocation of Christ not so much in terms of his humanity and solidarity with humankind, but rather with his divinity, as the Son and Word of God.

First of all, Origen offers his explanation of the text of Psalm 55.2, 'Have mercy on me, O Lord, for people trample on me; all day long fighters afflicted me'.[79] In the commentary he explicitly identifies Christ as the one who offers this prayer, with Christ emphasizing his divine nature: 'Christ says to the Father "Have mercy on me". For a person has trampled on me, who am God (Θεὸν γάρ με ὄντα ἄνθρωπος κατεπάτησε). And I think, from here that is taken to mean "He who has trampled down the Son of God"' (Ὁ τὸν Υἱόν τοῦ Θεοῦ καταπατήσας).[80]

This interpretation by Origen would appear to fly in the face of Philippians 2.6, one of the most widely used biblical texts in these psalm-commentaries. However, Origen seems to see no conflict between that kenotic reference and Christ's bold divine self-affirmation in this invocation.

78 PG 80, 1017C-1020A.

79 Ἐλέησόν με, ὁ Θεὸς, ὅτι κατεπάτησέ με ἄνθρωπος· ὅλην τὴν ἡμέραν πολεμῶν ἔθλιψέ με, κ.τ.ἑ.: PG 12, 1469B.

80 Ibid.

In his commentary on Psalm 108.25–9, Eusebius, on the other hand, underlines Christ's divinity in his interpretation of verse 26, precisely in order to affirm the kenotic nature of the Philippian hymn. He understands the prayer, 'Help me, O Lord; save me according to your steadfast love',[81] as a prayer of the Word of God. He interprets it in the light of Hebrews 12.2, and says that the hand of God is at work in the form of the only-begotten Word of God (τουτέστιν ὁ μονογενὴς αὐτοῦ Λόγος), who in anticipation of the resurrection of the dead 'endured the cross, despising the shame'.[82]

## *6. Christ as one*

The paucity of psalm-texts which emphasize the divinity of Christ is unsurprisingly surpassed by those which focus on the unity of Christ's person. Both Didymus and Eusebius display a clear interest in this subject. Didymus stands alone in interpreting the short invocatory prayers of Psalm 21.21–22 as pronouncements by Christ which point to his own integrity.[83] He writes, dismissing those who would interpret this text as evidence for a disconnection between the soul and the body in the composite humanity of Christ: 'Question: Who speaks? – These people uphold this: "If he speaks of his soul, who is the one who speaks? It is the body who speaks". But they are mistaken in saying that. In the composites, each one of the elements of the composition is said entirely for the composition'.[84]

He follows this theme of the integrity of Christ's person in his comment on Psalm 30.17, 'Let your face shine upon your slave; save me in your

81 Βοήθησόν μοι, Κύριε ὁ Θεός μου, καὶ σῶσόν με κατά τὸ ἔλεός σου: PG 23, 1340A.

82 PG 23, 1340B.

83 ῥῦσαι ἀπὸ ῥομφαίας τὴν ψυχήν μου ... καὶ ἐκ χειρὸς κυνὸς τὴν μονογενῆν μου...: *In Ps. Tura* 21.21, T 41, 18, Gronewald, 1, 166; and T 42, 29, Gronewald, 1, 172.

84 ἐν τοῖς συνθέτοις ἕκαστον τῶν ἐν τῇ συνθέσει ὅλης της συνθέσεως λέγεται': *In Ps. Tura* 21.21, T 42, 9, Gronewald, 1, 170; based on the translation of Rondeau, *Commentaires Patristiques du Psautier, Vol. II*, 239.

steadfast love'.[85] He does so in respect of the relationship between the divine and human natures in Christ rather than the relationship between the body and the soul in his manhood.

As we have seen in Chapter 8, Didymus comments on the text of the psalm, using a wealth of Scriptural references from Hebrews 1.3, Colossians 1.15, Philippians 2.7, and John 1.14, and speaking with the voice of Christ.[86] For Didymus, the speaker is not solely man nor solely God, but God who is made man. He goes on to say with regard to verse 18: 'Ah well, since he who says these words is not only man nor only God, but God who has made himself man, certain things are said as from the point of view of man, the others as from the point of view of God the Word... He does not therefore say: "Show your face to your servant" in the sense of: on one other than me, but: on me your servant'.[87]

Again in his comment on Psalm 24.16 and 20, 'Look upon me, and have mercy on me, for I am an only child and am poor... O guard my life and deliver me; may I not be put to shame for I hoped in you',[88] though with a greater degree of ambiguity, Didymus appears to highlight the connectedness of the two natures in his reflection. He links the cry in verse 16 with the cry of Elijah, as in Romans 11.3 and 1 Kings 19.10: 'He affirms himself as only-begotten, according to what is said. And I have been left alone, and they seek my life (Κἀγὼ ὑπελειφθην μόνος, καὶ ζητοῦσι τὴν ψυχήν μου). And therefore I am poor, not having the protection of those of like zeal'.[89]

He then goes on to appear to equate the only-begotten in the psalm with the person of Christ ('only-begotten of a father'). And, though there

85 ἐπίφανον τὸ πρόσωπόν σου ἐπὶ τὸν δοῦλόν σου, σῶσόν με ἐν τῷ ἐλέει σου: *In Ps. Tura* 30.17, T 149, 14, Gronewald, 3, 102.

86 *In Ps. Tura* 30.17, T: 149, 15–18, Gronewald, 3, 102; based on the translation of Rondeau, *Commentaires Patristiques du Psautier, Vol. II*, 236.

87 μὴ γὰρ τοῦτο λέγει· ἐπίφανον τὸ πρόσωπόν σου ἐπὶ τὸν δοῦλόν σου, τὸν ἄλλον ἐμοῦ· ἐμὲ τὸν δοῦλόν σου: *In Ps. Tura* 30.18, T 149, 30, Gronewald, 3, 104.

88 ἐπίβλεψον ἐπ' ἐμὲ καὶ ἐλέησόν με, ὅτι μονογενὴς καὶ πτωχός εἰμι ἐγώ.... φύλαξον τὴν ψυχήν μου καὶ ῥῦσαί με· μὴ καταισχυνθείην, ὅτι ἤλπισα ἐπί σέ.

89 *In Ps. caten.* 24, 16b-20, Mühlenberg, 1, 228, 248.

is some ambiguity, it is most likely that for Didymus the prayer is a prayer offered by Christ.[90]

There is here in this commentary an allusion to Christ's abandonment by his friends in the face of his enemies at the time of his passion. Didymus in this passage interprets the phrase 'only child and poor' (μονογενὴς καὶ πτωχός) as an affirmation of both the divinity and the humanity of the Son of God.

The relationship of the two natures in Christ is also a concern for Eusebius. He seeks to explain the text of Psalm 85.2–3, 'Preserve my life for I am devoted to you, save your slave who hopes in you, O my God. Have mercy on me, O Lord, for to you I cry all day long'.[91] This is the only psalm-text out of the fifty-eight which does not appear to be linked to the passion. Eusebius comments on verse 2, implying that the speaker is Christ, and appears to make a distinction between the man who speaks and the Word by whom he is assumed:

> And since he is not yet aware of being a son (συνῄδει ἑαυτῷ μηδέπω ὄντι υἱῷ), he naturally likens himself to a slave and says, 'Save your slave, O God, who hopes in you'. He is a slave of God who is not in servitude to sin, nor subdued by any passion, but who is in subjection to the only Word of God (μόνῳ δὲ Θεοῦ Λόγῳ ὑποτεταγμένος), and who has hope is no one else other than the one God.[92]

And he adds with regard to verse 3: 'I pray for and ask for your mercy: and this is my continual prayer (καὶ αὕτη μου ἐστιν ἡ διηνεκὴς προσευχή).... For it is necessary to pray not just for one day, but for the whole of one's life' (ἀλλὰ διὰ πάσης τῆς ἑαυτῶν ζωῆς).[93]

Again he speculates on the relationship between the two natures, with regard to Psalm 108.21–4. Eusebius sees Christ as the exclusive speaker of this psalm. He notes in his commentary on verses 2 and 3: 'The present

90 ὅπου γὰρ πρόσκειται τῷ μονογενεῖ υἱὸς ἢ παρὰ πατρὸς μονογενές, λέγεται τὸ μόνον ἐξ ἐκείνου τυγχάνον: ibid.

91 Φύλαξον τὴν ψυχήν μου, ὅτι ὅσιός εἰμι· σῶσον τὸν δοῦλον σου, ὁ Θεὸς, τὸν ἐλπίζοντα ἐπὶ σέ...Ἐλέησόν με, Κύριε, ὅτι πρὸς σέ κεκράξομαι ὅλην τὴν ἡμέραν: PG 23, 1029D–1032A.

92 Ibid.

93 PG 23, 1032A.

psalm refers to the person of Christ (Ὁ παρῶν ψαλμὸς ἀναφέρεται εἰς πρόσωπον τοῦ Χριστοῦ) and to the sufferings surrounding him'.[94] He goes on to say: 'In this beginning the Saviour asks his Father in a completely human way, as he is made man, but remains God, as he was…'.[95]

He makes no specific Christological reference to the prayers in verses 21 and 22. However, there is surely some justification for reading those psalm-prayers in the light of the above, wherein Eusebius, in contrast to Didymus, clearly sees within the psalm a witness to the distinctiveness rather more than to the unity of the two natures in Christ.

## *7. Ambiguous texts*

As has been indicated above, in four of the fifty-eight texts it is unclear as to whether the scholar is attributing the psalm-verse to the person of Christ or to some other speaker. We must now explore those texts in which the identity of the speaker is withheld, whether or not by the design of the exegete.

Ambiguity surrounds two texts which find themselves in Origen's commentary, both of which are considered to be from Evagrius' *Scholia ad psalmos*. Firstly, he lays out the text of Psalm 3.8, 'Rise up, O Lord! Save me, O my God! For you are the one who struck all who are hostile to me for nothing; you shattered the teeth of sinners'.[96] He interprets this plea in the light of the resurrection of Christ. The call to the Lord to 'arise (Ἀνάστα), and save me' is clearly linked to his resurrection (ἀνάστασις): 'How much more did he hand over the Saviour for us all. The Father put him to sleep. And he raised him, saving him and smiting his enemies (ἀνίσταται δὲ σώσων αὐτόν καὶ πατάσσων τοὺς ἐχθροὺς αὐτοῦ), whether those from the circumcision, or the unseen powers, enemies of the truth'.[97]

94 PG 23, 1333B.

95 Ὁ τοίνυν Σωτὴρ διὰ τῶν προκειμένων ἀρχόμενος ἀνθρωπίνως, ὡς γενόμενος ἄνθρωπος, μείνας δὲ Θεὸς, ὅπερ ἦν, ἱκετεύει τὸν ἑαυτοῦ Πατέρα… PG 23, 1333C.

96 Ἀνάστα, Κύριε, σῶσόν με, ὁ Θεός μου, ὅτι σὺ ἐπάταξας πάντας τοὺς ἐχθραίνοντάς μοι ματαίως, ὀδόντας ἁμαρτωλῶν συνέτριψας, κ.τ.έ.: PG 12, 1129B.

97 PG 12, 1129C.

It appears that the words of the psalm-verse may be spoken by Christ. Origen comments on the previous verse: '"I would not fear the myriads of people who hound me"... The Saviour, knowing in the Spirit the myriads of Jews who are clamouring for him to be crucified, and seeing his own lack of confusion (ὁρῶν τὸ ἀτάραχον αὐτοῦ) – according to the flesh, I would say, – can also say these words'.[98]

As to whether or not Psalm 3.8 is a prayer of Christ himself, therefore, Origen seems prepared to keeps his options open with. For him, Christ may be either the addressor or the recipient of the supplication in question.

Secondly, in much the same way, Origen, or rather Evagrius, comments on Psalm 4.2: 'When I would call, the God of my righteousness listened to me. In distress you gave me room. Have compassion on me and listen to my prayer'.[99] He adopts an approach with a similar ambiguity to that of his exegesis of Psalm 3.8. He says that the verse is spoken in the person of the prophet (David) or of Christ 'according to the economy which he assumes for us',[100] without committing himself to give a definitive explanation as to who the speaker is.

In a similar way, in his commentary on Psalm 40.11, 'But you, O Lord, be gracious to me, and raise me up, and I shall repay them', Cyril appears to affirm that this prayer to the Lord to be gracious and to 'raise me up' is also made BY Christ: 'These things are fitting for Christ through the mode of humanity'.[101] However, the commentary goes on to interpret the prayer in the light of the resurrection of Christ for us.[102] Here Cyril displays a similar ambiguity to that of Origen in his exegesis of Psalm 3.8. It is not absolutely clear whether Cyril understands this to be a prayer offered BY Christ or TO Christ.

Finally, we see a comparable uncertainty in Theodoret's commentary on Psalm 9.14, 'Have mercy on me, O Lord. See my humiliation at the hands

98 PG 12, 1129AB.

99 Ἐν τῷ ἐπικαλεῖσθαί με, εἰσήκουσέ μου ὁ Θεὸς τῆς δικαιοσύνης μου: PG 27, 72C; see also AS 2, 452.

100 κατὰ τὴν οἰκονομίαν ἣν ὑπὲρ ἡμῶν ἀνεδέξατο: PG 12, 1133D–1136A.

101 Ταῦτα ἁρμόττει τῷ Χριστῷ διὰ τὸ τῆς ἀνθρωπότητος μέτρον: PG 69, 997A.

102 PG 69, 997B-D.

of my enemies; you are the one who lifts me up from the gates of death':[103] '[T]his was the kind of cry of lament and wailing, as though containing some petition about the troubles besetting him'.[104]

The preceding commentary would seem to suggest that the speaker of this verse is the Saviour. Theodoret identifies the 'son's secrets' in the title of the psalm with the mystery of Christ's death, and agrees with other authorities that the psalm 'contains a prophecy of Christ the Lord's victory over death'. However, whether or not Theodoret intends to impute this prayer to the Son of God is far from clear, as he fails to nail his colours to the mast.

## *8. Miscellanea*

Five other texts give us a miscellany of insights into how the scholars in question understood the various invocations of Christ in the psalm-verses. Eusebius is content with a simple observation with regard to the text of Psalm 16.7, 'Wondrously show your steadfast love, you who save those that hope in you from those who withstand your right hand'.[105] He comments that Jesus saves, in a way that is different from the law of Moses, those who have hoped in him.[106] In the following verse, 'Guard me as the apple of an eye; you will shelter me under the shelter of your wings',[107] he treads a slightly different path. Here he brings out both the soteriological and ecclesiological aspects of Christ's cries of distress, where the prayers addressed to the Father are on behalf of the Church.[108]

103 Ἐλέησόν με, Κύριε, ἴδε τὴν ταπείνωσίν μου ἐκ τῶν ἐχθρῶν μου, PG 80, 928B.

104 Hill, Fathers of the Church 101, 92.

105 θαυμάστωσον τὰ ἐλέη σου, ὁ σώζον τοὺς ἐλπίζοντας ἐπὶ σὲ ἐκ τῶν ἀνθεστηκότων τῇ δεξιᾷ σου.

106 ἀλλ' ὥσπερ καινὴν ὁδὸν εὑράμενος, σώζων ἀνεφάνη τοὺς εἰς αὐτὸν ἠλπικότας: PG 23, 161C.

107 φύλαχον με ὡς κόραν ὀφθαλμοῦ· ἐν σκέπῃ τῶν πτερύγων σου σκεπάσεις με.

108 Ἀλλὰ καὶ ὁ Σωτὴρ ὑπὲρ τῆς αὐτοῦ Ἐκκλησίας, ἥτις ἐστὶν αὐτοῦ σῶμα, ταύτας ἀνέπεμπε πρὸς τὸν Πατέρα τὰς φωνάς: PG 23, 161D–164A.

Ecclesiology is also a key concern in Origen's treatment of Psalm 17.44, 'You will deliver me from disputes with people, you will make me head of nations'.[109] His commentary links the prayer to the New Testament teaching on the headship of Christ: 'Christ says these things as a sign to his opponents, he whom God has placed as head of the nations (ὅν ὁ Θεὸς κατέστησεν εἰς κεφαλὴν ἐθνῶν). For Christ is the Head of the Church'.[110]

As with Origen's reflection on Psalm 16.7, so simplicity is the order of the day with regard to Eusebius's reading of the text of Psalm 69.2, 'O God, attend to helping me'.[111] Eusebius links this prayer of David with the 'sayings of the Saviour'.[112] Here and in verse 5 it is clear that he understands Christ to be the speaker of the psalm.

Finally, though it makes few appearances in these psalm-texts, the ἀναστάσις is the focus of Cyril's interpretation of Psalm 68.15,[113] where, for Cyril, this prayer for mercy is linked to salvation through the resurrection of Christ (ὑπὲρ αὐτῶνἀποθανόντα με σώσας διὰ τῆς ἀναστάσεως), for, Christ says, 'for them I have taken upon myself life and salvation' (Ὑπὲρ αὐτῶν γὰρ ἀναδέχομαι ζωὴν καὶ σωτηρίαν).[114]

## II. Summary

As has been made clear, where the scholars interpret a particular psalm-verse to be a prayer offered by Christ, the dominant *motif* in his exposition has centred on Christ's humanity and his solidarity with the human race. The readers of these particular texts are therefore being encouraged to invoke

109 Ρύσαί με ἐξ ἀντιλογών λαού, καταστήσεις με εἰς κεφαλὴν ἐθνῶν, κ.τ.έ.: PG 12, 1240A.
110 PG 12, 1240A.
111 Ὁ Θεὸς, εἰς τὴν βοήθειαν μου πρόσχες: PG 23, 768B.
112 εἰς πρόσωπον ἀναφέρεται τὰ λεγόμενα τοῦ Σωτῆρος: PG 23, 768D.
113 σῶσόν με ἀπὸ πηλοῦ, ἵνα μὴ ἐνπαγῶ᾽ ῥυσθείην ἐκ τῶν μισούντων με καὶ ἐκ τοῦ βάθους τῶν ὑδάτων.
114 PG 69, 1165CD.

and to engage with Christ as a partner in prayer, taking his words upon their lips and into their hearts and minds, and, in the spirit advocated by Athanasius in *Epistola ad Marcellinum*, making the prayers of the Psalter, in this case the prayers of Christ, their own.

One of the surprising things about this collection of texts is that there appears to be very little Davidic reflection in the exegeses of the prayers credited to Christ, despite the fact that David is often portrayed as the mouthpiece of Christ by the writers in question. Nevertheless, the Christological interest in these passages surrounds the determination of the exegetes to affirm the true and full humanity of Christ. Jesus, in his κένωσις, in his descent from David, in the exercise of his free will, and in his experience of suffering and vulnerability is, without reservation, a 'man among men'.

Following on from this, as one who stands in solidarity with the human race, Christ prays, intercedes, fights, suffers, dies and rises again, as the representative of corporate humanity before God. The soteriological dynamic arises easily from the establishment of the Christological base, with the ecclesiological interest playing a relatively minor role.

For the Greek Fathers of the fourth and fifth centuries, as for the Eastern Church as a whole, the recitation of psalmody therefore involved an encounter with Christ himself, in which the individual or the community would be standing alongside Christ and praying with him in partnership with a fellow human being, a suffering intercessor on behalf of an afflicted human creation and a comrade-in-arms in spiritual warfare.

Whether as inspired poetic works, or as a collection of songs, or as a hymn book of the Second Temple, or as a Psalter of the Church, the Fathers encouraged the communities of their day to use the psalms as a way of joining their prayers with those of Christ, who, in the much quoted words of Paul the Apostle, 'emptied himself, taking the form of a servant, being born in human likeness'.

CHAPTER TEN

# The Invocation of Christ as Deliverer

We now turn our attention to what Andrew Louth in his article has described as the second of the 'two predominant Christian ways of understanding the psalms', whereby the recitation of the psalm-verses is to be understood as an activity involving praying TO Christ for divine assistance. Thus our focus shifts from the invocation of Christ as partner to the invocation of Christ as deliverer.

In his opening comment on Psalm 79.2–4 Didymus the Blind boldly declares, 'The shepherd of Israel is none other than he who said, "I am the good shepherd"'.[1] It follows that, for Didymus, the psalm is addressed to the person of Christ, and, furthermore, that the short invocatory prayer, 'Stir up your sovereign power and come in order to save us',[2] is a prayer whereby the psalmist directly calls upon Christ for the salvation of his people.

The purpose of this chapter is to explore the extent to which and the manner in which the exegetes understood such short invocatory prayers, which occur in the Septuagint Psalter, as either direct appeals to the Saviour for deliverance, or as pleas made to God the Father for aid through the intervention of his Son. The short invocatory prayers in question include such personal phrases as those listed in the previous chapter, as well as some more corporate usages, such as οἰκτειρῆσαί ἡμᾶς, and ἐλθὲ εἰς τὸ σωσαι ἡμᾶς.

The commentaries selected for this part of the investigation are those which demonstrate the keenest interest in the matter under discussion. For that reason, with regard to those of Didymus the Blind, the relevant texts are drawn exclusively from Mühlenberg's edition of the *catenae*, rather than from the Tura commentary, edited by Gronewald. The latter provides no

1 *In Ps. caten.* 79.2–4, Mühlenberg 2, 825, 136.

2 ἐξέγειρον τὴν δυναστείαν σου καὶ ἐλθὲ εἰς τὸ σῶσαι ἡμᾶς.

useful material for our purpose here. In the works under discussion there is a total of forty-one texts in which it is possible to establish an intention on the part of the exegete to identify the person of Christ as either the direct or indirect recipient of the short invocatory prayer. In addition to these texts there are others where the exegete stops short of making such a specific identification, but where he makes some unequivocal Christological reflection upon the prayer.[3] In other words, the tendency of the Fathers not only to read the psalms from a general Christological perspective, but, more specifically, to understand them as prayers for salvation, mercy, etc. from Christ himself is firmly rooted in the works which they produced for the edification of the faithful, including the monastic communities.

A total of twenty-two psalms provide the passages for the forty-one texts. Of these, Psalm 79 is the most widely used, accounting for seven of the texts in question. Following this, Psalm 30 features in five of the texts, Psalms 3, 53 and 66 in three each, and Psalms 27, 59 and 85 in two each. Those providing only one text are Psalms 6, 7, 16, 34, 35, 42, 43, 70, 84, 107, 117, 118, 142 and 143.

Eleven different imperatives or their equivalents call the Son of God to action within the forty-one texts. Sometimes the imperative stands on its own, and at other times it is coupled with another. According to the works under consideration, the phrases in the Psalter which are most likely to commit the commentator to identify the prayer as an invocation of Christ is σῶσόν με/ἡμᾶς or its equivalents. With twenty-three references, it appears in more than half of the total number of texts.

The prayer ἐλέησόν με/ἡμᾶς and its equivalents form the imperative in nine of the psalm-verses in question. The combined plea of ῥῦσαι με καὶ ἐξελοῦ με is to be found in five texts, with these imperatives appearing together rather than separately, though in Psalm 7 ῥῦσαί με is combined

3 See, for example, Athanasius' treatment of Psalm 11.2, where the prayer for salvation, 'because the holy man has failed and truth is diminished among the children of men', is seen in the light of the Jews' rejection of Jesus; and Origen's and Cyril's exegeses of Psalm 50.3, where the prayer for mercy is linked to the great mercy of Christ which wipes out every sin from the world (PG 27, 93C; PG 12, 1453D–1456A; PG 69, 1088CD).

with σῶσόν με. Four references to κρίνόν με feature in the texts, three of which relate to the commentaries on Psalm 53, while οἰκτειρήσαί ἡμᾶς makes a total of three appearances, all within the coverage of Psalm 66. While εἰς τήν βοήθειάν μου and βοήθησόν ἡμῖν are recorded in the commentaries on Psalms 34 and 43 respectively, ζωώσεις ἡμᾶς makes one solitary entrance, in Origen's commentary on Psalm 79.

## I. Themes

What were the connecting links which led the exegetes to look beyond the outer letter of the psalm-verse to the inner spiritual meaning of the text? What were the themes which enabled and encouraged the authors of the works in question to hear the voice of the psalmist appealing either directly or indirectly to Christ for help? In some of the passages before us more than one theological connection comes into play. However, in the exploration which follows we will endeavour to identify seven key theological themes which emerge from the commentaries, which are by no means mutually exclusive, but which, nevertheless, encapsulate much of the inspiration behind the drive of the fourth- and fifth-century Greek Fathers to see the presence of Christ in this particular aspect of the Psalter.

### *1. Gegonen Anthrōpos*

In his commentary on Psalm 79.3, 'Before Ephraim, Benjamin and Mannaseh, stir up your sovereign power and come in order to save us', Cyril says, 'These things are said prophetically... For in the last times the only-begotten Word of God is made man (γέγονεν ἄνθρωπος)'.[4] For Cyril,

4 Ἐν ἐσχάτοις γὰρ τοῦ αἰῶνος καιροῖς γέγονεν ἄνθρωπος ὁ μονογενὴς τοῦ Θεοῦ Λόγος: PG 69, 1197B.

then, this prayer is grounded in the simple truth of the incarnation, which is the fulfilment of the prophecy of the psalm-verse. The verse, Ἐλθὲ εἰς τὸ σῶσαι ἡμᾶς,[5] is therefore either a plea to the Father that he will send his Word to take on human flesh, or, more likely, to the Son that he will come in person 'to save us'.

While Cyril focuses on the incarnation itself as the key to understanding the psalm-verse, in five other passages, one from Athanasius and four from Eusebius, the spotlight is placed on particular aspects of the incarnation, which become foci for Christological interpretation.

The identification of the Son with a divine attribute is made by Athanasius in his commentary on the text of Psalm 118.76, 'Let your steadfast love come to comfort me'.[6] He writes, 'The Son is the mercy of the Father, even he who comforted our hearts, which were oppressed by Satan'.[7] Thus this prayer, 'Let your mercy be a comfort to me' is identified as a prayer that the Son, 'who is the mercy of the Father', should be sent as a comforter.

Following a similar pattern, Eusebius comments on the passage, Psalm 34.1–2, 'Render judgment, O Lord, on those who do me injustice; fight against those who fight against me! Take hold of circular shield and oblong shield, and rise up to help me!'[8] Here Eusebius identifies Christ as the embodiment of the salvation of God. This prayer to God to arise to help, followed by the invocation 'Say to my soul, I am your salvation',[9] is a prayer linked to Paul's words about Christ in Galatians 2.20, 'I have been crucified with Christ; it is no longer I who live, but Christ who lives in me'. Eusebius adds, with reference to Christ, 'For he is our salvation'.[10] The God invoked here is therefore Christ.

5 Ibid.

6 Γενηθήτω δὴ τὸ ἔλεός σου τοῦ παρακαλέσαι με: PG 27, 493B.

7 Ἔλεος τοῦ Πατρὸς ὁ Υἱὸς, ὅς καὶ παρεκάλεσεν ἡμῶν τὰς καρδίας τυρρανουμένας ὑπὸ τοῦ Σατανᾶ: PG 27, 493B.

8 Δίκασον, Κύριε, τοῦς ἀδικοῦντας με, πολέμησον τοῦς πολεμοῦντας με. Ἐπιλαβοῦ ὅπλου καὶ θυρεοῦ· καὶ ἀνάστηθι εἰς βοήθειάν μοι: PG 23, 296D.

9 Εἶπον τῇ ψυχῇ μου· Ζωτηρία σου ἐγώ εἰμι: ibid.

10 Αὐτὸς γάρ ἐστιν ἡ σωτηρία ἡμῶν: PG 23, 297AB.

In the same vein, he also reflects on Psalm 84.8, 'Show us your steadfast love, O Lord, and may you grant us your salvation'.[11] This prayer for mercy and salvation is linked directly to the prophecy of Christ's coming, that is, the prophecy of Simeon. With regard to the words, 'and may you grant us your salvation', Eusebius comments, 'Simeon in the Gospels clearly taught that Christ was this salvation'.[12] It therefore follows that 'Show us your mercy, Lord, and may you grant us your salvation' is a plea either to Christ that he may come as Saviour, or possibly to the Father to send his Son as the embodiment of his saving love.

In two further passages, less obviously related to the incarnation theme, Eusebius seizes upon a key concept in order to identify the recipient of the invocation as the Person of Christ.

Firstly, he comments on the text of Psalm 6.2–4: 'Have mercy on me, Lord, for I am weak; heal me, Lord, for my bones are troubled'.[13] This prayer for mercy and healing is linked to a flight to the 'Saviour and Physician, the Son of God'.[14] Hence the invocation is made directly to the Son of God, the Great Physician, and source of healing.

Secondly, with regard to Psalm 27.9, 'O save your people and bless your heritage',[15]he writes, 'What the inheritance of Christ is like is declared in the second psalm: "Ask of me", he says, "And I will give you the nations as your inheritance, and the ends of the earth as your possession"'.[16] This prayer for salvation and blessing for the Lord's people is understood in the light of a prayer addressed to Christ in Psalm 2.8. 'Your inheritance' (τὴν κληρονομίαν σου) therefore indicates that this prayer is also addressed to Christ.

11 Δεῖξον ἡμῖν, Κύριε, τὸ ἔλεός σου καὶ τὸ σωτήριόν σου δῷης ἡμῖν: PG 23, 1021A.

12 τὸ σωτήριον αὐτὸν εἶναι τὸν Χριστὸν ἐδίδαξεν ὁ Συμεὼν ἐν τοῖς Εὐαγγελίοις: PG 23, 1021A.

13 Ἐλέησόν με, Κύριε, ὅτι ἀσθενής εἰμι· ἴασαί με, Κύριε, ὅτι ἐταπάχθη τὰ ὀστᾶ μου: PG 23, 120B.

14 καταφεύγει πρὸς τὸν Σωτῆρα καὶ ἰατρὸν, τον Υἱὸν τοῦ Θεοῦ: PG 23, 120B.

15 Σῶσον τὸν λαὸν σου, καὶ εὐλόγησον τὴν κληρονομίαν σου, PG 23, 249C.

16 Ποία δὲ τοῦ Χριστοῦ ἡ κληρονομία δείκνυται ἐν τῷ δευτέρῳ ψαλμῷ· Αἴτησαι γὰρ, φησὶν, καὶ δώσω σοι ἔθνη τὴν κληρονομίαν σου, καὶ τὴν κατάσχεσίν σου τὰ πέρατα τῆς γῆς:¨PG 23, 249CD.

Origen also comments on this verse. For him, the prayer to the Lord to save his people and to bless his inheritance should be seen in the light of Christ pasturing his people (Αὐτὸς ὁ Χριστὸς ἡμᾶς ποιμανεῖ τοὺς εἰς αὐτὸν πεπιστευκότας) and sending to them the Paraclete, the Spirit of Truth. Christ as pastor and as sender of the Spirit is therefore invoked as Saviour.

## 2. *Dikaiosynē*

The passages above feature various aspects of the incarnation, whereby Christ is identified as the embodiment of a particular attribute of divinity. Divine righteousness (δικαιοσύνη) is one such attribute which plays a key role in five of the texts under investigation.

Psalm 30.2 provides rich pickings for us in this present quest. In each of the commentaries of Origen, Cyril and Didymus the commentator makes a link between the δικαιοσύνη of the psalm-verse and the destination of the short invocatory prayer contained therein.

Origen records the Septuagint text, 'In you, O Lord, I hoped; may I never be put to shame; in your righteousness deliver me and rescue me'.[17] In a subsequent passage, attributable to Evagrius, the prayer to the Lord to 'deliver me and rescue me' in his righteousness is understood in the light of Christ (Ἡ τάχα δικαιοσύνην λέγει τὸν Χριστὸν) who is the wisdom and righteousness, the sanctification and the redemption of God, according to 1 Corinthians 1.30.[18] Through the identification of Christ with divine righteousness, Christ is therefore invoked as an agent of God's will to free and to rescue the supplicant.

Cyril similarly identifies Christ with the righteousness of God. He begins his commentary on the verse by saying, 'That is, in Christ deliver me from the captivity of the devil'.[19] And he makes this identification

17 Ἐπι σοι, Κύριε, ἤλπισα, μὴ καταισχυνθείην εἰς τὸν αἰῶνα, ἐν τῇ δικαιοσύνῃ σου ῥῦσαί με καὶ ἐξελοῦ με, κ.τ.ἑ.: PG 12, 1297C.

18 PG 12, 1297D–1300A.

19 Τουτέστιν ἐν τῷ Χριστῷ ῥῦσαί με ἀπὸ τῆς αἰχμαλωσίας τοῦ διαβόλου, PG 69, 857C.

clear as he goes on to say, with a little help from Acts 4.12 (and with John 10.9 and 15.5 thrown in for good measure!).[20] The equation of 'in your righteousness' (ἐν τῇ δικαιοσύνῃ σου) with 'in Christ' (ἐν τῷ Χριστῷ), and with the saving name of Christ, confirms that Cyril interprets this psalm as a prayer for deliverance through the medium of the divine righteousness, which is Christ.

Didymus offers a different perspective on his exegesis of this verse, though with the same result as that of the two previous interpretations. For him, the psalmist is asking God to deliver him 'in his righteousness', which is 'not another than your only-begotten' (οὐκ ἄλλη οὔσῃ τοῦ μονογενοῦς σου).[21] This seems to be a statement of Alexandrian Christology, affirming the unity of Christ's person. Christ is therefore invoked as an expression of divine righteousness and as an instrument of deliverance.

Eusebius sets down the text of Psalm 35.11, 'O extend your steadfast love to those who know you, and your righteousness to the upright of heart!'[22] This prayer for mercy is addressed directly to the Saviour. For Eusebius begins his commentary on the verse: 'Saviour, extend your mercy and your righteousness to those who will know you.'[23] He therefore understands the prayer as a direct appeal to Christ 'in his righteousness'.

Psalm 70.2, 'In your righteousness rescue me and deliver me; incline your ear to me and save me',[24] provides Cyril with an opening to acknowledge Christ as the indirect addressee of the trilogy of calls for assistance in the psalm-text. This prayer for deliverance and mercy 'in your righteousness' is made to the Son of the Father, for he says, 'The Son is the righteousness of the Father'.[25] The Son is therefore invoked as the Father's agent.

20 Γέγονε γὰρ ἡμῖν δικαιοσύνην· οὐκ ἔστιν γὰρ ὄνομα ἕτερον τὸ δεδομένον ἐν ἀνθρώποις, ἐν ᾧ δεῖ σωθῆναι ἡμᾶς: PG 69, 857D.

21 *In Ps. caten.* 30.2–3b, Mühlenberg 1, 268, 264.

22 Παράτεινον τὸ ἔλεός σου τοῖς γινώσκουσί σε, καὶ τὴν δικαιοσύνην σου τοῖς εὐθέσι τῇ καρδίᾳ: PG 23, 321C.

23 τοῖς δὲ γινώσκουσί σε, Σῶτερ, παράτεινον τὸ ἔλεός σου καὶ τὴν δικαιοσύνην σου, PG 23, 321C.

24 Έν τή δικαιοσύνή σου ρύσαί με καί έξελού με: PG 69, 1180A.

25 Έστι δικαιοσύνη τού Πατρὸς ὁ Υἱὸς: ibid.

### 3. *Dynamis*

As the short invocatory prayers are all calling for some kind of exercise of divine potency, it is not surprising to find that power (δύναμις), like righteousness, is also an important theological theme in these texts.

Didymus specifically focuses on 'your power' in the text of Psalm 53.3, 'Save me O God, in your name, and you will judge me in your power'.[26] For him, this prayer for divine judgment and salvation is made to the power of the Father, who is Christ. He says, 'Christ is the power of the Father. And he judges the hidden things of men…'.[27] The psalmist is therefore understood to be invoking Christ, as the power of God.

Athanasius also reflects on Psalm 53.3. And in his reflection this prayer to God to 'save me in your name',[28] is accompanied by the request that this should be done 'in your power, that is, in your Son'.[29] Christ, as the embodiment of the power of God, is therefore invoked as the instrument for giving salvation and justice to the supplicant.

The same psalm-verse is treated rather differently by Theodoret. This prayer to God for salvation 'in your name' is specifically interpreted as an invocation in the name of Christ. Here we have a classic example of a tendency on the part of the commentators in question to equate the divine name in the psalms with the name of Christ, as we have seen in Chapter 7.

In a similar spirit, Theodoret interprets Psalm 53.3 in the light of Acts 3.6: '"In the name of Jesus Christ", Scripture says, "get up and walk"'.[30] Therefore the prayer 'O God, in your name save me' is a prayer addressed to Christ, the power of whose name can bring salvation.

Origen's, or rather Evagrius', exegesis of Psalm 79 yields an abundance of useful material to our enquiry, especially with regard to the power theme.

26 ὁ θεὸς, ἐν τῷ ὀνόματί σου σῶσόν με, καὶ ἐν τῇ δυνάμει σου κρῖνόν με.

27 Δύναμις τοῦ πατρὸς ὁ Χριστός. οὗτος δὲ κρινεῖ τὰ κρυπτὰ τῶν ἀνθρώπων: *In Ps. caten.* 53.3b, Mühlenberg 2, 566, 7.

28 PG 27, 249B.

29 ἐν δυναστείᾳ σου, τουτέστι τῷ Υἱῷ σου: PG 27, 249CD.

30 Ἐν τῷ ὀνόματι γὰρ, φησὶν, Ἰησοῦ Χριστοῦ ἔγειραι, καὶ περιπάτει: PG 80, 1265A; Hill, Fathers of the Church 101, 311–12.

He begins with verse 3, 'Stir up your sovereign power, etc.'.[31] In the commentary which immediately follows, Origen says: 'Christ the power of God and the wisdom of God'.[32] This establishes the Christological context of the psalm, and Christological interpretations follow in verses 8, 18 and 19. Verse 3 is thus identified as an appeal to God to stir up his power, his Son, for the salvation of his people.

The commentary on verse 18, which itself contains no short invocatory prayer, reflects on the words, 'Let your hand be upon the man of your right hand' (ἐπ' ἄνδρα δεξιᾶς σου, κ. τ. ἑ.). Origen observes that the psalmist 'calls the man of the right hand Christ (Ἄνδρα δεξιὸν λέγει τὸν Χριστὸν), who is the Son of Man'.[33] The concept of the 'man of the right hand', or the 'right hand' as a symbol of the power and authority of God, is featured in three of the texts. It carries with it in the ensuing exegeses undertones of the ascension of Christ.

Eusebius offers a similar interpretation of Psalm 107.7 'Save with your right hand and hearken to me'.[34] This is a prayer for salvation 'by your right hand' to the 'God who has spoken in his holy one' (Ὁ Θεὸς ἐλάλησεν ἐν τῷ ἁγίῳ αὐτοῦ). Who is this God? It is the only-begotten Son: 'Who was the holy one of God, if not the only-begotten Son (ἤ ὁ μονγενὴς Παῖς...), who is truly holy and beloved.?'. The equation of the divine right hand with the 'holy one' and their mutual identification with the only-begotten Son places Eusebius in the tradition of Origen in interpreting such a psalm-verse as an invocation of the power of God through the action of Christ.

Theodoret comments on Psalm 59.7, 'Save with your right hand and listen to me'.[35] On the prayer, he says, in an insertion from the longer text, 'May none of those believing in him doubt that his only-begotten Son is called right hand of God and Father'.[36] Origen's and Eusebius's identification

31 Ἐξέγειρον τὴν δυναστειάν σου, κ. τ. ἑ. PG 12, 1544B.

32 Χριστὸς Θεοῦ δύναμις καὶ Θεοῦ σοφία: PG 12, 1544B.

33 PG 12, 1544C.

34 Σῶσον τῇ δεξιᾷ σου, καὶ ἐπακουσόν μου: PG 23, 1329B.

35 Σῶσον τῇ δεξιᾷ σου, καὶ ἐπάκουσόν μου: PG 80, 1317D.

36 ὅτι δὲ δεξιὰ τοῦ Θεοῦ καὶ Πατρὸς ὁ μονογενὴς αὐτοῦ Υἱὸς ὀνομάζεται: PG 80, 1320A; Hill, Fathers of the Church 101, 345.

of Christ with this symbol of power is thus followed, and the intervention of Christ is thus invoked.

Similarly, with regard to the same psalm-verse, Cyril writes, 'We say that the Son is the right hand of the Father (Δεξιὰν εἶναί φαμεν τοῦ Πατρὸς τὸν Υἱὸν), through whom all things were made'.[37] Like Theodoret he understands the prayer 'save by your right hand' as an appeal to God to effect salvation through the action of his Christ.

## 4. *Epiphaneia*

In a significant number of passages an epiphanic or revelatory theme functions as the connecting link between the psalm-verse and the commentary. In Chapter 8 we have seen how the commentaries of Origen, Theodoret and Cyril on Psalm 66.2 make great play on a psalm-verse which includes the phrase, 'display his face to us' (ἐπιφάναι τὸ πρόσωπον αὐτου ἐφ' ἡμᾶς), thus associating Christ with the πρόσωπον of God in the psalm-verse.[38] We have also seen how Origen (Evagrius), Theodoret and Cyril, in their commentaries on Psalm 79.3–4 and 8, make a similar association with regard to the text, 'show your face, and we shall be saved'.[39] The effect of these associations is to identify Christ as the recipient of the prayers contained within the psalm-verses.

Eusebius also reflects on this Psalm 79.3–4: 'Stir up your sovereign power, and come in order to save us ... show your face, and we shall be saved' (Ἐξέγειρον τὴν δυναστείαν σου, καὶ ἐλθὲ, εἰς τὸ σῶσαι ἡμᾶς...Ἐπίφανον τὸ πρόσωπόν σου, καὶ σωθησόμεθα).[40] Who is the God invoked here? Eusebius's commentary focuses on the glory of God, which he goes on to identify with that of the 'only-begotten Word of God' (ἢ ὁ μονογενὴς τοῦ Θεοῦ Λόγος).[41] Christ is therefore invoked as the bringer of salvation, either directly or as an agent of the Father.

37 PG 69, 1113A.
38 PG 12, 1504B; PG 80, 1372B; PG 69, 1140C.
39 PG 12, 1544B; PG 80, 1513B; PG 69, 1197C.
40 PG 23, 952CD.
41 PG 23, 956B.

As we have seen in the introduction to this chapter, Didymus offers an explicit interpretation of this verse. For him, this prayer for salvation is made against the background of the 'light of the knowledge of the glory of Christ'.[42] Didymus makes it clear in his opening comment on verses 2–4 that this invocation of the 'shepherd of Israel' is a prayer to the one who said, 'I am the good shepherd'.

Athanasius comments on the text of Psalm 42.1, 'Vindicate me, O God, and defend my cause'.[43] This prayer to God to 'judge me' is a prayer for those of Israel seeking salvation through Christ. 'Send out your light and your truth', with an allusion to the transfiguration,[44] is a direct reference to Christ. The agency of Christ is thus invoked.

Meanwhile Cyril approaches Psalm 30.10 from the perspective of the revelation of the grace of Christ, 'Have mercy on me, O Lord, for I am being afflicted'.[45] He observes concerning the psalmist: 'What, then, do we say? He senses grace through Christ, and he wonders at the way in which he is helped'.[46] Christ is therefore invoked either as the source or the bearer of the mercy sought.

Theodoret speaks to the text of Psalm 117.25, 'Ah, Lord, do save us! Ah, Lord, do give us success'.[47] In this prayer to God for salvation the invocation refers back to the 'Sun of Righteousness' in verse 24: 'In a particular sense, however, he said this day was made by God, since God in the beginning made the light on it, and it also received the resurrection of our Saviour and dispatched the rays of the Sun of Righteousness to the whole world'.[48]

42 πρὸς φωτισμὸν τῆς γνώσεως τῆς δόξης τοῦ Χριστοῦ: *In Ps. caten.* 79.2–4, Mühlenberg 2, 825, 136.

43 Κρῖνόν με, ὁ Θεὸς, καὶ δίκασον: PG 27, 204B.

44 Αὐτὸς γὰρ αὐτοὺς καὶ εἰς τὸ ἅγιον ὄρος εἰσάγειν ἔμελλε: PG 27, 204C.

45 Ἐλέησόν με, Κύριε, ὅτι θλίβομαι: PG 69, 860C.

46 Τί οὖν ἐροῦμεν; Αἰσθάνεται μὲν τῆς χάριτος τῆς διὰ Χριστοῦ, καὶ δὴ τεθαύμακε τῆς ἐπικουρίας τὸν τρόπον: PG 69, 860D.

47 Ὦ Κύριε, σῶσον δὴ, ὦ Κύριε, εὐόδωσον δή: PG 80, 1817B.

48 Διαφερόντως δὲ ταύτην ὑπὸ τοῦ Θεοῦ γεγενῆσθαι τῆν ἡμέραν ἔφη. Ἐπειδὴ γὰρ ἐξ ἀρχῆς τὸ φῶς ἐν αὐτῇ πεποίηκεν ὁ Θεὸς, καὶ τὴν του Σωτῆρος ἡμῶν ἀνάστασιν δεξαμένη, τοῦ τῆς δικαιοσύνης ἡλίου τὰς ἀκτῖνας εἰς πᾶσαν τὴν οἰκουμέντην κατέπεμψε: PG 80, 1817A; Hill, Fathers of the Church 102, 242.

Furthermore, it looks ahead to the routine Christological interpretation of verse 26,[49] and to the explicit celebration of Christ's divinity in the commentary on verse 27.[50] The commentary on verse 25 also includes the tell-tale title Δέσποτα,[51] indicating that Theodoret understands that the Lord who is invoked is Christ: 'In the future, O Lord, provide salvation'.[52]

## 5. *Anastasis*

It is not surprising that the Fathers are eager to make a connection between the invocation 'Rise up, O Lord' (Ἀνάστα, Κύριε) in the psalm-verse and the resurrection (ἀνάστασις) of Christ, in the subsequent commentary. Psalm 3, in particular, provides them with a golden opportunity for such Christological reflection, and they do not shirk it.

Origen, or rather Evagrius, lays out the text of Psalm 3.8, 'Rise up, O Lord! Save me, O my God! For you are the one who struck all who are hostile to me for nothing; you shattered the teeth of sinners'.[53] He interprets this plea in the light of the resurrection of Christ. The call to the Lord to 'arise, and save me' is clearly linked to his ἀνάστασις: 'How much more did he hand over the Saviour for us all.

The Father put him to sleep. And he raised him, saving him and smiting his enemies (ἀνίσταται δὲ σώσων αὐτὸν καὶ πατάσσων τοὺς ἐχθροὺς αὐτοῦ), whether those from the circumcision, or the unseen powers, enemies of the truth'.[54] As the one who rose, Christ would appear to be the recipient of this prayer, though it is important to remember the ambiguity inherent in this exegesis, as was noted in Chapter 9.

49 PG 80, 1817BC.

50 PG 80, 1817D.

51 See under δεσπότης 2.c. in Lampe, *Patristic Greek Lexicon*, 339.

52 Καὶ εἰς τὸν ἔπειτα χρόνον, ὦ Δέσποτα, παράσχου τὴν σωτηρίαν...: PG 80, 1817B; Hill, Fathers of the Church 102, 242.

53 Ἀνάστα, Κύριε, σῶσόν με, ὁ Θεός μου, ὅτι σὺ ἐπάταξας πάντας τοὺς ἐχθραίνοντάς μοι ματαίως, ὀδόντας ἁμαρτωλῶν συνέτριψας, κ. τ. ἑ.: PG 12, 1129B.

54 PG 12, 1129C.

Similarly, Eusebius sees in this text a prayer to the Lord Christ to arise and 'save me' on account of his resurrection, though from a different perspective:

> This, he says, I seek only so that I may be saved, lest my enemies destroy me. He takes his stand on nothing other than the resurrection of the Saviour, and consequently prays for the resurrection of the Lord to be hastened (ἀκολούθως εὔχεται ἐπιταχῦναι τοῦ Κυρίου τὴν ἀνάστασιν), on account of his favour and of his salvation. Therefore he says, 'Arise, Lord, save me, O my God'.[55]

Cyril, on the other hand, in his commentary on this psalm-verse does not directly refer to the resurrection, but to a prophecy of Christ's descent into Hades. However, the connecting link and the thrust and direction of the invocation are the same as those of Origen (Evagrius) and Eusebius: 'And how much more does the Prophet, seeing that Christ risen from the dead will set free his soul which has been held back in Hades (εἰδὼς ὅτι τὴν ψυχὴν αὐτοῦ ἐν ᾅδου κατασχεθεῖσαν ὁ Χριστὸς ἐκεῖθεν ἐλευθεπώσει ἐκ νεκρῶν ἀναστὰς), foretell what is to come'[56]

In a rare example of the βοήθησον imperative in the texts under discussion, Origen sets out the psalm-verse 43.27, 'Rise up, O Lord, come to our help. Redeem us for the sake of your name'.[57] Again the ἀνάστασις is not specified, with the emphasis being this time on the burial and the passion of Christ. This prayer to the Lord is seen as a prayer offered to the Saviour who through his passion gives redemption to many: 'Such things as these may be said to the Saviour as he lies in the heart of the earth at the time of his sufferings (κατὰ τὸν τοῦ πάθους καιρόν). He it is who gives his life as ransom for many, and does these things for the glory of his name'.[58]

We return to an explicit reference to the resurrection as Athanasius sets out the text of Psalm 142.8, 'Make me hear of your steadfast love in the

55 PG 23, 97B.

56 PG 69, 729B.

57 Ἀνάστα, Κύριε, βοήθησον ἡμῖν, καὶ λύτρωσαι ἡμᾶς ἕνεκεν τοῦ ὀνόματός σου, κ. τ. ἑ.: PG 12, 1428B.

58 PG 12, 1428BC.

morning'.[59] This prayer for mercy is linked to the 'early resurrection of the Lord'.[60] Athanasius therefore understands this prayer as an invocation to God for Christ's resurrection, as an act of mercy (ἐλεούμεθα).

### *6. Zōē*

It is interesting to note that while the word 'waters' in the Psalter generally carries with it a negative connotation, representing chaos or danger, in their commentaries the Fathers introduce the same word when seeking to emphasize the positive, life-giving nature of what is asked for in the short invocatory prayers.

Thus Didymus sees fit to tackle the passage, Psalm 143.7–8, 'Send out your hand from on high; deliver me and rescue me from many waters, from the hand of the aliens, whose mouths spoke vanity, and whose right hand was a right hand of injustice'.[61] This prayer for salvation from 'the many waters' is interpreted in the light of the story of Jesus and the woman at the well. There is an implication that he who gives the water of eternal life (εἰς ζωὴν αἰώνιον) in John 4.14 is the same one who is invoked to give salvation from the 'many waters' of destruction in Psalm 143.7–8.[62]

Eusebius reflects upon the verse, Psalm 30.10, 'Have mercy on me, O Lord, for I am being afflicted; my eye was troubled because of vexation, my soul and my belly also'.[63] This prayer to the Lord for mercy is linked with the words of Christ in John 7.38, 'Out of his *belly* (κοιλίας) will flow rivers of living water'. Eusebius moves easily from the invocation of the Lord in the psalm to the words of Jesus in the Gospel: 'And therefore the Saviour called the power of memory, or even the authoritative part of the soul, "the

59 Ἀκουστὸν ποίησόν μοι τὸ πρωί τὸ ἔλεός σου: PG 27, 541C.

60 Τὴν πρωϊνὴν ἀνάστασιν τοῦ Κυρίου λέγει: ibid.

61 ἐξελοῦ με καὶ ῥῦσαί με ἐξ ὑδάτων πολλῶν ἐκ χειρὸς υἱῶν ἀλλοτρίων, ὧν τὸ στόμα ἐλάλησεν ματαιότητα, καὶ ἡ δεξιὰ αὐτῶν δεξιὰ ἀδικίας.

62 *In Ps. caten.* 143.7–8, Mühlenberg 2, 1248, 344–5.

63 Ἐλέησόν με, Κύριε, ὅτι θλίβομαι: PG 23, 268C.

belly"'.[64] His love of irony here, with regard to κοιλίαν, does not mask his interest in identifying Christ as the giver of the water of life, which clearly represents the mercy, for which the supplicant asks from the Lord.

And once again we find Origen (Evagrius) resorting to Psalm 79, the Aladdin's Cave for Christ-directed invocations in the Psalter. He sets out the text of verse 19, 'You will revive us, and we will call upon your name',[65] a verb expressed in the form of an indicative (Ζωώσεις), but contextually bearing the force of an imperative. Here the prayer 'you will revive us', or 'give us life', is qualified by the observation that no one can give us life except him who said 'I am the life', as in John 14.6.[66] The invocation is therefore clearly addressed to Christ.

## *7. Elpizō*

The final theme through which the Fathers in these works link the short invocatory prayers of the psalm-verses to invocation of the person of Christ is that of hope. The prayers often consist of an imperative, followed by a statement as to why God should act in the way requested, which normally begins with the preposition ὅτι. One of the grounds for divine assistance most frequently expressed is that of the hope of the person or persons offering the prayer. In four of the texts under consideration it is the ground of such hope which leads the supplicant to call upon the person of Christ.

The text of Psalm 16.7 is quoted by Origen, 'Wondrously show your steadfast love, you who save those that hope in you from those who withstand your right hand'.[67] He links the plea to God to show the marvels of his mercy to the words of Jesus in response to the cry for mercy from a leper in Matthew 8.3, 'I will (it), be clean'.[68] The invocation in the psalm is

64 Κάνταῦθα τοίνυν τὴν μνημονικὴν δύναμιν, ἤ καὶ αὐτὸ τὸ ἡγεμονικὸν τῆς ψυχῆς, κοιλίαν ὠνόμασεν ὁ Σωτήρ: PG 23, 269A.

65 Ζωώσεις ἡμᾶς, καὶ τὸ ὄνομά σου ἐπικαλεσόμεθα, κ. τ. ἐ.: PG 12, 1544C.

66 Οὐδεὶς δύνασται ζωοποιῆσαι ἡμᾶς, εἰ μὴ ὁ εἰπών· <Ἐγώ εἰμι ἡ Ζωή.>: ibid.

67 Θαυμάστωσον τὰ ἐλέη σου, ὁ σώζων τοὺς ἐλπίζοντας ἐπὶ σὲ, κ. τ. ἐ.: PG 12, 1217D.

68 Θέλω, καθαρίσθητι, PG 12, 1220A.

therefore linked directly to an invocation of Christ in the Gospel, where Christ responds positively to those who hope (τοὺς ἐλπίζοντας) in him.

For Theodoret also this is the basis for his commentary on the passage Psalm 85.2–3, 'Preserve my life, for I am devoted to you; save your slave who hopes in you, O my God. Have mercy on me, O Lord, for to you I will cry all day long'.[69] This prayer for salvation is offered to Δέσποτα, one of Theodoret's titles for Christ. On the words 'Save your servant, O my God, who has hoped in you', he comments, 'I hoped in you, O Lord (Δέσποτα), save [me]; grant salvation in return for hope'.[70] The prayer is therefore made directly to Christ.

Similarly, the same text is a source for Didymus. This prayer for salvation is linked to Christ. Didymus refers to James' and Paul's self-description as a 'slave of Christ' in James 1.1 and Romans 1.1 (δοῦλος Ἰησοῦ Χριστοῦ), thus implying that it is Christ who is invoked in the prayer in which 'my God' is called upon to 'save your slave'.[71]

Finally, Didymus also offers his commentary on the passage Psalm 7.2–3, 'O Lord my God, in you I hoped; save me from all my pursuers, and deliver me, or like a lion they will seize me, with no one to redeem or save'.[72] On the grounds that 'I have hoped in you', his prayer for salvation is made through the Son, whose saving action he thus invokes, with allusions to the words of the Lord God in Hosea 13.4, but also to the words of Jesus in Luke 19.10 and Matthew 20.28: 'And who is this who says, "There is no Saviour besides me", and who comes to seek and save the lost, and to give his life as a ransom for many?'[73]

69 <Σῶσον τὸν δοῦλόν σου, ὁ Θεός μου, τὸν ἐλπίζοντα ἐπὶ σέ.>…<Ἐλέησόν με, Κύριε, ὅτι πρὸς σε κεκράξομαι ὅλην τὴν ἡμέραν.>: PG 80, 1556B.

70 Ἐγὼ ἤλπισά σοι, Δέσποτα, σῶσον· δὸς τῇ ἐλπίδι τῆς σωτηρίας ἀντίδοσιν, PG 80, 1556B; Hill, Fathers of the Church 102, 73.

71 Ἰάκωβος γὰρ θεοῦ καὶ κυρίου Ἰησοῦ Χριστοῦ δοῦλος, καὶ Παῦλος δοῦλος Ἰησοῦ Χριστοῦ: *In Ps. caten.* 85.2b-3, Mühlenberg 2, 858, 155.

72 Κύριε, ὁ Θεός μου, ἐπὶ σοὶ ἤλπισαι· σῶσόν με ἐκ πάντων τῶν διωκόντων με καὶ ῥῦσαί με.

73 Τίς δὲ οὗτος ἢ ὁ εἰπὼν Σῴζων οὐκ ἔστιν πάρεξ ἐμοῦ, ὁ ἐληλυθὼς Ζητῆσαι καὶ σῶσαι τὸ ἀπολωλός, καὶ Δοῦναι τὴν ψυχὴν αὐτοῦ ἀντίλυτρον ἀντὶ πολλῶν': *In Ps. caten.* 7.2–3, Mühlenberg 1, 40, 140.

## II. Summary

It is clear from this study that the Greek Fathers in question interpreted a significant number of the short invocatory prayers to be found in the Psalter as either appeals to Christ in person for his deliverance or as pleas to the Father to come to their aid through the action of his Son.

In so doing, they bear testimony to the wider principle enunciated by the 'learned old man', who is the source of the wisdom which Athanasius imparts to Marcellinus: 'When you desire, in private, to extol the events concerning the Savior, you find such things in nearly every psalm'.[74] The identification of Christ as the object of invocation in the Psalter is thus but one particular, though profoundly significant, manifestation of the broader exegetical approach.

It is also clear that in making the link between the text of the psalm-verse and the Christological interpretation the Fathers had recourse to several different and, at times, overlapping theological themes. What is particularly striking from that list of themes is the virtual absence of references to the passion, the cross and the atonement, and the recurring preference for such subjects as the incarnation, the epiphany, the transfiguration, the resurrection, the ascension and the life-giving and hope-fulfilling power of Jesus.

The fact that the passion finds serious expression only in Origen's treatment of Psalm 43.27 (κατὰ τὸν τοῦ πάθους καιρόν) stands in stark contrast to the abundant use which is made of it in those same commentaries where the Fathers in question are interpreting other psalm-verses, not as prayers offered TO Christ, but as prayers offered BY Christ. This is clear from Rondeau's study, as has been shown in Chapter 9. This contrast bears witness to a clear distinction between the invocation of a Christ who is at one with suffering humanity and the invocation of a Christ who is the embodiment or manifestation of divine power.

74 τὰ περὶ τοῦ Σωτῆρος ψάλλειν, *Epist. Marcell.* 26, PG 27, 37B; Gregg, *Letter to Marcellinus*, 123.

That both of these forms of invocation are present in the various commentaries, with the exception of Didymus' Tura commentary, is evidence of their complementarity in the understanding of the authors. The Christ who is invoked as a partner is the same Christ who is invoked as a deliverer, and the authors move easily from praying with him to praying to him, and back again, in the course of the commentaries.

What, again, is also somewhat surprising is the paucity of references in the various texts to the person of David. Although two-thirds of the psalms which contain invocations of Christ bear a Davidic ascription, theological reflection upon the ancestor of Jesus in the comments on the relevant psalm-verses is, in the main, conspicuous by its absence.

To conclude, the thrust of these commentaries, in identifying Christ as the addressee of the psalmist's short prayers for salvation, mercy, rescue, release, help, justice, life and so on, is to imprint upon the hearts and minds of those studying the texts the truth that in reciting the psalmody, in making the psalmists' prayers their own, monastic communities are invoking, either directly or indirectly, the divine deliverance of Jesus himself, who is called upon in a wide variety of ways to 'Stir up your sovereign power and come in order to save us'.

# Conclusion

The picture which emerges from this extensive investigation presents us with an intriguing alternative to the narrow depiction of the monastic *milieu* as presented by Hausherr. In this picture words such as dialogue, partnership, and meeting-place play significant roles, both in relation to the Psalter and to the Christ who lies hidden among so many of its verses.

On the basis of what has been unearthed in this excavation, it is possible to describe a spiritual and theological environment which was particularly conducive to the emergence of a prayer which was centred on the invocation of Christ and a plea for divine assistance. A re-evaluation of Hausherr's *Noms du Christ et voies d'oraison* is certainly in order. On the one hand, we may reaffirm his basic hypothesis that the Jesus Prayer developed from within desert monasticism as a result of a similar quest to that which gripped the author of *The Way of a Pilgrim*. However, on the other hand, we need to draw on the wealth of insights generated by subsequent publications, and allow them to provide us with a broader understanding of the background and context of that quest, thereby correcting the omissions which have been identified in Hausherr's work.

We may therefore conclude that the Jesus Prayer developed from within a culture in which late fourth- and early fifth-century Eastern monastic psalmody:

1. played a crucial role with regard to monastic discipline and formation, as an encapsulation and summary of the whole of Scripture and as a proclamation of Christ;
2. formed a symbiotic partnership with prayer, which was characterized by a mutualism which ensured the exchange of spiritual impulses from each to the other;
3. formed a symbiotic partnership with prayer, which originated within anencounter between the monastic and Christ in the chanting of the

psalms, inwhich the Word of God addressed the human person, and offered instruction, healing and deliverance in the ascetic struggle with the demons;

4. gave birth, through this symbiotic partnership with prayer, to a dialogue between the divine and the human, where, psalmody, as 'spiritual teaching' was the divine input, and prayer, as 'conversation of the intellect with God', was the human response;
5. facilitated, through this symbiotic partnership with prayer, a gradual spiritual progression from ascetic practice (πρακτική) and natural contemplation (φυσική) to theology (θεολογία) and the deeper knowledge of God (γνῶσις);
6. provided texts through which Christ could be encountered as the meeting-place between God and humanity, as the divine-human deliverer and as the pathway to the true γνῶσις;
7. provided texts through which Christ could be persistently invoked as the divine name (ὄνομα), and thus as the Lord of glory, the Lord whose coming is prophesied, the Second Person of the Trinity, the bringer of salvation, the Lord of the Church and the God of Battles;
8. provided texts through which Christ could be persistently invoked as the divine face, countenance, manifestation and outward appearance (πρόσωπον), and thus as the embodiment of divine light, the agent of divine salvation, the dispenser of divine justice, the bringer of divine joy and as the divine object of human longing;
9. provided texts of short prayers through which Christ could be persistently invoked as a partner in prayer, and thus as a fellow human being, a suffering intercessor on behalf of an afflicted human creation and as a comrade-in-arms in spiritual warfare;
10. provided texts of short prayers through which Christ could be persistently invoked as a deliverer, and thus as the one who embodies and manifests divine righteousness, power, life and hope and as the one who rises to liberate the suppliant soul.

The weight of evidence assembled in this study would suggest that when Diadochus of Photice sought to promote a new form of contemplative prayer, based on the continual recitation of τὸ Κύριε Ἰησοῦ, he was pushing at an open door. He was addressing an audience whose practice of psalmody made available a regular and habitual pattern of worship, in which Jesus was persistently invoked, and in which the saving help or solidarity of Jesus was constantly sought. As this study has shown, this was a key characteristic of the environment generally accredited with providing the setting for the emergence and eventual establishment of the prayer, which *par excellence* relates to the invocation of Christ: 'Lord Jesus Christ, Son of God, have mercy on me'.

# Bibliography

## Primary sources

*Apothegmata partum*, Jean Baptiste Cotelier, ed., *Ecclesiae Graecae monumenta, Vol. I* (Paris: Muguet, 1677). Reprinted in Jacques-Paul Migne, *Patrologiae cursus completus. Series Graeca, Vol. LXV* (Paris: 1864). Supplemented by Jean-Claude Guy in *Recherches sur la tradition grecque des Apophthegmata Patrum. Subsidia Hagiographica* 36 (Brussels: Société des Bollandistes, 1962).

——, Luciana Mortari *Vita e detti dei padri del deserto, Vols I and II* (Rome: Città Nuova, 1971).

——, Lucien Regnault, *Les sentences des pères du désert* (Sablé-sur-Sarthe: Solesmes, 1981).

——, Benedicta Ward, trans., *The Sayings of the Desert Fathers: The Alphabetical Collection*, Cistercian Studies Series 59 (Kalamazoo, Michigan: Cistercian Publications, 1975).

Athanasius, *Epistola ad Marcellinum*, Jacques-Paul Mignes, ed., *Patrologiae cursus completus. Series Graeca, Vol. XXVII* (Paris: 1857); Robert C. Gregg, trans., *Athanasius: The Life of Anthony and the Letter to Marcellinus* (Mahway, New Jersey: Paulist Press, 1980).

——, *Expositiones in psalmos*: Jacques-Paul Migne, ed., *Patrologiae cursus completus. Series Graeca, Vol. XXVII* (Paris: 1857).

Basil of Caesarea, *Homiliae in psalmos*, Jacques-Paul Migne, ed., *Patrologiae cursus completus. Series Graeca, Vol. XXIX* (Paris: 1857).

Cassian, John, *Conlationes*, Michael Petschenig, ed., *Corpus Scriptorum Ecclesiasticorum Latinorum* 13 (Vienna: Publications Universitaires, 1886); Boniface Ramsey, *John Cassian: The Conferences, translated and annotated* (New York/Mahwah: The Newman Press, 1997).

——, *De institutis coenobiorum et de octo principalium vitiorum remediis*, Jean-Claude Guy, ed., *Jean Cassien Institutions Cénobitiques*, Sources Chrétiennes 109 (Paris: Les Éditions du Cerf, 1965); Boniface Ramsey, *John Cassian: The Institutes, translated and annotated* (New York and Mahwah, New Jersey: The Newman Press, 2000).

Chrysostom, John, *Exposition in psalmos*: Jacques-Paul Migne, ed., *Patrologiae cursus completus. Series Graeca, Vol. LV* (Paris: 1862).

*Constitutiones apostolicorum*, Alexander Roberts and James Donaldson, eds, *Ante-Nicene Christian Library, Vol. XVII* (Edinburgh: T. & T. Clark, 1870), 187–99.

Cyril of Alexandria, *Explanatio in psalmos*, Jacques-Paul Migne, ed., *Patrologiae cursus completus. Series Graeca, Vol. LXIX* (Paris: 1864).

Diadochus of Photice, *Capita centum de perfectione spirituali*, Édouard des Places, ed., *Oeuvres spirituelles, Diadoque de Photicé, introduction, texte critique, traduction et notes*, Sources Chrétiennes 5 (Paris: Éditions du Cerf, 1955); Gerald E. H. Palmer, Philip Sherrard and Kallistos Ware, ed. and trans., *The Philokalia. The Complete Text, compiled by St Nikodimos of the Holy Mountain and St Makarios of Corinth, Vol. I* (London: Faber and Faber, 1979), 251–96.

Didymus the Blind, *Commentarii in psalmos*, Michael Gronewald, ed., *Didymos der Blinde, Psalmenkommentar (Tura-Papyrus), Vols I–V* (Bonn: R. Habelt, 1968–70); Ekkehard Mühlenberg, ed., *Psalmenkommentare aus der Katenenüberlieferung, Vols I, II and III* (Berlin: De Gruyter, 1975–8).

Eusebius of Caesarea, *Commentarii in psalmos*, Jacques-Paul Migne, ed., *Patrologiae cursus completus. Series Graeca, Vols XXIII and XXIV* (Paris: 1857).

Evagrius of Pontus, *Ad monachos*, Hugo Gressmann, ed., *Nonnensspiegel und Mönchsspiegel des Evagrios Pontikos, Texte und Untersuchungen* 39.4 (Leipzig: Hinrich, 1913), 152–65; Jeremy Driscoll, *Evagrius Ponticus: Ad Monachos, Translation and Commentary* (New York and Mahwah, New Jersey: The Newman Press, 2003).

——, *Ad virginem*, Hugo Gressmann, ed., *Nonnensspiegel und Mönchsspiegel des Evagrios Pontikos, Texte und Untersuchungen* 39.4 (Leipzig: Hinrich, 1913), 146–51.

——, *Antirrhētikos*, Wilhelm Frankenberg, ed., *Evagrius Ponticus*, Abhandlungen der königlichen Gesellschaft der Wissenschaften zu Göttingen, Phil.-hist. Klasse, Neue Folge, 13.2 (Berlin: Weidmannche Buchhandlung, 1912); David Brakke, trans., *Talking Back: a monastic handbook for combating demons*, Cistercian Studies Series 229 (Collegeville, Minnesota: Liturgical Press, 2009).

——, *De oratione, Philokalia tōn Ierōn Nēptikōn, Vol. I* (Athens: Astir Publishing Company, 1957); John Eudes Bamberger, *Evagrius Ponticus: The Praktikos & Chapters on Prayer, Translated with an introduction and notes* Cistercian Studies Series 4 (Kalamazoo, Michigan: Cistercian Publications, 1981); Gerald. E. H. Palmer, Philip Sherrard and Kallistos Ware, *The Philokalia. The Complete Text, compiled by St Nikodimos of the Holy Mountain and St Makarios of Corinth, translated from the Greek, Vol. I* (London: Faber and Faber, 1979), 55–71; Simon Tugwell, ed., *Evagrius Ponticus: De oratione* (Oxford: Oxford Faculty of Theology, 1981).

——, *Epistola 11*: Wilhelm Frankenberg, ed., *Evagrius Ponticus*, Abhandlungen der königlichen Gesellschaft der Wissenschaften zu Göttingen, Phil.-hist. Klasse, Neue Folge, 13.2 (Berlin: Weidmannche Buchhandlung, 1912).

——, *Kephalaia Gnostika*, Wilhelm Frankenberg, ed., *Evagrius Ponticus*, Abhandlungen der königlichen Gesellschaft der Wissenschaften zu Göttingen, Phil.-hist. Klasse, Neue Folge, 13.2 (Berlin: Weidmannche Buchhandlung, 1912).

——, *Peri Logismōn*, Paul Géhin, ed. and trans., *Évagre le Pontique Sur les Pensées*, Sources Chrétiennes 438 (Paris: Les Éditions du Cerf, 1998).

——, *Praktikos*, John Eudes Bamberger, *Evagrius Ponticus: The Praktikos & Chapters on Prayer, Translated with an introduction and notes*, Cistercian Studies Series 4 (Kalamazoo, Michigan: Cistercian Publications, 1981); Antoine and Claire Guillaumont, ed. and trans., *Évagre le Pontique: Traité Pratique ou Le Moine*, Sources Chrétiennes 170 and 171 (Paris: Les Éditions du Cerf, 1971).

——, *Scholia ad proverbia*, Paul Géhin, ed. and trans., *Évagre le Pontique Scholies aux Proverbes*, Sources Chrétiennes 340 (Paris: Les Éditions du Cerf, 1987).

——, *Scholia ad psalmos*, Jacques-Paul Migne, ed., *Patrologiae cursus completus. Series Graeca, Vols. XII and XXVII* (Paris: 1862 and 1857); Joannes Baptista Pitra, ed., 'Origenes in Psalmos', in *Analecta sacra spicilegio solesmensi parata, Vol. II* (Paris: Tusculum, 1884), and *Vol. III* (Venice: St Lazarus Monastery, 1883); Luke Dysinger, trans., *Selected Scholia on the Psalms*, Greek Text based on Migne (PG), Pitra (AS), and the collation of M.-J. Rondeau, accessed on 20 December, 2010 at <http://www.ldysinger.com/Evagrius/08_Psalms/00a_start.htm>.

——, *Skemmata (Capita Cogniscitiva)*, Joseph Muyldermans, ed., 'Evagriana', in *Le Muséon: revue d'études orientales* 44 (Louvain: 1931), 37–68, 369–83.

*Historia monachorum in Aegypto*, Norman Russell, trans., *The Lives of the Desert Fathers*, Cistercian Studies Series 34 (Kalamzoo, Michigan: Cistercian Publications, 1981).

Jerome, *Pachomiana Latina*, Amand Boon, ed., *Pachomiana Latina, Règle et Épitres de S. Pachôme, Épitre de S. Théodore et 'Liber' de S. Orsiesius, Texte latin de S. Jerôme* (Louvain: Bureaux de la Revue, 1932); Armand Veilleux, trans., *Pachomian Koinonia, Vol. II: Pachomian Chronicles and Rules*, Cistercian Studies Series 46 (Kalamazoo, Michigan: Cistercian Publications, 1981).

Origen, *Excerpta in psalmos*, Jacques-Paul Migne, ed., *Patrologiae cursus completus. Series Graeca, Vol. XVII* (Paris: 1857); Joannes Baptista Pitra, ed., 'Origenes in Psalmos', in *Analecta sacra spicilegio solesmensi parata, Vol. II* (Paris: Tusculum, 1884); and *Vol. III* (Venice: St Lazarus Monastery, 1883).

——, *Selecta in psalmos*, Jacques-Paul Migne, ed., *Patrologiae cursus completus. Series Graeca, Vol. XII* (Paris: 1862).

Palladius, *Historia Lausiaca*, Cuthbert Butler, ed. and trans., *The Lausiac History of Palladius: a critical discussion together with notes on early Egyptian monachism, Vols I and II* (Cambridge: Cambridge University Press, 1898–1904); William Kemp Lowther Clarke, trans., *The Lausiac History of Palladius* (London: SPCK, 1918); Meyer, Robert T., trans., *Palladius: The Lausiac History* (London: Longmans, Greens and Co., 1965).

*Peri tou Abba Philēmon, Philokalia tōn Ierōn Nēptikōn, Vol. II* (Athens: Astir Publishing Company, 1959); Gerald E. H. Palmer, Philip Sherrard and Kallistos Ware, ed. and trans., *The Philokalia. The Complete Text compiled by St Nikodimos of the Holy Mountain and St Makarios of Corinth, Vol. II* (London: Faber and Faber, 1981), 343–57.

*Septuagint*: Lancelot C. L. Brenton, ed., *The Septuagint with Apocrypha: Greek and English* (London: Samuel Bagster and Sons, 1851).

——, Alfred Rahlfs, ed., *Septuaginta. Vetus Testamentum Graecum Auctoritate Academiae Litterarum Gottingensis editum, Vol. X* (Göttingen: Vandenhoeck and Ruprecht, 1931–93).

——, Henry Barclay Swete, ed., *The Old Testament in Greek according to the Septuagint, Vol. II, Pt. 1* (Cambridge: Cambridge University Press, 1891).

——, Albert Pietersma, trans., *A New English Translation of the Septuagint and other Greek translations traditionally included under that title, The Psalms* (Oxford and New York: Oxford University Press, 2000).

——, Edwin Hatch and Henry A. Redpath, ed., *Concordance to the Septuagint and other Greek versions of the Old Testament, including the Apocryphal books* (Oxford: Clarendon Press, 1897).

Theodoret of Cyrrhus, *Commentarii in psalmos*, Jacques-Paul Migne, ed., *Patrologiae cursus completus. Series Graeca, Vol. LXXX* (Paris: 1864); Robert C. Hill, trans., *Theodoret of Cyrrhus, Commentary on the Psalms, Psalms 1–72* and *Psalms 73–150*, The Fathers of the Church, a New Translation 101 and 102 (Washington D.C.: Catholic University of America Press, 2000 and 2001).

*Vita Pachomii*, François Halkin, ed., *Le corpus athénien de saint Pachôme*, with a French translation by André-Jean Festugière, Cahiers d'orientalisme 2 (Geneva: Patrick Cramer, 1982).

## Secondary sources

Alfeyev, Hilarion, *Le Nom grand et glorieux. La vénération du Nom de Dieu et la prière de Jésus dans la tradition orthodoxe.* Traduction du russe par Claire Jounievy, Hieromoine Alexandre [Siniakov] et Dom André Louf (Paris: Les Éditions du Cerf, 2007).

Amélineau, Emile, *De Historia Lausiaca quaenam sit hujus ad Monachorum Aegyptiorum historiam utilitas: adjecta sunt quaedam hujus Historiae coptica fragmenta inedita* (Paris: E. Leroux, 1887).

Ballard, Harold Wayne, Jr., *The Divine Warrior Motif in the Psalms*, BIBAL Dissertation Series 6 (North Richland Hills, Texas: BIBAL Press, 1999).

Bradshaw, Paul, *The Search for the Origins of Christian Worship: Sources and Methods for the Study of Early Liturgy* (Oxford and New York: Oxford University Press, 2002).

Bunge, Gabriel, *Das Geistgebet: Studien zum Traktat, De Oratione des Evagrios Pontikos* (Cologne: Luthe-Verlag, 1987); English translation by Luke Dysinger, *Spritiual Prayer*, accessed on 25 August, 2010 at <http://ldysinger.stjohnsem.edu/@texts2/1985_bunge/01_GGB-pref_ch1.htm>.

Burton-Christie, Douglas, *The Word in the Desert: Scripture and the Quest for Holiness in Early Christian Monasticism* (Oxford and New York: Oxford University Press, 1993).

Casiday, Augustine, *Reconstructing the Theology of Evagrius Ponticus: Beyond Heresy* (Cambridge: Cambridge University Press, 2012).

Chitty, Derwas J., *The Desert a City: An Introduction to the Study of Egyptian and Palestinian Monasticism under the Christian Empire* (Crestwood, New York: St Vladimir's Seminary Press, 1995).

De Vogüé, Adalbert, *De Saint Pachômien à Jean Cassien: Études littéraires et doctrinales sur le monachisme égyptien à ses débuts*, Studia Anselmiana 120 (Rome: S. Anselmi de Urbe, 1996).

——, *La Règle de saint Benoit, Vol. VII, Commentaire Doctrinal et Spirituel* (Paris: Les Éditions du Cerf, 1977); English translation by John Baptist Hasbrouk, *The rule of Saint Benedict, a doctrinal and spiritual commentary*, Cistercian Studies Series 54 (Kalamazoo, Michigan: Cistercian Publications, 1983).

——, 'Psalmodie n'est pas prier', in *Ecclesia Orans* 6 (Rome: Pontificio Istituto Liturgico, 1989) 7–32.

Driscoll, Jeremy, *Evagrius Ponticus: Ad Monachos, Translation and Commentary* (New York and Mahwah, New Jersey: The Newman Press, 2003).

Du Roy, Olivier, *Moines aujourd'hui: une experience de réforme institutionelle* (Paris: Épi Édition, 1972).

Dysinger, Luke, *Psalmody and Prayer in the Writings of Evagrius Ponticus* (Oxford and New York: Oxford University Press, 2005).

Fiensy, David A., *Prayers Alleged to be Jewish: An Examination of the Constitutiones Apostolorum*, Brown Judaic Studies 65 (Chico, California: Scholars Press, 1985).

French, Reginald M., *The Way of a Pilgrim* (London: SPCK, 1954).

Gesché, Adolphe, 'L'âme humaine de Jésus dans la christologie du IVe siècle. Le témoignage du Commentaire sur les Psaumes découvert à Toura', in *Revue d'Histoire Ecclésiastique* 54 (Louvain: Université catholique de Louvain, 1959), 385–425.

——, *La christologie du Commentaire sur les Psaumes découvert à Toura* (Gembloux: Éditions J. Duculot, 1962).

Goehring, James E., ed., *Ascetics, Society and the Desert: Studies in Early Egyptian Monasticism* (Harrisburg, Pennsylvania: Trinity Press International, 1999).

Guillaumont, Antoine, *Les 'Kephalaia Gnostica' d'Évagre le Pontique et l'histoire de l'Origénisme chez les Grecs et chez les Syriens*, Patristica Sorbonensia 5 (Paris: Éditions du Seuil, 1962).

Guy, Jean-Claude, *Les Apophtegmes des Pères. Collection systématique, Vol. I*, Sources Chrétiennes 387 (Paris: Les Éditions du Cerf, 1993).

——, 'Cassian, St John', in Aziz S. Atiya, ed., *Coptic Encyclopedia Vol. II* (New York: Macmillan, 1991), 461–4.

——, 'Jean Cassien, historien du monachisme égyptien?', in *Studia Patristica* 8, Texte und Untersuchungen 93 (Berlin: Akademie Verlag, 1966), 363–72.

Harmless, William, *Desert Christians: An Introduction to the Literature of Early Monasticism* (Oxford and New York: Oxford University Press, 2004).

Hausherr, Irénée, *Hésychasme et prière*, Orientalia Christiana Analecta 176 (Rome: Pontificium Institutum Orientalium Studiorum, 1966).

——, 'Le Traité de l'Oraison d'Évagre le Pontique', in *Revue d'Ascétique et de Mystique, Vol. XV* (Brussels: Culture et Civilisation, 1934), 34–93, 113–70.

——, *Noms du Christ et voies d'oraison*, Orientalia Christiana Analecta 157 (Rome: Pontificium Institutum Orientalium Studiorum, 1960); English translation by Charles Cummings, *The Name of Jesus*, Cistercian Studies Series 44 (Kalamazoo, Michigan: Cistercian Publications, 1978).

——, *Penthos: La doctrine de compunction dans l'Orient Chrétien*, Orientalia Christiana Analecta 132 (Rome: Pontificium Institutum Orientalium Studiorum, 1944).

Hayward, C. T. Robert, 'Memra and Shekhina: A Short Note', in *Journal of Jewish Studies* 31 (Oxford: Oxford Centre for Postgraduate Hebrew Studies, 1980), 210–13.

Hester, David, 'Diadochos of Photiki: The Memory and its Purification', in *Studia Patristica* 23 (Leuven: Peeters Press, 1989), 49–52.

*Jewish Encyclopedia, Vol. VIII* (New York and London: Funk and Wagnalls, 1904).

Kok, Frans, 'L'Office Pachômien: Psallere, Orare, Legere', in *Ecclesia Orans* 9 (Rome: Pontificio Istituto Liturgico, 1992), 69–95.

Kolbet, Paul R., 'Athanasius, the Psalms and the Reformation of the Self', in *Harvard Theological Review* 99 (Cambridge, Massachusetts: Harvard Divinity School, 2006), 85–101.

Konstantinovsky, Julia S., *Evagrius Ponticus: The Making of a Gnostic* (Farnham: Ashgate Publishing, 2009).

Lampe, Geoffrey W. H., *A Patristic Greek Lexicon*, Seventeenth Impression (Oxford and New York: Oxford University Press, 2003).

Longman, Tremper, III, 'The Divine Warrior: The New Testament Use of an Old Testament Motif', in *Westminster Theological Journal* 44 (Philadelphia: Westminster Theological Seminary, 1982), 209–307.

Louth, Andrew, 'Inspiration of the Scriptures'. A paper given at the first colloquy of the Orthodox Theological Research Forum at Cuddesdon in August, 2003, and published in *Sobornost* 31:1 (Oxford: Fellowship of St Alban and St Sergius, 2009), 29–44.

——, *The Origins of the Christian Mystical Tradition*, Second Edition (Oxford and New York: Oxford University Press, 2007).

Mckinnon, James W., 'Desert Monasticism and the Later Fourth-Century Psalmodic Movement', in *Music and Letters* 75, No. 4, November, 1994 (Oxford: Oxford University Press, 1994), 505–21.

Madden, Nicholas, 'Αἴσθησις νοερά (Diadochus-Maximus)', in *Studia Patristica* 23 (Leuven: Peeters Press, 1989), 53–60.

Monk of the Eastern Church, A, *The Jesus Prayer* (Crestwood, New York: St Vladimir's Seminary Press, 1987).

Muyldermans, Joseph, ed., *A travers la tradition manuscrite d'Évagre le Pontique: essai sur les manuscrits grecs conservés à la Bibliothèque nationale de Paris*, Bibliothèque du Muséon 3 (Louvain: Bureaux du Muséon, 1932), 47–8.

Plested, Marcus, *The Macarian Legacy: the place of Macarius-Symeon in the Eastern Christian tradition* (Oxford and New York: Oxford University Press, 2004).

Polyzogopoulos, Theodoritus, 'The Anthropology of Diadochus of Photice,' in *Theologia: Hiera Synodos tēs Ekklēsias tēs Hellados* 55 (Athens: Brabeion Akadēmias Athēōn, 1984), 1072–101.

Regnault, Lucien, *The Day-to-Day Life of the Desert Fathers in Fourth-Century Egypt* (Petersham, Massachusets: St Bede's, 1999).

Reitzenstein, Richard, *Hellenistichen Wundererzählungen* (Stuttgart: Teubner, 1906).

Rondeau, Marie-Josèphe, *Les Commentaires Patristiques du Psautier (IIIe-Ve siècles), Vol. I, Les Travaux des pères grecs et latins sur le psautier. Recherches et bilan; Vol. II, Exégèse prosopologique et théologie*, Orientalia Christiana Analecta 219 and 220 (Rome: Pontificium Institutum Studiorum Orientalium, 1982 and 1985).

——, 'Le Commentaire sur les Psaumes d'Évagre le Pontique', in Orientalia Christiana Periodica 26 (Rome: Pontificium Institutum Orientalium Studiorum, 1960), 307–48.

Sinkewicz, Robert E., *Evagrius of Pontus: the Greek Ascetic Corpus, Translated with Introduction and Commentary* (Oxford and New York: Oxford University Press, 2003).

Stec, David M., trans., *Targum Psalms* (London: T. & T. Clark, 2004).

Stewart, Columba, *Cassian the Monk* (Oxford and New York: Oxford University Press, 1998).

Taft, Robert F., *The Liturgy of the Hours in East and West: the origins of the Divine Office and its meaning for to-day* (Collegeville, Minnesota: Liturgical Press, 1986).

——, 'Praise in the Desert: The Coptic Monastic Office Yesterday and Today', in *Worship* 56, No.2 (Collegeville, Minnesota: St John's Abbey, 1982), 513–36.

Van der Mensbrugghe, Alexis, 'Prayer-time in Egyptian Monasticism', in *Studia Patristica* 2 (Leuven: Peeters Press, 1957).

Veilleux, Armand, *La Liturgie dans le cénobitisme pachômien au quatrième siècle*, Studia Anselmiana 57 (Rome: S. Anselmi de Urbe, 1968).

Von Balthasar, Hans Urs, 'Die Hiera des Evagrius Pontikus', in *Zeitschrift für katholische Theologie* 63 (Innsbruck: Theologische Fakultät, 1939), 86–106, 181–206.

Weingarten, Hermann, *Der Ursprung des Mönchtums im nachconstantinischen Zeitalter* (Gotha: F. A. Perthes, 1877).

Wellington, James F., 'Encountering Christ in the Psalms: Antecedents of the Jesus Prayer in Eastern Monastic Psalmody c.350-c.450', in *Studia Patristica* 52 (Leuven: Peeters Press, 2012), 19–26.

——, 'From Cantor to Contemplative: Evagrian Psalmody and the Invocation of Jesus in the *Capita centum de perfectione spirituali* of Diadochus of Photice', in *Studia Patristica* 72 (Leuven: Peeters Press).

Woolfenden, Gregory W., *Daily Liturgical Prayer: Origins and Theology* (Aldershot: Ashgate Publishing, 2004) 88–94.

——, 'The Use of the Psalter by Early Monastic Communities', in *Studia Patristica* 26 (Leuven: Peeters Press, 1993), 88–94.

# General Index

# Biblical Reference Index

# *Studies in Eastern Orthodoxy*

Edited by GRAHAM SPEAKE and RENÉ GOTHÓNI

This series is concerned with Eastern Orthodox Christianity in its various manifestations. Originating as the church of the East Roman or Byzantine empire, Eastern Orthodoxy comprises the group of churches that owe allegiance to the Ecumenical Patriarchate in Constantinople. The Orthodox Church has exercised unparalleled influence over the history, thought, and culture of the region and remains one of the most dynamic and creative forces in Christendom today. The series will publish studies in English, both monographs and edited collections, in all areas of social, cultural, and political activity in which the Orthodox Church can be seen to have played a major role.

Vol. 1 Forthcoming

Vol. 2 James F. Wellington
Christe Eleison!: The Invocation of Christ in Eastern Monastic Psalmody c.350–450.
2014. ISBN 978-3-0343-1789-4